Film – Television – Sound Archive Series

Papers and Reference Tools for Film Archivists
Dealing with Audiovisual Material

Vol 5

Fédération Internationale des Archives du Film (FIAF)
International Association of Sound Archives (IASA)
International Council on Archives (ICA)
International Federation of Library Associations (IFLA)
International Federation of Television Archives (IFTA)

World Directory of Moving Image and Sound Archives

Edited by
Wolfgang Klaue

K · G · Saur
München · New Providence · London · Paris 1993

The directory was compiled with financial assistance
from UNESCO

Die Deutsche Bibliothek – CIP-Einheitsaufnahme

World directory of moving image and sound archives /
Fédération Internationale des Archives du Film (FIAF) ... Ed.
by Wolfgang Klaue. – München ; New Providence ; London ;
Paris : Saur, 1993
(Film, television, sound archive series ; Vol. 5)
ISBN 3-598-22594-6
NE: Klaue, Wolfgang [Hrsg.]; International Federation of Film
Archives; GT

Gedruckt auf säurefreiem Papier
Printed on acid-free paper

Alle Rechte vorbehalten / All Rights Strictly Reserved
K.G. Saur Verlag GmbH & Co KG, München 1993
A Reed Reference Publishing Company
Printed in the Federal Republic of Germany

Data preparation and automatic data processing
by Microcomposition, Wittmar
Printed and bound by Strauss Offsetdruck, Hirschberg 2

ISBN 3-598-22594-6

Contents

Introduction	7	HONG KONG	88
		HUNGARY	89
Directory		ICELAND	90
ABU DHABI	11	INDIA	90
ALBANIA	11	INDONESIA	92
ALGERIA	12	IRAN	92
ANGOLA	12	IRELAND	93
ARGENTINIA	12	ISRAEL	94
AUSTRALIA	13	ITALY	96
AUSTRIA	20	JAMAICA	100
BANGLADESH	24	JAPAN	101
BELGIUM	24	JORDAN	102
BERMUDA	27	KENYA	102
BOLIVIA	28	KIRIBATI	103
BOTSWANA	28	KOREA, DEMOCRATIC	103
BRAZIL	29	KOREA, REPULIC OF	103
BRUNEI	30	LESOTHO	104
BULGARIA	30	LIECHTENSTEIN	104
BURKINA FASO	32	LUXEMBOURG	105
CANADA	32	MALAWI	105
CHILE	40	MALAYSIA	105
CHINA, PEOPLE'S REPUBLIC	41	MARSHALL ISLANDS	107
COLOMBIA	43	MAURITIUS	107
CONGO	44	MEXICO	108
COSTA RICA	44	NAMIBIA	110
CROATIA	44	NETHERLANDS	110
CUBA	45	NEW ZEALAND	116
CZECH REPUBLIC	48	NIGERIA	118
DENMARK	50	NORWAY	119
ECUADOR	53	PAPUA NEW GUINEA	123
ESTONIA	54	PERU	124
FIJI	54	PHILIPPINES	125
FINLAND	54	POLAND	125
FRANCE	60	PORTUGAL	126
GERMANY	76	ROMANIA	127
GREECE	87	RUSSIA	128
GUINEA	87	SAUDI ARABIA	129
GUINEA-BISSAU	88	SEYCHELLES	130

Contents

SINGAPORE	130	TUNISIA	147
SLOVAK REPUBLIC	131	TURKEY	147
SLOVENIA	132	UNITED KINGDOM	148
SOLOMON ISLANDS	132	U.S.A	162
SOUTH AFRICA	133	URUGUAY	180
SPAIN	134	VATICAN CITY	180
SRI LANKA	138	VENEZUELA	181
SUDAN	139	VIETNAM	182
SWEDEN	139	YUGOSLAVIA	182
SWITZERLAND	142	ZAMBIA	183
SYRIA	146	ZIMBABWE	184
TANZANIA	146		
THAILAND	146	Index	185

Introduction

The idea for this publication arose during one of the annual meetings of the International Round Table on Audiovisual Records, a co-ordinating forum which brings together those international organizations concerned with the preservation of the audiovisual heritage: the Fédération Internationale des Archives du Film (FIAF), the International Association of Sound Archives (IASA), the International Council on Archives (ICA), the International Federation of Library Associations (IFLA), the International Federation of Television Archives (IFTA).

Because of the growing importance of audiovisual media in all spheres of communication, the demand for information about audiovisual collections is ever increasing. The international audiovisual organizations consequently felt that there was an urgent need to provide a directory of such collections to help all categories of users – researchers, students, programmers, broadcasters, film and television makers. The directory would attempt to include collections worldwide, so closing a gap in information about audiovisual resources.

The project was only made possible as a result of a grant from Unesco, the enthusiasm and co-operation of international organizations concerned, the support from the Bundesarchiv Koblenz (Germany) and the enormous amount of secretarial assistance given by Mrs. Brigitte van der Elst, Executive Secretary of FIAF.

The Directory is based on the results of a joint survey undertaken by all the international organizations mentioned above. A questionnaire was designed so that it could be completed quickly (under 30 minutes) as the project leaders recognized the pressure under which recipients are working and it was feared that a longer and more detailed form might result in more returns. Only basic information was requested. The data in the Directory are based solely on the information supplied from this survey. No other information was added. Only editorial or technical corrections have been made. Omissions relate to those institutions with no audiovisual collections (yet which participated in the survey) and those organizations failing to return their questionnaires, even where it is known that audiovisual collections exist.

As with all directories, the information is out-of-date by the time of publication. Too many political and institutional changes have taken place and it is impossible to accommodate all these in the Directory. Nor can this Directory replace the more detailed handbooks specializing in film and video collections within a country, e.g. USA, the Netherlands, Austria, United Kingdom or the membership of international organizations.

Those who worked on the project are well aware of the gaps in this first attempt at a world directory. It requires updating, additions, more comprehensive entries, and even a revised plan for a next edition. In order to achieve these improvements, also users are invited to send their comments, ideas, additions and corrections to the FIAF Secretariat, 190 Rue Franz Merjay, 1180 Bruxelles, Belgium.

Wolfgang Klaue, Editor

Introduction

Directory

ABU DHABI

ABU DHABI

_____ 001
THE NATIONAL LIBRARY – CULTURAL FONDATION
Zaid the Second Street
ABU DHABI 2380
ABU DHABI

Member of IFLA.

Collections
Collections of Video, Sound, Slides.
Documentary, cultural, educational, scientific.
Video 2000
Sound 2500

Access
Catalogue published, on cards.
Access to catalogue.
Access to materials.
Access by purchase.

Fees – Copyright
Fees for research for reuse and production purposes, research by archive staff, facilities and handling, other.
Institution holds no copyright.

ALBANIA

TIRANA

_____ 002
ARKIVA E VIDIO-FILMO-FONO E RTSH
VIDEO-FILM-SOUND ARCHIVES OF THE R.T.SH.
Pr. Ismail Qemali RTSH.
TIRANA
ALBANIA

Tel.: 355-42-230 46
Fax.: 355-42-236 50, 355-42-26 583
Telex: 2216 R.T.V.SH. AB

Member of IFTA.

Collections
Collections of Film, Video, texts of TV-programmes.
Political, cultural (historical), musical (classical, folk and pop music), scientific, artistic (films, theaters), educational (education, sport) osv local and foreign programmes and materials.
Films 21500
Video 5200

Access
Catalogue indexed on cards.
Acces to catalogue: limited.
Access to materials: limited. In general, for the employees at RTSH.
Access by purchase.

Fees – Copyright
Fees: Up to now everything has been free of charge. In the future we think to change this practice.
Copyright holder is the institution.
The conditions for copyright-access are not yet defined.

_____ 003
ARKIVI SHTETËROR I FILMIT I REPUBLIKËS SË SHQIPËRISË
ARCHIVES D'ETAT DU FILM DE LA REPUBLIQUE D'ALBANIE
rue Aleksander Moisiu 76
TIRANA
ALBANIA

Tel.: 355-42-327 33
Fax.: 355-42-327 33

Member of FIAF.

Collections
Collections of Film, Sound, scripts, filmmusic, documents, photos, books, magazines.
Collection of feature films, short films, documentaries, newsreels, animation films of national and international production.
Films 5669 titles
Sound 2432 titles

Access
Catalogue on database.
Access to catalogue.
Access to materials.
Access on archives premises, by loan.

Fees – Copyright
Fees for research for reuse and production purposes, research by archive staff, facilities and handling.
Copyright holder is the institution.

ALGERIA

ALGERS

_____ **004**
CENTRE DES ARCHIVES NATIONALES
B.P. 38 Birkhadem
ALGER
ALGERIA

Tel.: 213-2-56.61.62
Telex: 62524

Member of ICA.

Collections

Collections of Film, Video, Sound.

Political events, history, economy, sports, culture.
Documentaries.
Films 7100 reels
Video 303 cassettes
Sound 206 tapes

Access

Catalogue on database.

Access to catalogue.

Access to materials: limited. Only through specialized personnel for the AV-collection ; for reasons of security.
Access on archives premises.

Fees – Copyright

Copyright conditions are defined in a law for the Centre des Archives Nationales (N° 88-09, 26 Jan 1988).

ANGOLA

LUANDA

_____ **005**
CINEMATECA NACIONAL DE ANGOLA
place Luther King 4
3512
LUANDA
ANGOLA

Tel.: 244-330918
Telex: 3398 EDECINE AN

Member of FIAF.

Collections

Collections of Film, related materials.

Nearly all nationally produced films ; selection of international films.
Films 643

Access

Catalogue indexed on cards.

Access to catalogue.

Access to materials: limited, for reasons of preservation.
Access on archives premises.

Fees – Copyright

Fees for research by archive staff.
Pricelist and conditions for use available.
Institution holds no copyright.
Renting and selling of material depends on right holders agreement.

ARGENTINIA

BUENOS AIRES

_____ **006**
FUNDACION CINEMATECA ARGENTINA
Lavalle 2092, 2nd floor
BUENOS AIRES 1045
ARGENTINA

Tel.: 54-1-953/3755-7163
Fax.: 54-1-311.0562
Telex: 24569 SICVIL AR

Member of FIAF.

Collections

Collections of Film, Video, books, magazines, photos, slides, posters.

Fiction, documentaries, experimental, art, newsreels.
Films 11000
Video 500

Access

Catalogue on database.

Acces to catalogue: limited, colleagues and researchers.

Access to materials: limited, colleagues, researchers, film directors, students.
Access on archives premises.

Fees – Copyright

Fees for research for reuse and production purposes, facilities and handling.
Pricelist and conditions for use available.
Institution holds no copyright.
Theoretically, copyright expires after 30 years but in each case the producers or their descendants must be consulted.

AUSTRALIA

ADELAIDE

_____ 007
CORPORATION OF THE CITY OF ADELAIDE
ADELAIDE CITY ARCHIVES
Topham Mall, off 54 Waymouth Street
G.P.O. Box 2252
ADELAIDE, SOUTH AUSTRALIA, 5001
AUSTRALIA

Tel.: 61-8-203 7439
Fax.: 61-8-231 5838

Member of ICA.

Collections
Collections of Sound.

Recordings of meetings of the Adelaide City Council and its committees. Oral history recordings of former Council members, former members of (senior) staff, and elderly people with longstanding associations with the City of Adelaide.
Sound About 6 shelf metres

Access
Access to materials: limited. Access in accordance with Council's policies (some materials restricted), and for oral histories, the wishes of the interviewees.
Access on archives premises.

Fees – Copyright
Fees and copyright conditions advised for individual items after individual application.

CALLAGHAN

_____ 008
UNIVERSITY OF NEWCASTLE
UNIVERSITY ARCHIVES, AUCHMUTY LIBRARY, UNIVERSITY OF NEWCASTLE
University Drive
CALLAGHAN 2308
AUSTRALIA

Tel.: 61-49-21 5820
Fax.: 61-49-21 5833

Collections
Collections of Video, Sound.

Newcastle University Medical School Teaching and Public Relations videos (1970s-1980s). Newcastle University Oral History tapes (1970s-1980s): history of Newcastle University.
Video 20 videos
Sound 180 tapes

Access
Catalogue on database.
Access to catalogue.
Access to materials.
Access on archives premises.

Fees – Copyright
Copyright holder is the institution.
Almost all of the above material may be accessed for research purposes, but is not available for commercial use.

CANBERRA

_____ 009
AUSTRALIAN INSTITUTE OF ABORIGINAL AND TORRES STRAIT ISLANDER STUDIES
Acton House, Marcus Clarke St, Acton, Act
G.P.O. Box 553
CANBERRA, ACT, 2601
AUSTRALIA

Tel.: 61-6-246 1111
Fax.: 61-6-249 7310

Member of IASA.

Collections
Collections of Film, Video, Sound, production documentation, transcripts, stills, field notes, books.

Australian Aboriginal and Torres Strait Islander cultures including ethnography, languages, music, oral history, contemporary social conditions.
Films 7000 hours (films + videos)
Sound 17000 hours

Access
Catalogue on database.

Acces to catalogue: limited. Staff assistance required.

Access to materials: limited, for preservation; limited facilities; cultural restrictions on use of information content; depositors' conditions.
Access on archives premises.

Fees – Copyright
Fees for research by archive staff, broadcasting and publication.
Pricelist and conditions for use available.
Copyright may be held by the institute, depositors or others; permission may be required from the copyright holder for access.

_____ 010
AUSTRALIAN WAR MEMORIAL
Anzac Parade
G.P.O. Box 345

CANBERRA 2601
AUSTRALIA

Tel.: 61-6-243 4211
Fax.: 61-6-243 4325

Member of IASA, ICA, IFLA.

Collections

Collections of Film, Video, Sound.

Material covers Australians involvement in World War I, World War II, Korea, Malaya, Vietnam and the Gulf war.
Films More than 4000 titles consisting of over 1000 km of footage (films + videos)
Sound over 5000 discrete items

Access

Catalogue on database.

Access to database for items that have been through the copying program.

Access to materials.
Access on archives premises.

Fees – Copyright

Fees for research for reuse and production purposes, facilities and handling.
Pricelist and conditions for use available.
Copyright holder is the institution.
1% of copyright of the collection lies with individuals.

_____ 011
NATIONAL FILM AND SOUND ARCHIVE
McCoy Circuit, Acton
G.P.O. Box 2002
CANBERRA, ACT, 2600
AUSTRALIA

Tel.: 61-6-267 1711
Fax.: 61-6-247 4651
Telex: AA 61930

Member of FIAF, IFTA, IASA.

Collections

Collections of Film, Video, Sound, objects/artefacts, photographs, posters, scripts, publicity items, newspaper clippings, literature.

Australian feature films (1910-present), documentary films, newsreels, TV programmes ; some foreign feature films ; Australian folk music, and history, radio programmes ; international classical, jazz and popular music.
Films 225000 cans
Video 240000 reels/cassettes
Sound 900000 carriers

Access

Catalogue on database.

Access to catalogue.

Access to materials.
Access on archives premises, by loan, by hire, by purchase.

Fees – Copyright

Fees for research, for reuse and production purposes, research by archive staff, facilities and handling, Licensing fees for materials for which Archive holds copyright.
Pricelist and conditions for use available.
Institution holds no copyright.
Copyright clearance not required for viewing or auditioning on premises. Otherwise prior copyright clearance required.

_____ 012
NATIONAL LIBRARY OF AUSTRALIA, FILM-VIDEO LENDING COLLECTION
Parkes Place
CANBERRA 2600
AUSTRALIA

Tel.: 61-6-262 1361
Fax.: 61-6-262 1634

Member of IFLA.

Collections

Collections of Film, Video. Also large holding of monographs and serials on cinema and television as part of the Library's print collection.

Primarly for tertiary level educational use and community groups as Film Societies. Includes a large screen studies component (4500 titles) and informational educational films and videocassettes.
Films 21200 16mm prints
Video 5000 videocassettes (4200 VHS, 800 U-Matic)

Access

Catalogue on database.

Access to catalogue.

Access to materials.
Access on archives premises, by loan.

Fees – Copyright

Fees for handling and outwards freight recovery.
Pricelist and conditions for use available.
Copyright holder is the institution.
Non-exclusive rights for lending only (rent free).
Films and videocassettes available only for screening not copying. For copying permission is required from the copyright owner.

_____ 013
NATIONAL MUSEUM OF AUSTRALIA
Yarramundi, Lady Denman Drive
P.O. Box 1901

CANBERRA, ACT, 2601
AUSTRALIA

Tel.: 61-6-256 1111
Fax.: 61-6-256 1233

Member of IASA.

Collections

Collections of Film, Sound, cinematographic equipment, production stills, posters, radio and television equipment.

NMA collects in 3 broad areas : Australian Social History, Australian Aboriginal Culture, Human Interaction with the Environment. Film and sound objects are representative of this rather than comprehensive. A collection of OH (75) tapes complements other holdings.
Films 1042 film related ojects, inc. 22 films
Sound 816 sound related objects, inc. 138 discs, 21 cylinders

Access

Catalogue on cards.

Acces to catalogue: limited. Museum-based rather than archive/library.

Access to materials: limited. Limited facilities. Access on archives premises, by loan.

Fees – Copyright

Fees for research for reuse and production purposes, facilities and handling, copyright, loan. Copyright holder is the institution.

CAULFIELD

_____ 014

MONASH UNIVERSITY LIBRARY, CAULFIELD/FRANKSTON BRANCH
Queens Avenue
CAULFIELD EAST, VICTORIA, 3145
AUSTRALIA

Tel.: 61-3-573 2272
Fax.: 61-3-573 2323

Collections

Collections of Film, Video, Sound.

Cinema, marketing, business, literature, education, sociology are the major areas covered.
Films 590 items
Video 1624 items
Sound 2642 items

Access

Catalogue on database.

Access to catalogue on sites or through ABN.

Access to materials: limited. Sound cassettes only for loan.

Fees – Copyright

Institution holds no copyright.
Films and video not available for loan or use outside the Branch Library.

CLAYTON

_____ 015

MONASH UNIVERSITY
HUMANITIES & SOCIAL SCIENCES LIBRARY (AUDIO VISUAL)
Monash University
CLAYTON, VICTORIA, 3168
AUSTRALIA

Tel.: 61-3-565 2627
Fax.: 61-3-565 2610

Member of IFLA.

Collections

Collections of Film, Video, Sound, slide/tape kits, some literature, journals & catalogues.

History, politics, social issues, environmentalism, library studies, psychology, education, strong visual arts collection.
Films 562 titles (16mm)
Video 211 titles (VHS & U-Matic)
Sound 214 kits (including slide/tape kits)

Access

Catalogue on database.

Access to catalogue.

Access to materials: limited. Film restricted to avoid damage.
Access on archives premises, by loan.

Fees – Copyright

Fees for Post & pack for inter library loan.
Copyright holder is the institution.
Some items are Monash copyright, most not.
Access is free unless specified by copyright holder.
Nothing may be copied.

_____ 016

MONASH UNIVERSITY, MUSIC LIBRARY, MUSIC DEPARTMENT
Wellington Road
CLAYTON, VICTORIA, 3168
AUSTRALIA

Tel.: 61-3-565 3239, 61-3-565 3236, 61-3-565 3230
Fax.: 61-3-565 3241
Telex: AA 32691

Member of IASA.

Collections

Collections of Film, Video, Sound, slides, scores.

World music : field recordings + records, cassettes, compact discs, videos + slides. Western popular music : as above. Western classical music : as above.
Films 3
Video About 200
Sound About 13000

Access

Catalogue on database.

Acces to catalogue: limited. On request (payment required).

Access to materials.
Access on archives premises.

Fees – Copyright

Fees for catalogues/discographies.
Institution holds no copyright.
Only on archive premises.

DARWIN

_____ 017

NORTHERN TERRITORY ARCHIVES SERVICE
Corner Carey & McMinn Streets
G.P.O. Box 874
DARWIN, NORTHERN TERRITORY, 0801
AUSTRALIA

Tel.: 61-89-89 5188
Fax.: 61-89-41 1458

Collections

Collections of Sound.

Oral history audio cassette recordings.
Sound About 2000 audio cassettes

Access

Catalogue on database.

Access to catalogue.

Access to materials. Most recordings have been transcribed to the written word – access to transcripts preferred.
Access on archives premises, by purchase.

Fees – Copyright

Fees for copying.
Institution holds no copyright.
Conditions for access are imposed by the interviewee although the NT Archives owns the recordings and transcripts.

_____ 018

STATE LIBRARY OF THE NORTHERN TERRITORY. NORTHERN AUSTRALIA COLLECTION
25 Cavenagh Street
G.P.O. Box 42
DARWIN, NT, 0800
AUSTRALIA

Tel.: 61-89-89 7364
Fax.: 61-89-41 1375

Collections

Collections of Film, Video, Sound.

Material relating to the Northern Territory. Documentary films/videos. Records cassettes of Aboriginal music and western music by Northern Territory artists.
Films 325
Video 918
Sound 200

Access

Catalogue on database.

Access to catalogue.

Access to materials: limited.
Access on archives premises.

Fees – Copyright

No fees.
Institution holds no copyright.

ENFIELD

_____ 019

ROYAL BLIND SOCIETY OF NEW SOUTH WALES
4 Mitchell Street
P.O. Box 176, BURWOOD, NSW, 2134
ENFIELD, NSW, 2134
AUSTRALIA

Tel.: 61-02-334 3333
Fax.: 61-02-747 5993

Member of IFLA.

Collections

Collections of Sound.

Talking books in 4 track 15/16 ips and 2 track 7/8 ips cassette format. For use of blind and print handicapped readers only.
Sound 10000 titles

Access

Catalogue on database.

Access to catalogue. Available in large print and through Australian Bibliographic Network (ABN) administered by National Library of Australia.

Access to materials: limited. Blind & print handicapped readers only.
Access by loan, by purchase.

Fees – Copyright

Fees for facilities and handling.
Pricelist and conditions for use available.
Copyright holder is the institution.
Restricted to blind and print handicapped readers in Australia and New Zealand.

HOBART

_____ 020

STATE LIBRARY OF TASMANIA
TASMANIANA LIBRARY
91 Murray Street
HOBART, TASMANIA, 7000
AUSTRALIA

Tel.: 61-02-30 7474
Fax.: 61-02-31 0927

Member of IFLA.

Collections

Collections of Film, Video, Sound.

The Tasmaniana Library is a permanent collection of all material in all formats published in, or relating to the State of Tasmania. Its resources include film, video and all forms of sound recordings which relate to Tasmania or are by Tasmanian artists.
Films 200
Video 150
Sound 200

Access

Catalogue on cards.

Access to catalogue.

Access to materials.
Access on archives premises.

Fees – Copyright

Pricelist and conditions for use available.
Institution holds no copyright.
Copying for study and research or for publication of any item which is in copyright will only be permitted with the permission of the owner of copyright.

LINDFIELD

_____ 021

FILM AUSTRALIA PTY LTD
Eton Road
P.O. Box 46, LINDFIELD
LINDFIELD, N.S.W
AUSTRALIA

Tel.: 61-2-413 8777
Fax.: 61-2-416 5672
Telex: 21734

Collections

Collections of Film, Video.

Mainly Australiana, street scenes, wildlife, industry, rural. Plus 40000 ft archival Australian 1920-1935.
Films 7 million feet 35mm, 16mm, orig. negative with matching work print
Video 1 inch Betacam with viewing cassettes

Access

Catalogue on database.

Access to catalogue.

Access to materials.

Fees – Copyright

Fees for research for reuse and production purposes, research by archive staff, facilities and handling, Copyright fee.
Pricelist and conditions for use available.
Copyright holder is the institution.
All clients pay copyright fee (per second used) depending on end use.

MELBOURNE

_____ 022

PERFORMING ARTS MUSEUM, VICTORIAN ARTS CENTRE
100 St Kilda Road
MELBOURNE, VICTORIA, 3004
AUSTRALIA

Tel.: 61-3-684 8325
Fax.: 61-3-682 1507

Member of IASA.

Collections

Collections of Film, Video, Sound, Documentation.

Material relating to all forms of the performing arts with specialisation in Australian relevance.
Films 100 titles
Video 1500 titles
Sound 5000 titles

Access

Collection largely uncatalogued.

Access to materials.
Access on archives premises.

Fees – Copyright

Fees for research for reuse and production purposes.
Pricelist and conditions for use available.
Institution holds no copyright.

AUSTRALIA – MELBOURNE / 023

_____ 023
STATE LIBRARY OF VICTORIA
THE AUDIO-VISUAL SERVICES UNIT, STATE LIBRARY OF VICTORIA
328 Swanston Street
MELBOURNE, VICTORIA, 3000
AUSTRALIA

Tel.: 61-3-669 9977
Fax.: 61-3-663 1480
Telex: AA 38104

Member of IFLA.

Collections
Collections of Video, Sound.

Videos primarily support existing collection strengths in art, music and performing arts, Australian literature and humour with local emphasis. Recorded music collection aims for a general coverage of all periods, places styles and movements in western and non-western music, with particularly strong emphasis on Australian music. Non-music recordings include poetry, plays and oral history interviews.
Video 200 VHS videos
Sound 4000 sound recordings, 1000 cassette tapes, 200 CDs, 400 kits, 1200 reel tapes

Access
Catalogue on database.

Access to catalogue. Restricted access to some of the oral history tapes.

Access to materials: limited. Collections on closed access, available on request through enquiry desk.
Access on archives premises.

Fees – Copyright
Institution holds no copyright.

NEW SOUTH WALES

_____ 024
MACQUARIE UNIVERSITY LIBRARY
N.S.W. 2109
AUSTRALIA

Tel.: 61-2-805 7511
Fax.: 61-2-805 7568
Telex: AA 10716392
Electronic mail: gfleet@mars.mqcc.mq.oz.au

Collections
Collections of Film, Video, Sound.

Working collection of resources to serve teaching and research needs of all disciplines of the University. Housed in Library's audiovisual services department.
Films 689
Video 1745
Sound 22523

Access
Catalogue on database.

Access to catalogue.

Access to materials. Film & video replays to Macquarie University Library card holders only; interlibrary loan to other universities, public libraries & government departments.
Access on archives premises, by loan.

Fees – Copyright
Institution holds no copyright.
Most material is from normal commercial sources.
Note : This reply relates to the Audiovisual Collection of the Library. The only true "archives" are not part of the Library's collection.

PERTH

_____ 025
CURTIN UNIVERSITY OF TECHNOLOGY
Kent Street
G.P.O. U 1987
PERTH
WESTERN AUSTRALIA

Tel.: 61-9-351 7388
Fax.: 61-9-351 2424
Telex: AA 92983

Member of IFLA.

Collections
Collections of Film, Video, Sound, published materials.

A collection to support the teaching and research needs of the academic community. Business, science, technology, art, humanities, social sciences.
Films 556 (16mm)
Video 1809
Sound 2988

Access
Catalogue on database.

Access to catalogue Via AARNET in person.

Access to materials in person or via inter library loan.
Access by loan.

Fees – Copyright
Fees for Inter library loan only, standard ALIA charges.
Copyright holder is the institution.

026
THE LIBRARY BOARD OF WESTERN AUSTRALIA
THE STATE FILM ARCHIVES OF WESTERN AUSTRALIA
Alexander Library Building, Perth Cultural Centre
PERTH
WESTERN AUSTRALIA

Tel.: 61-9-427 3310
Fax.: 61-9-427 3256
Telex: WAINF 92231

Member of FIAF.

Collections
Collections of Film, Video, posters, cue sheets, brochures, press cuttings, etc.

Any film gauge relating to Western Australia or made by a West Australian. Includes private and amateur footage.
Films 2000 titles
Video 250 titles

Access
Catalogue on database.

Access to catalogue.

Access to materials: limited. Access is limited to items copied onto a video or duplicate format. Access on archives premises.

Fees – Copyright
Institution holds no copyright.
Access rights are determined by donor or physical constraints of the item. Only available on the premises.

SOUTH MELBOURNE

027
BROKEN HILL PROPRIETARY COMPANY LIMITED
BHP ARCHIVES
209 Normanby Road
SOUTH MELBOURNE, VICTORIA, 3205
AUSTRALIA

Tel.: 61-3-645 3011
Fax.: 61-3-645 3378

Collections
Collections of Film, Video, Sound, transcripts of oral history sound tapes.

Audiovisual material produced by the BHP Co Ltd, or about the operations of the company. Also some general films and videotapes about industries with which BHP is involved. Material covers mining, steelmaking, oil exploration and drilling, 1918-1988.

Films 700 items
Video 600 items
Sound 150 items

Access
Catalogue on database.

Access to catalogue after consultation with Archives staff.

No on-site playback equipment. Access/viewing by arrangement if condition of item allows.
Access by loan.

Fees – Copyright
Fees for reproduction costs plus service fee if required. Costs involved in viewing to be met by researcher privately.
Copyright holder is the institution.
In cases where copyright not held by BHP, researcher must discover and meet conditions for use and/or reproduction. No restrictions for viewing material.

SYDNEY

028
AUSTRALIAN BROADCASTING CORPORATION, RADIO ARCHIVES
700 Harris St. Ultimo
Box 9994
SYDNEY, NEW SOUTH WALES, 2001
AUSTRALIA

Tel.: 61-2-394 2513
Fax.: 61-2-394 2525

Member of IASA.

Collections
Collections of Sound, Scripts held by ABC Document Archives.

Broadcast programs of ABC Radio.
Sound 100 shelf metres

Access
Catalogue on database.

Access to catalogue: no.

Access to materials: limited.
Access by purchase.

Fees – Copyright
Fees for research for reuse and production purposes, research by archive staff, facilities and handling.
Pricelist and conditions for use available.
Copyright holder is the institution.

AUSTRALIA – SYDNEY / 029

029
AUSTRALIAN BROADCASTING CORPORATION, TELEVISION ARCHIVES
Pacific Highway
P.O. Box 9994
SYDNEY, NEW SOUTH WALES, 2001
AUSTRALIA

Tel.: 61-2-437 8000
Fax.: 61-2-950 4885

Member of IFTA.

Collections
Collections of Film, Video, stills, slides.

Australian Wildlife and Archival footage. Stock shots material – Australian Program and News/Public Affairs program.
Films Dating from 1956 – recent, about 35000000 feet
Video Dating from 1970 – recent, about 100000 videos

Access
Catalogue on database.

Acces to catalogue: limited. By staff only.

Access to materials: limited. Limitation for reasons of preservation, copyright restrictions or legal problems.
Access on archives premises, by purchase.

Fees – Copyright
Fees for research for reuse and production purposes, research by archive staff, facilities and handling.
Pricelist and conditions for use available.
Copyright holder is the institution.
Subject to copyright clearance the material is supplied on a strictly non-exclusive basis for use in one specified production only.

030
AUSTRALIAN RECORD INDUSTRY ASSOCIATION
NATIONAL FILM & SOUND ARCHIVE
9th Floor, 263 Clarence Street
P.O. Box 020, OVB, SYDNEY
SYDNEY
AUSTRALIA

Tel.: 61-2-267 7996
Fax.: 61-2-264 5589

Member of IASA.

Collections
Collections of Sound.

List of all sound recording titles available in Australia.
Sound 49000 titles

Access
Catalogue published.
Acces to catalogue: limited. By subscription only.
Access by purchase.

Fees – Copyright
Pricelist and conditions for use available.
Copyright holder is the institution.
This is a catalogue of titles available in Australia, available by subscription only.

031
STATE LIBRARY OF NEW SOUTH WALES
Macquarie Street
SYDNEY 2000
AUSTRALIA

Tel.: 61-2-230 1414
Fax.: 61-2-233 2003
Electronic mail: MLN000001

Member of IFLA.

Collections
Collections of Film, Video.

Collection strengths include Australiana, Management, the Environment and "how to" videos. The collection is selected in accordance with the Library's Collection Development Policy with its target audience being the "independent learner".
Films 13059 (films are not purchased now) – last purchased in 1985 – 16mm
Video VHS : 3505

Access
Catalogue on database.

Access to catalogue. On site access only at present.

Access to materials. On site and inter library loan.
Access by loan.

Fees – Copyright
Fees for Standard ILL charges apply.
Institution holds no copyright.

AUSTRIA

GRAZ

032
LANDESMUSEUM JOANNEUM, ABT. BILD- UND TONARCHIV
Sackstrasse 17
A – 8010 GRAZ
AUSTRIA

Tel.: 43-316-83 03 35, 43-316-82 53 17, 43-316-82 21 53

Member of IASA.

Collections

Collections of Film, Video, Sound, photographies.

Regional collection of AV-materials concerning historical, cultural, artistic, topografic facts.
Films 130
Video 1500
Sound 10000

Access

Catalogue on database.

Access to catalogue.

Access to materials. We don't give outside original materials, only copies.

Fees – Copyright

Fees for research by archive staff.
Pricelist and conditions for use available.
Copyright holder is the institution.

_____ 033
STUDIENBIBLIOTHEK DER PÄDAGOGISCHEN AKADEMIE DES BUNDES IN DER STEIERMARK UND DER BERUFSPÄDAGOGISCHEN AKADEMIE DES BUNDES IN GRAZ
STUDY LIBRARY OF THE COLLEGE OF EDUCATION IN STEIERMARK
Theodor-Körner-Strasse 38/E
A – 8020 GRAZ
AUSTRIA

Tel.: 43-316-67 23 60

Member of IASA.

Collections

Collections of Film, Video, Sound, related materials.

Films 1220
Video 840
Sound 1530

Access

Catalogue on database.

INNSBRUCK

_____ 034
UNIVERSITÄTSBIBLIOTHEK
Innrain 50
A – 6010 INNSBRUCK
AUSTRIA

Tel.: 43-512-507 2070
Fax.: 43-512-507 2307
Telex: 53 37 08

Member of IFLA.

Collections

Collections of Video, Sound.

No separate AV-collection, but integrated in the general library holdings. Additional material to books, languages, literature, tirolensies.
Video 3
Sound About 90 discs, about 10 tapes

Access

Catalogue on database.

Access to catalogue.

Access to materials: limited.
Access on archives premises, by purchase.

Fees – Copyright

No fees.
Institution holds no copyright.

LINZ

_____ 035
ARCHIV DER STADT LINZ
Hauptstrasse 1-5
LINZ
AUSTRIA

Tel.: 43-732-2393, 43-732-2961

Collections

Collections of Film, Video, photographs, slides.

Important persons, events, topographic motives of the town.
Films 760 (16mm)
Video 30 (own prod.), 150 VHS cassettes, 300 U-Matic cassettes (reprod.)

Access

Catalogue on cards.

Access to catalogue.

Access to materials.
Access on archives premises.

Fees – Copyright

Copyright holder is the institution.
Permission of direction of archives is needed for publication.

SALZBURG

_____ 036
INTERNATIONALE STIFTUNG MOZARTEUM
INTERNATIONAL FOUNDATION MOZARTEUM
MOZART TON- UND FILM-MUSEUM
Getreidegasse 14/II
A – 5020 SALZBURG

AUSTRIA

Tel.: 43-662-84 13 69
Fax.: 43-662-89 19 89

Member of IASA.

Collections

Collections of Video, Sound.

Collection of video- and sound-recordings of the works of Mozart.
Video 200 (in preparation)
Sound 3000 (in preparation)

Access

Catalogue on database.

Access to catalogue: no.

Access to materials.
Access on archives premises.

Fees – Copyright

No fees required.
Copyright holder is the institution.

037
LANDESSTELLE FÜR AUDIO-VISUELLE LEHRMITTEL
CENTER FOR AUDIO-VISUAL MEDIA FOR SCHOOLS
Mozartplatz 8
P.O. B. 527
A – 5010 SALZBURG
AUSTRIA

Tel.: 43-662-8042 2103
Fax.: 43-662-8042 2916
Telex: 63 30 28

Collections

Collections of Film, Video, Sound.

All titles are specially for introduction in schools in all subjects.
Films 1304 titles
Video 840 titles
Sound 3013 titles

Access

Catalogue on database.

Access to catalogue. Only for schools.

Access to materials. Only for schools.
Access by loan.

Fees – Copyright

No fees.
Copyright holder is the institution.
Only for use for schools, without copyright conditions.

VIENNA

038
ÖSTERREICHISCHE PHONOTHEK
Webgasse 2a/Annagasse 20
A – 1060 VIENNA/A-1010 VIENNA
AUSTRIA

Tel.: 43-222-597 36 69/43-222-512 14 43
Member of IASA.

Collections

Collections of Video, Sound.

40% music, mainly western classical music ; 60% spoken word ; historical recordings, literature, political events and documentation, recordings showing every day life.
Video 1500 VHS cassettes
Sound 15000 LP, 50000 78e discs, 12000 tapes, 8000 CDs

Access

Catalogue on database.

Access to catalogue.

Access to materials: limited, according to copyrights.
Access on archives premises.

Fees – Copyright

Fees for copying.
Pricelist and conditions for use available.
Institution holds no copyright.
Listening and watching on the premises nearly for all our holdings possible. Copying depends.
Copying of published recordings is possible (we have a treaty with the copyright organisations and are paying an annual fee).

039
ÖSTERREICHISCHER RUNDFUNK (ORF) – FERNSEHARCHIV
AUSTRIAN BROADCASTING CORPORATION – TELEVISION ARCHIVES
Würzburggasse 30
A – 1136 VIENNA
AUSTRIA

Tel.: 43-1-87878 2380
Fax.: 43-1-87878 2739
Telex: 133601 orfz a

Member of IFTA, IASA, ICA, IAMHIST.

Collections

Collections of Film, Video, Sound, photographs.

Television Archives of ORF, collections of TV-materials dating back until 1956 on the main technicals carriers used since then (16 and 35mm film, 2" tape, 1" tape, BVU and MII cassettes) ; since 1988 cataloguing by computerized data-base ; separated sound collection (with data-base).

Films About 300000 titles
Video About 200000 titles
Sound About 60000 titles

Access

Catalogue on database.

Acces to catalogue: limited. Very limited for external users depending on free capacities.

Access to materials: limited. Very limited for external users depending on free capacities and full clearance of copyright questions.
Access on archives premises, by purchase.

Fees – Copyright

Fees for research for reuse and production purposes, research by archive staff, facilities and handling.
Copyright held by institution or outside producers.

040
ÖSTERREICHISCHES FILMARCHIV
Rauhensteingasse 5
P.O.B. 253
A – 1015 WIEN (VIENNA)
AUSTRIA

Tel.: 43-222-512 99 36
Fax.: 43-222-513 53 30

Member of FIAF.

Collections

Collections of Film, posters, stills, production documents, books and periodicals.

Austriaca.
Films 105371 reels

Access

Catalogue on cards.

Acces to catalogue: limited. By staff only.

Access to materials: limited. By staff only.
Access on archives premises, by hire.

Fees – Copyright

Fees for research for reuse and production purposes, research by archive staff, facilities and handling.
Pricelist and conditions for use available.
The right holder's permission is needed on each use outside the archive.

041
PHONOGRAMMARCHIV DER ÖSTERREICHISCHEN AKADEMIE DER WISSENSCHAFTEN
PHONOGRAPHIC ARCHIVES OF THE AUSTRIAN ACADEMY OF SCIENCES
Liebiggasse 5
A – 1010 WIEN
AUSTRIA

Tel.: 43-1-40103 2734
Telex: 01-12628
Electronic mail: v4110dab at awiunillbit.net

Member of IASA.

Collections

Collections of Sound.

Collection of soundrecordings, mainly fieldrecordings, made for research purposes, in the areas of linguistics/dialectology, cultural anthropology, (ethno)musicology, oral history, wild life recordings.
Sound About 43000 items

Access

Catalogue on database.

Acces to catalogue: limited. For qualified academic research purposes.

Access to materials: limited. For qualified academic research purposes.
Access on archives premises.

Fees – Copyright

Fees depending on nature and size of request.
Copyright depending on contractual situation.

042
WIENER STADT- UND LANDESARCHIV
MUNICIPAL ARCHIVES OF VIENNA
Felderstrasse 1
A – 1082 WIEN
AUSTRIA

Tel.: 43-222-4000 84808
Fax.: 43-222-4000 7100
Telex: 114735

Member of ICA.

Collections

Collections of Film, Sound, photographs.

News casts, tapes from City meetings.
Films 373
Sound 197

Access

Catalogue on database.

Access to catalogue.

Access to materials.

Fees – Copyright

Fees for reproduction.
Copyright holder is the institution.

WIENER NEUSTADT

043

STADTARCHIV WIENER NEUSTADT
Petersgasse 2
A – 2700 WIENER NEUSTADT
AUSTRIA

Tel.: 43-2622-23531 341
Fax.: 43-2622-23531 498
Telex: 0/16/688

Collections
Collections of Film, Video, Sound.

Films and videos about the history of Wiener Neustadt. Sound-recordings from the municipal-sessions as like recordings from famous people of Wiener Neustadt.
Films 42
Video 6
Sound 87

Access
Catalogue on database.

Acces to catalogue: limited.

Access to materials: limited.

Fees – Copyright
Fees for research by archive staff.
Copyright holder is the institution.

BANGLADESH

DHAKA

044

BANGLADESH FILM ARCHIVE
Block No.3, Ganabhaban, Sher-e-Bangla Nagar
DHAKA 1207
BANGLADESH

Tel.: 880-2-814816, 880-2-323727

Member of FIAF.

Collections
Collections of Film, Video, scripts, stills, posters, books, magazines and other related materials.
Films 1650
Video 100

Access
Catalogue indexed on cards.

Access to catalogue.

Access to materials.
Access on archives premises.

Fees – Copyright
No fees.

BELGIUM

ANTWERP

045

ARCHIEF EN MUSEUM VOOR HET VLAAMSE CULTUURLEVEN
ARCHIVES AND MUSEUM OF FLEMISH CULTURE
Minderbroedersstraat 22
B – 2000 ANTWERPEN
BELGIUM

Tel.: 32-3-233.26.06
Fax.: 32-3-220.86.57
Telex: 33610 stbian b

Member of ICOM.

Collections
Collections of Film, Video, Sound.

Persons and institutions related to the cultural life of Flanders, Flemish (social) movement.
Films 80
Video 50
Sound 150

Access
Catalogue on database.

Access to catalogue.

Access to materials on demand.
Access on archives premises.

Fees – Copyright
Fees for research by archive staff, copies.
Copyright holder is the institution.

046

UNIVERSITEIT ANTWERPEN, AV CENTRE
UNIVERSITY OF ANTWERPEN, AV CENTRE
Universiteitsplein 1
B – 2610 ANTWERP (WILRIJK)
BELGIUM

Tel.: 32-3-820.22.22
Fax.: 32-3-820.22.49
Telex: 33646

Member of IFLA.

Collections
Collections of Video.

General academic collection of video-tapes mainly in the following domain : medecine, language and literature, biology, physics, theatre.
Video 3000 titles

Access

Catalogue on database.

Acces to catalogue: limited. Access via the UA-library database (X, 25 or dial up) ; password can be obtained by applying to the UIA-library (same address).

Access to materials: limited.
Access on archives premises, by loan.

Fees – Copyright

Fees for research for reuse and production purposes, facilities and handling.
Copyright clearance has to be sought by applying to the AV-Centre. Viewing of AV-Materials of which the university has not the copyright is limited to own premises ; other use of this material is not allowed.

047

UNIVERSITEIT ANTWERPEN, BIBLIOTHEEK UFSIA
UNIVERSITY OF ANTWERP, UFSIA LIBRARY
Prinsstraat 9
B – 2000 ANTWERPEN
BELGIUM

Tel.: 32-3-220.49.96
Fax.: 32-3-220.44.37

Member of IFLA.

Collections

Collections of Video.

Programmes from open television broadcast, relevant for a university public.
Video 1300 tapes

Access

Catalogue on database.

The tapes are described in the online catalogue ; they are retrievable by producer, title and subject.

Access to materials. Shelved in open access according to broad UDC classes.
Access by loan.

Fees – Copyright

No fees.
Institution holds no copyright.

BRUSSELS

048

CENTRE DU FILM SUR L'ART (C.F.A.)
rue Joseph II, 18
B – 1040 BRUXELLES
BELGIUM

Tel.: 32-2-217.28.92
Fax.: 32-2-217.28.92

Collections

Collections of Film, Video.

Films about art, artists and animation films.
Films 130 titles
Video 10 titles

Access

Catalogue published.

Access to catalogue.

Access to materials.
Access on archives premises, by hire.

049

CENTRE UNIVERSITAIRE DU FILM SCIENTIFIQUE DE L'UNIVERSITE LIBRE DE BRUXELLES
avenue F. Roosevelt 50
P.O.B. 165
B – 1050 BRUXELLES
BELGIUM

Tel.: 32-2-650.31.10
Fax.: 32-2-650.30.96
Telex: 23069 UNILIB B

Collections

Collections of Film, Video.

Chemistry, physics, astronomy, mathematics, biology, botanics, psychology, medicine, archeology, geography, geology, applied sciences.
Films 450
Video 90

Access

Catalogue published.

Access to catalogue.

Access to materials: limited. For teachers of the university.
Access by hire, by purchase.

Fees – Copyright

Fees for loan 200 BF per week per document.
Copyright holder is the institution.
Copyright only for films produced by the university.

050

CINEMATHEQUE ROYALE DE BELGIQUE/KONINKLIJK FILMARCHIEF
Palais des Beaux-Arts, rue Ravenstein 23
B – 1000 BRUXELLES
BELGIUM

Tel.: 32-2-507.83.70
Fax.: 32-2-513.12.72

Member of FIAF.

Collections

Collections of Film, Documentation centre : books, periodicals, press clippings.

Feature films, documentaries.
Films About 40000 titles

Access

Catalogue on database.

Access to catalogue: no.

Access to materials for researchers, students, teachers and professionals in cinema.
Access on archives premises.

Fees – Copyright

Fees for research by archive staff, facilities and handling, For possible reproduction.
Pricelist and conditions for use available.
Institution holds no copyright.
Access to films : only with written agreement of right holders. Access to documentation material : for consultation, without right for reproduction.

_____ 051

RADIO-TELEVISION BELGE DE LA COMMUNAUTE FRANÇAISE, RTBF
boulevard Auguste Reyers 52
B – 1040 BRUXELLES
BELGIUM

Tel.: 32-2-737.21.11
Fax.: 32-2-737.41.02
Telex: 21437

Member of IFTA.

Collections

Collections of Film, Video.

Any subjects.
Films About 300000 items
Video About 20000 items (videocassettes)

Access

Catalogue on cards.

Acces to catalogue: limited. By staff of the archive, by researchers of the institute, by external researchers, with authorization of the Program Director, with educational or cultural purpose.

Access to materials: limited. By staff of the archive, internal re-users, customers.
Access on archives premises, by purchase.

Fees – Copyright

Fees for research by archive staff, copyright.
Copyright holder is the institution.
Authorization of copyright holder is required for non RTBF material. RTBF owns the worldwide rights to all RTBF pictures only.

HASSELT

_____ 052

PROVINCIALE CENTRALE OPENBARE BIBLIOTHEEK
CENTRAL PUBLIC COUNTY LIBRARY
Martelarenlaan 17
B – 3500 HASSELT
BELGIUM

Tel.: 32-11-21.28.92
Fax.: 32-11-24.22.60

Collections

Collections of Video, Sound.

The collection of the P.C.O.B. consists largely, besides printed books, of LP's, CD's and cassettes, supplemented by videotapes. This collection is intended for general public use. LP's, CD's and MC's cover classical, jazz, pop and some ethnic music. A wide variety of language training cassettes is also available. Videotapes are mostly non-fiction, covering all popular topics presented on this medium.
Video 900 VHS videotapes
Sound 30000 LP's, 7000 CD's, 2500 cassettes

Access

Catalogue on cards.

Access to catalogue.

Access to materials.
Access on archives premises.

Fees – Copyright

Fees for facilities and handling, Hire of videotapes only.
Pricelist and conditions for use available.
Institution holds no copyright.

HEVERLEE

_____ 053

KANDIDATUURCENTRUM (TOND)
K.U.LEUVEN CAMPUS OF EXACT SCIENCES.
UNDERGRADUATE CENTRE
Celestijnenlaan 200 A
B – 3001 HEVERLEE
BELGIUM

Tel.: 32-16-20.06.56

Collections

Collections of Film, Video.

Didactic material complementary to lectures on mathematics, physics and chemistry for 1st year students in engineering.
Films 51
Video 170

Access

Access to catalogue.

Access to materials: limited.

Fees – Copyright

Pricelist and conditions for use available.
Institution holds no copyright.

LEUVEN

_____ 054
FACULTEITSBIBLIOTHEEK LETTEREN/WIJSBEGEERTE/ AGGREGATIEBIBLIOTHEEK
FACULTY LIBRARY OF LETTERS, LIBRARY OF TEACHER'S EDUCATION
Blijde-Inkomststraat 21
B – 3000 LEUVEN
BELGIUM

Tel.: 32-16-28.49.90
Fax.: 32-16-28.50.25

Collections

Collections of Video.

Mainly literature, history, art history.
Video 1500 videos

Access

Catalogue on database.

Access to catalogue.

Access to materials on the spot.

_____ 055
K.U.LEUVEN, DEPARTEMENT PEDAGOGIE
K.U.LEUVEN, DEPARTMENT EDUCATIONAL SCIENCES
Vesaliusstraat 2
B – 3000 LEUVEN
BELGIUM

Collections

Collections of Video.

Education (very large sense) : didactics ; research.
Video 200

Access

Catalogue on database.

Access to catalogue.

Access to materials: limited for academic staff.
Access on archives premises.

_____ 056
K.U.LEUVEN, RECHTSFACULTEIT
K.U.LEUVEN, FACULTY OF LAW
Tiensestraat 41
B – 3000 LEUVEN
BELGIUM

Collections

Collections of Video.

Criminology, sociology of law.
Video U-Matic : 150, VHS : 200

Access

Catalogue on database.

Access to catalogue.

Access to materials: limited for academic staff.
Access on archives premises.

BERMUDA

HAMILTON

_____ 057
BERMUDA GOVERNMENT ARCHIVES
30 Parliament Street
HAMILTON HM12
BERMUDA

Tel.: 1-809-297-7833
Fax.: 1-809-292-2349

Member of ICA.

Collections

Collections of Film, Video, Sound.

Bermuda Archives is a small local archives mandated to document the social history of the Island. The Archives collects material in all formats, including moving image and sound archives. The film and sound collection dating from as early as 1929 primarily documents tourism, the mainstay of the local economy.
Films 16mm : about 100 reels
Video VHS & Beta video cassettes : 50 but new accessions about 150 p.a.
Sound RPM records : about 50 (from 50's and 60's)

Fees – Copyright

The collection has remained uncatalogued and current policy is to prohibit public use until preservation measures may be taken to conserve the originals.

BOLIVIA

LA PAZ

058

CINEMATECA BOLIVIANA
Pichincha Esq. Indaburo s/n
P.O.B. 9933
LA PAZ
BOLIVIA

Tel.: 591-1-325346
Telex: 3288 CORMESA BV

Member of FIAF.

Collections
Collections of Film, Video, books, periodicals, posters, stills, press clippings.

Mostly historical. Also general subjects.
Films 6200 titles
Video 350 titles

Access
Catalogue on database.

Access to catalogue: no.

Access to materials: limited. Only for those materials whose physical state it permits.
Access on archives premises.

Fees – Copyright
Copyright holder is the institution.

BOTSWANA

GABORONE

059

BOTSWANA NATIONAL ARCHIVES AND RECORDS SERVICES
Government Enclave – Khama Crescent/State Drive
P.O. Box 239
GABORONE
BOTSWANA

Tel.: 267-3601000
Fax.: 267-313584
Telex: 2994BD

Member of ICA.

Collections
Collections of Film, Video, Sound.

National occasions, cultural activities, radio broadcasts, oral traditions, conference proceedings, traditional music.
Films 34 titles
Video 8 titles
Sound 75 cassette tapes, 1134 reel to reel tapes

Access
Catalogue indexed on cards.
Access to catalogue.

Access to materials. Collection still new therefore there is lack of training and experience on handling and preservation.
Access on archives premises.

Fees – Copyright
No fees.
Institution holds no copyright.
Creators and depositors set the conditions of access.

060

INFORMATION AND BROADCASTING DEPT OF BOTSWANA
Private Bag 0060
GABORONE
BOTSWANA

Tel.: 267-352861
Fax.: 267-357138
Telex: 2394 BD

Collections
Collections of Film, Video, Sound.

79 video tapes about Botswana recorded in Botswana on various subjects, 5000 recorded speeches, interviews of Presidents, Vice-Presidents, Ministers of Botswana, Heads of other states and other international/local programmes on sound tape reels, 27000 records (music) on different types of music, 12 films on Botswana on various subjects, e.g. Independence Day, Agriculture, Religious, Ceremonies, etc.
Films 12
Video 79
Sound 32000

Access
Catalogue on cards.
Acces to catalogue: limited.
Access to materials: limited.
Access by loan.

Fees – Copyright
No fees.
Conditions for use available.
Institution holds no copyright.
The Government is the copyrights holder. The Government Departments and Ministries can borrow any cassettes/films locally and these can also be recorded for them. Individuals/researchers can not borrow any material but may come to the Department for viewing/listening to any cassettes/tapes and these can be recorded/dubbed for them on provision of an empty cassette/tape if it is not confidential.

BRAZIL

RIO DE JANEIRO

_____ 061
ARQUIVO NACIONAL
DIVISAO DE DOCUMENTOS AUDIOVISUAIS E CARTOGRAFICOS (AUDIOVISUAL & CARTOGRAPHIC DIVISION)
rua Azeredo Coutinho, 77/6° andar
20230 RIO DE JANEIRO, RJ
BRAZIL

Tel.: 55-21-252.2766
Fax.: 55-21-232.8430
Telex: 21.34103

Member of ICA.

Collections
Collections of Film, Video, Sound, production papers, scripts and censorship documents.

80% of the collections of films and sound records are from official origin, generated mainly by the extinguished "Agencia Nacional" (press and advertising medium of the Brazilian governement, until 1979). The other 20% are output of the Arquivo Nacional, or unmatched material. The collections of magnetic tapes (audio & video) simply copies the contends of the major part of films and sound records.
Films 2400 titles (about 3000 reels)
Video 250 tapes (VHS and U-Matic)
Sound 15000 sound records

Access
Catalogue indexed on cards.

Access to catalogue.

Access to materials.
Access on archives premises.

Fees – Copyright
Fees for research for reuse and production purposes.
Pricelist and conditions for use available.
Copyright holder is the institution.
As the origin of our collection – governmental or from the Arquivo Nacional itself -, there aren't restrictions for copyright. We only demand the user to mention the Arquivo Nacional to each utilisation of the reproduced record.

_____ 062
CINEMATECA DO MUSEU DE ARTE MODERNA
av. Infante D. Henrique 85
Caixa Postal 44
20000 RIO DE JANEIRO
BRAZIL

Tel.: 55-21-210.2188

Member of FIAF.

Collections
Collections of Film, Video, photos, posters, apparatus, books, scripts, censorship documents, periodicals.

All categories.
Films about 15000 titles
Video about 300 titles

Access
Catalogue indexed on cards.

Access to catalogue.

Access to materials for research approved by the Cinemateca.
Access on archives premises.

Fees – Copyright
Fees for research for reuse and production purposes.
Institution holds no copyright.
Copyright with right holders.

_____ 063
TV GLOBO – DOCUMENTATION CENTER
rua Pacheco Leao, 204 J. Botanico
22460 RIO DE JANEIRO, RJ
BRAZIL

Tel.: 55-21-259.5795
Fax.: 55-21-274.8088

Member of IFTA.

Collections
Collections of Film, Video, scripts, stills, books, magazines, clippings, newspapers.

News.
Films 29500
Video 42000

Access
Catalogue on database.

Acces to catalogue: limited, by staff only.

Access to materials: limited.
Access on archives premises.

Fees – Copyright
Fees for research for reuse and production purposes.
Pricelist and conditions for use available.
Copyright holder is the institution.

SAO PAULO

_____ 064
CINEMATECA BRASILEIRA
Parque Conceiçao s/n
Caixa Postal 12900
CEP 04092 SAO PAULO, s.p.
BRAZIL

Tel.: 55-11-577.4666
Fax.: 55-11-577.7433
Telex: 11-53.714 CNTB-BR

Member of FIAF.

Collections

Collections of Film, Video, photos, posters, scripts, books, production papers, catalogues, periodicals.

Mostly Brazilian cinema since the beginning of the century (about 80% of the collection).
Films about 150000 reels, about 50000 titles
Video 6500 reels

Access

Catalogue on database.

Access to catalogue.

Access to materials: limited due to legal problems and physical condition.
Access on archives premises, by loan.

Fees – Copyright

Fees for research for reuse and production purposes, facilities and handling, for copyright.
Pricelist and conditions for use available.
The institution has the copyright for some materials. For the major part agreement of right holder necessary for usage and production purposes.

_____ 065
MUSEU DA IMAGEM E DO SOM
avenida Europa 158
01449 SAO PAUL, SP
BRAZIL

Tel.: 55-11-280.0896, 55-11-881.4417

Collections

Collections of Film, Video, Sound, scripts, photographs, slides, appparatusses, related library.

Themes on Brazilian culture and art. Regional culture. Popular and contemporary music. Cinema. Photography. Graphic arts ; Brazilian studies ; Arts ; Cultural movements.
Films 500 titles (10000 titles to be indexed)
Video 1200 titles
Sound 2000 titles

Access

Catalogue on database.

Access to catalogue.

Access to materials: limited for preservation reasons.
Access on archives premises, by loan.

Fees – Copyright

Consultation of archive on the spot. Limited loan for legal reasons. Only for educational, cultural and non-commercial purposes.

BRUNEI

BRUNEI

_____ 066
BRUNEI NATIONAL ARCHIVES
Brunei Museums, Ministry of Culture Youth & Sports
BRUNEI DARUSSALAM
BRUNEI DARUSSALAM

Tel.: 637-2-244545/6
Fax.: 44047
Telex: BRUART 2655

Member of ICA.

Collections

Collections of Film, Video, Sound.

Films 1299 16mm
Video 321
Sound 239

Access

Catalogue indexed on cards.

Access to catalogue.

Access to materials.
Access on archives premises.

Fees – Copyright

Fees for facilities and handling.
Pricelist and conditions for use available.

BULGARIA

SOFIA

_____ 067
BULGARSKA NACIONALNA FILMOTEKA
BULGARIAN NATIONAL FILM ARCHIVE
Gourko 36
1000 SOFIA
BULGARIA

Tel.: 359-2-876004

Member of FIAF.

Collections

Collections of Film, production-papers, scripts, censorship documents, stills, posters, books, magazines, post-production scripts.

Bulgarian and foreign documentaries, newsreels, non-fictions, feature-films, animated films.
Films 3600 feature films, 7600 non-fiction films

Access

Catalogue indexed on cards.

Acces to catalogue: limited. Access to catalogues on cards and catalogues indexed on cards is free on the archive premises.

Access to materials: limited. No access to orig. neg. for preservation reasons. Limited facilities. Access on archives premises, by loan, by hire, by purchase.

_____ 068
BULGARSKA TELEVIZIJA
BULGARIAN TELEVISION
TELEVISION FOND, BULGARIAN TELEVISION
29 San Stephano str.
1504 SOFIA
BULGARIA

Tel.: 359-2-443 421
Fax.: 359-2-871 871

Member of IFTA.

Collections

Collections of Film, Video, Sound, scripts, production papers, stills.

Fiction, serials, documentaries, plays, educational programmes, shows, sports, cultural programmes, animation, shows and programmes for children, newsreels, feature-films, musical programmes, etc.
Films 50000 film programmes and films, 150000 film sujets
Video 12000 video programmes, 30000 video sujets, 14000 video cassettes
Sound 30000 sound recordings

Access

Catalogue on database.

Access to catalogue.

Access to materials: limited according to Archival Legislation and Copyright Legislation.
Access on archives premises, by loan, by hire.

Fees – Copyright

Fees for research for reuse and production purposes, research by archive staff, with the permission of the chief of the company, access to copies of programmes of archival value.
Copyright holder is the institution.

Consultations on the content of the archives are free for everyone at any time – they are part of the National Archives. In case of purchase the permission of the Archive is required if the film is not a property of the Bulgarian Television.

_____ 069
BULGARSKO RADIO
BULGARIAN RADIO
GOLDEN FOND, BULGARIAN RADIO
No 4 Dragan Tzankov blv.
1000 SOFIA
BULGARIA

Tel.: 359-2-8541
Fax.: 359-2-665103
Telex: 22557 and 22305

Collections

Collections of Sound, speach recordings transferred on paper.

Documentary (authentic) and art sound recordings conected with all aspects of human life.
Sound 14608 magnetic tapes, 576 plates, 605 matrixes

Access

Catalogue on database.

Access to catalogue.

Access to materials: limited in case of poor physical condition and lack of copies.
Access on archives premises.

Fees – Copyright

Fees for research for reuse and production purposes, production of radio broadcasts, TV programmes, cinema films.
Pricelist and conditions for use available.
Copyright holder is the institution.
Access according to Archival and Copyright Legislation and the regulations issued by Bulgarian Radio.

_____ 070
INSTITUT PO PROBLEMITE NA IZKUSTVOZNANIETO PRI BAN
INSTITUTE ON THE PROBLEMS OF ART AT THE BULGARIAN ACADEMY OF SCIENCE, MUSICAL ARCHIVE
No 11 Evlogi Georgiev str.
1504 SOFIA
BULGARIA

Tel.: 359-2-44 19 01

Collections

Collections of Film, Video, Sound, text and tune desiphers.

Bulgarian folk songs, orchestra music, dances and traditional folklore music, folklore costumes all recorded "in life" and stage performances.
Films 716 films, 10, 20, 25 minutes length
Video 71 cassettes, 60 minutes length
Sound 4153 magnetic tapes, 560 plates (text), 214000 songs and melodies

Access

Catalogue indexed on cards.

Acces to catalogue: limited, depends on physical conditions and degree of processing.

Access on archives premises.

Fees – Copyright

Fees for research for reuse and production purposes, research by archive staff.
Pricelist and conditions for use available.
Copyright holder is the institution.
Access according to the copyright legislation and Archival legislation.

___

071

NARODNA BIBLIOTEKA SV.SV. KIRIL I METODIJ
NATIONAL LIBRARY ST.ST. CYRIL AND METHODIUS, MUSIC EDITIONS AND SOUND RECORDINGS
11 General Toulbuhin blv.
1504 SOFIA
BULGARIA

Tel.: 359-2-88 28 11
Telex: 22432

Collections

Collections of Sound.

The national production of discs, foreign discs mainly of classic music. Part of the collection is ensured on cassettes.
Sound 26152 discs, 860 cassettes, 420 tapes (data from 1990)

Access

Catalogue indexed on cards.

Access to catalogue.

Access to materials.

Fees – Copyright

Fees for research for reuse and production purposes, services to the public.
Copyright holder is the institution.
Access according to legislation and regulations issued by the National Library St.St. Cyril and Methodius.

BURKINA FASO

OUAGADOUGOU

___

072

SECRETARIAT GENERAL PERMANENT DU FESTIVAL PANAFRICAIN DU CINEMA ET DE LA TV DE OUAGADOUGOU
CINEMATHEQUE AFRICAINE
P.O. Box 01 BP 2505
OUAGADOUGOU 01
BURKINA FASO

Tel.: 226-35-30 75 38
Fax.: 226-35-31 25 09
Telex: 5255 BF

Collections

Collections of Film, Video, Sound, old projection apparatus. Database on African cinema (production, distribution, filmmakers, actors, photos, posters).

African feature film and short films of all genre (fiction, documentaries, newsreels).
Films 500 titles
Video 100 cassettes

Access

Catalogue on database.

Acces to catalogue: limited.

Access to materials.
Access on archives premises.

Fees – Copyright

No fees.
Institution holds no copyright.
Agreement of right holders is necessary for lending films to cultural manifestations around the world.

CANADA

CALGARY

___

073

UNIVERSITY OF CALGARY, COM/MEDIA FILM LIBRARY
2500 University Drive Nw
CALGARY, ALBERTA
CANADA

Tel.: 1-403-220-3721
Fax.: 1-403-282-4497

Member of IAMHIST.

Collections

Collections of Film, Video, slidesets.
University-level, all subjects.
Films 3000
Video 3200

Access
Catalogue on database.
Access to catalogue by DOBIS.
Access by loan.

Fees – Copyright
Fees for facilities and handling.
Institution holds no copyright.

EDMONTON

_____ 074
PROVINCIAL ARCHIVES OF ALBERTA
12845 – 102 avenue
EDMONTON, ALBERTA
CANADA

Tel.: 1-403-427-1750
Fax.: 1-403-454-6629
Member of IFTA.

Collections
Collections of Film, Video, Sound.

Material relating to history and development of Alberta-strengths of collection, films produced by and for the government of Alberta, broadcast archives relating to activities of Alberta radio/television stations.
Films 2800 cans
Video 500 reels
Sound 7200 reels

Access
Catalogue on cards.
Access to catalogue.
Access to materials.
Access on archives premises.

Fees – Copyright
No fees.
There are no restrictions on access to holdings. Depending on the copyright status of a particular collection on item, there may be restrictions on duplication.

HALIFAX

_____ 075
CANADIAN BROADCASTING CORPORATION
CBHT BROADCAST MATERIAL ARCHIVES
5600 Sackville St., Box 3000
HALIFAX, NS B3J 3E9
CANADA

Tel.: 1-902-420-4160
Fax.: 1-902-420-4010
Member of IFTA.

Collections
Collections of Film, Video, Sound, related materials.
Films 10000 cans
Video 10000 videotapes

Access
Catalogue on database.
Acces to catalogue: limited.
Access to materials: limited. Stock shot sales, and public viewing on per occasion basis.
Access on archives premises, by purchase.

Fees – Copyright
Fees for research for reuse and production purposes, research by archive staff, facilities and handling.
Pricelist and conditions for use available.
Copyright holder is the institution.
Access according to journalistic & sales policies and Canadian copyright legislation.

_____ 076
PUBLIC ARCHIVES OF NOVA SCOTIA, FILM AND SOUND DIVISION
6016 University avenue
HALIFAX, NOVA SCOTIA B3H 1W4
CANADA

Tel.: 1-902-424-6070, 1-902-424-6077
Fax.: 1-902-424-0516
Member of IASA.

Collections
Collections of Film, Video, Sound, textual support documentation.

Sound and moving image material made by, about and for Nova Scotians which has enduring historical, sociological, cultural, technological and artistic value.
Films 4622 items
Video 1335 items
Sound 10971 items

Access
Catalogue on database.
Acces to catalogue: limited.
Access to materials depends upon donor restrictions.
Access on archives premises.

Fees – Copyright
Fees for duplication costs, shipping & handling.
Institution holds no copyright.
Donor agreements must be consulted for details. However, most material is open for consultation on the archives premises.

MONCTON

_____ 077

UNIVERSITE DE MONCTON
BIBLIOTHEQUE CHAMPLAIN
Centre universitaire de Moncton
MONCTON, N.-B. E1A 3E9
CANADA

Tel.: 1-506-858-4012
Fax.: 1-506-858-4086

Member of IFLA.

Collections

Collections of Video, Sound.

Video : mostly a French language course ; also some nursing and education. Sound : classical music.
Video 160 videotapes
Sound 1500 titles

Access

Catalogue on database.

Acces to catalogue: limited. Being an on-line catalogue access is limited to the library's terminals, and to persons who have access to a personal computer equipped with a modem.

Access to materials: limited to faculty students, alumni and friends of the library, students who are registered in a post-secondary institution.
Access on archives premises, by loan.

Fees – Copyright

Fees for research by archive staff, ILL at cost.
Pricelist and conditions for use available.
Institution holds no copyright.

MONTREAL

_____ 078

BIBLIOTHEQUE MUNICIPALE DE MONTREAL, PHONOTHEQUE ET CINEMATHEQUE
880 rue Roy Est
MONTREAL, QC H2L 1E6
CANADA

Tel.: 1-514-872-3680
Fax.: 1-514-872-7735
Electronic mail: Envoy PEB-QMBM

Member of IFLA.

Collections

Collections of Film, Video, Sound, slides.

Audio collection consists of vinyl discs, audiocassettes and CD's mostly on jazz and classical music. Videocollection on 3/4" is reserved for screening on the premises.

Films 14111 (film and video)
Sound discs (20475), CD's (2000), audiocassettes (93579)

Access

Catalogue published, on cards.

Access to catalogue.

Access to materials.
Access on archives premises, by loan.

Fees – Copyright

Fees for rent of apparatus and 16mm films.
Pricelist and conditions for use available.
Institution holds no copyright.

_____ 079

BIBLIOTHEQUE NATIONALE DU QUEBEC, SECTEUR DES COLLECTIONS SPECIALES, SECTION MUSIQUE
125 rue Sherbrooke Ouest
MONTREAL, QUEBEC H2X 1X4
CANADA

Tel.: 1-514-873-1100
Fax.: 1-514-873-4310

Collections

Collections of Sound.

Sound about 80000 discs

Access

Access to catalogue: no. Catalogue still to be done.

Access to materials: no. Due to lack of equipment.
Access on archives premises.

_____ 080

CINEMATHEQUE QUEBECOISE
335 boulevard de Maisonneuve est
MONTREAL, QUEBEC H2X 1K1
CANADA

Tel.: 1-514-842-9763
Fax.: 1-514-842-1816

Member of FIAF.

Collections

Collections of Film, Video, Sound, photos, posters, scripts, clippings, apparatus, costumes, various documents.

Collection consists mainly of films from Quebec and Canada and also includes a special department for animation films (with more than 4000 titles on international production) and a French fond.
Films 25000 titles
Video 2000 titles
Sound undetermined number of reels

Access

Catalogue on database.

Acces to catalogue: limited. Depends on agreement by curator for exceptional cases of research.

Access to materials: limited. Depends on purpose of research.

Access on archives premises.

Fees – Copyright

Fees for research for reuse and production purposes, projection.
Pricelist and conditions for use available.
Institution holds no copyright.
Copyright must be obtained by users from right holders.

081

CONCORDIA UNIVERSITY, CENTRE FOR BROADCASTING STUDIES

1455 de Maisonneuve blvd. west
MONTREAL, QUEBEC H3G 1M8
CANADA

Tel.: 1-514-848-7719

Member of IFTA.

Collections

Collections of Sound, Mainly paper records of Canadian broadcasting, from 1927 to the present. Majority are related to radio drama ; but some TV and 16 complete personal collections.

Some sound records on tape and on cassette. Includes 15000 radio-drama scripts ; access by the two Radio Drama Bibliographies and Complete finding aids. NB : our CBC collection is the official repository of all CBC radio drama ongoing.
Sound 350 programs

Access

Catalogue on database.

Access to catalogue.

Access to materials for all bonafide scholars, with permission.
Access on archives premises, by loan.

Fees – Copyright

Fees for research by archive staff, facilities and handling, reproduction.
Pricelist and conditions for use available.
Institution holds no copyright.
Programs are copyright the CBC ; script-texts copyrights owned by original authors. No copyright permission necessary for access, consultation or fair-dealing quotation. Copyright-owners' permission necessary for quotation of large passages, in publication ; also necessary for reproduction or re-boadcast.

OTTAWA

082

NATIONAL ARCHIVES OF CANADA, AUDIO-VISUAL AND CARTOGRAPHIC ARCHIVES

395 Wellington Street
OTTAWA, ONTARIO K1A ON3
CANADA

Tel.: 1-613-995-1311
Fax.: 1-613-995-6575

Member of FIAF, IFTA, IASA, ICA, IFLA, IAMHIST.

Collections

Collections of Film, Video, Sound, stills, posters, books, periodicals, vertical files – all related to moving image and sound recordings.

The collection consists of nationally significant a-v records produced by private as well as public sector. It comprises a wide variety of subjects, mainly related to Canada.
Films 60000 hours
Video 110000 hours
Sound 100000 hours

Access

Catalogue on database.

Access to catalogue.

Access to materials.
Access on archives premises.

Fees – Copyright

Fees for copying for re-use and production purposes.
Pricelist and conditions for use available.
Institution holds no copyright.
Consultation : majority of holdings is available for research on archives' premises. Copying : records that are under copyright or donor/depositor restrictions can be copied for a client only when he/she obtains the copyright/restriction clearance.

083

NATIONAL LIBRARY OF CANADA – RECORDED SOUND COLLECTION, MUSIC DIVISION

395 Wellington Street
OTTAWA, ONTARIO K1A ON4
CANADA

Tel.: 1-613-996-3377
Fax.: 1-613-996-4424
Telex: 053-4311
Electronic mail: OONL.MUS Envoy 100

Member of IASA, IFLA.

Collections

Collections of Video, Sound.

Recordings of mostly Canadian interest from ca.1890 to the present, including cylinders, 78-, 45- and 33 1/3 rpm. discs, cassettes, 8-track cartridges, compact discs and piano rolls. Most are commercial releases, including material received on legal deposit since its extension to sound recordings in 1969, but some are private recordings and masters. There are also some early 5" Berliner discs.
Video 143 items
Sound 121500 items

Access

Catalogue on database.

Access to catalogue.

Access to materials: limited. Dependant on condition of materials and donor agreements.
Access on archives premises.

Fees – Copyright

No fees at present.
Institution holds no copyright.
Commercial recordings are available for on-site consultation (when conditions of materials permit). Copyright permissions and/or donor agreements required for access to some non-commercial recordings, and for dubbing material to which copyright restrictions apply.

084

UNIVERSITY OF OTTAWA
65 University
OTTAWA, ONTARIO K1N 9A5
CANADA

Tel.: 1-613-564-6893
Fax.: 1-613-564-9886
Telex: 0533338
Electronic mail: OOU.ILL.OOU

Collections

Collections of Film, Video, Sound, slides.

This is a teaching and research collection, not an archival collection in the strict sense.
Films 16mm = 1442
Video 2011
Sound 9421 (audiocassettes, records)

Access

Catalogue on database.

Access to catalogue.

Access to materials.
Access on archives premises, by loan.

Fees – Copyright

Institution holds no copyright.
Loans on a reciprocal basis from institution to institution.

REGINA

085

PROVINCIAL LIBRARY
1352 Winnipeg Street
REGINA, SASKATCHEWAN S4P 3V7
CANADA

Tel.: 1-306-787-2980
Fax.: 1-306-787-8866
Electronic mail: ILL.SRP

Member of IFLA.

Collections

Collections of Video, Sound.

Library Science.
Video 150 titles
Sound 210 titles

Access

Catalogue on database.

Access to catalogue through the UTLAS database.

Access to materials through interlibrary loan.
Access by loan.

Fees – Copyright

Institution holds no copyright.
May not be copied.

SCARBOROUGH

086

THE CITY OF SCARBOROUGH PUBLIC LIBRARY BOARD
1076 Ellesmere Road
SCARBOROUGH, ONTARIO M1P 4P4
CANADA

Tel.: 1-416-396-8800
Fax.: 1-416-396-8808
Electronic mail: ENVOY : SPLB.ADMIN

Member of IFLA.

Collections

Collections of Video, Sound.

Video-features, instructional, documentaries, travel, curriculum support, multilingual. Sound-popular, multilingual, international, classics, instructional, fiction.
Video 6356 items
Sound 124286 items

Access
Catalogue on database.

Acces to catalogue: limited. Access to sound material in a database limited to those that are catalogued.

Access to materials.
Access by loan.

Fees – Copyright
Institution holds no copyright.

STE-FOY

_____ **087**
ARCHIVES NATIONALES DU QUEBEC, ARCHIVES AUDIOVISUELLES
1210 avenue du Séminaire
STE-FOY, QC G1V 4N1
CANADA

Tel.: 1-418-643-1904
Fax.: 1-418-646-0868

Member of ICA.

Collections
Collections of Film, Video, Sound, production papers, photos.

Documentaries on Quebec : history, geography, tourism, agriculture, sports, transport, education, music. Documentaries on travel, arts, technics. Private and governmental films.
Films 4500 items
Video 1200 items
Sound 15000 hours

Access
Catalogue on database.

Access to catalogue.

Access to materials.
Access on archives premises, by purchase.

Fees – Copyright
Fees for research for reuse and production purposes.
Copyright holder is the institution.
The documents can be consulted free of charge. For certain documents for the sales of copies agreement of copyright holder is necessary.

TORONTO

_____ **088**
ARCHIVES OF ONTARIO, SOUND AND MOVING IMAGE PORTFOLIO
77 Grenville Street
TORONTO, ONTARIO M7A 2R9
CANADA

Tel.: 1-416-327-1600
Fax.: 1-416-324-3600

Collections
Collections of Film, Video, Sound, accompanying textual documentation may include production files, scripts, transcripts, etc.

The acquisition mandate fo the SMI Portfolio at the Archives of Ontario is to acquire film, video and sound documents significant to the history of the province of Ontario. As the official repository for the Ontario government, the Portfolio's holdings include Ministry productions, Royal Commission proceedings and Hansard. In addition to public documents, we also acquire private material some of which includes home movies and oral history projects.
Films about 4000 cans
Video about 1900 units
Sound about 7830 units

Access
Catalogue on cards.

Access to catalogue: This card catalogue is both title and subject.

Access to materials: limited. Material is made available to researchers on the premises depending upon individual donor restrictions.
Access on archives premises.

Fees – Copyright
Fees: Researchers are required to supply blank tapes for sound and video copies made on the Archives' premises. Researchers are also required to assume all costs incurred for copies of film and for film to video transfers which are made off-site. The Archives of Ontario does not hold the copyright for all the sound and moving image material in its holdings. Each request for copies is considered on an individual basis.

_____ **089**
JACK CHISHOLM FILM PRODUCTIONS LTD
CHISHOLM STOCKFOOTAGE LIBRARY
99 Atlantic Ave. #301
TORONTO, ONTARIO M6K 3J8
CANADA

Tel.: 1-416-588-5200
Fax.: 1-416-588-5324

Member of IFTA.

Collections
Collections of Film, Video.

Archival world events from 1896 to present. Extensive newsreel collection encompassing major world events and personalities. Many subjects : art, entertainment, industry, sports, scenics, personalities, social issues, education, communication, environment, medicine and health, fads and stunts, recreation, wildlife, transportation, across Canada scenics, major events (world wide).
Films 12 million feet 16/35mm
Video 9000 hours

Access

Catalogue on database.

Access to catalogue: no. Librarian access only.

Access to materials: limited. Librarian access only.
Access on archives premises, by purchase.

Fees – Copyright

Fees for research for reuse and production purposes, research by archive staff, facilities and handling, Footage supplied anywhere in world upon prepayment of research unless other arrangement are made.
Pricelist and conditions for use available.
Copyright holder is the institution.
Some exceptions for collections being held for marketing purposes. In these cases rights holders permission required.

_____ 090
METROPOLITAN TORONTO REFERENCE LIBRARY
789 Yonge St.
TORONTO, ONTARIO
CANADA

Tel.: 1-416-393-7107
Fax.: 1-416-393-7229

Member of IFLA.

Collections

Collections of Film, Video, Sound.

Films & videos produced by the Non Theatrical Industry in all subject areas, purchased to support and enhance the subject collections ; special audio-visual language learning collection with emphasis on English-as-a-second-language.
Films 8000
Video 3000
Sound 20000 LPs, 4000 CDs

Access

Catalogue on database.

Access to catalogue: At present, staff only on film & video databases ; sound recordings now on line for public & staff as well as audio-visual materials for language learning.

Access to materials.
Access on archives premises.

Fees – Copyright

Institution holds no copyright.
We purchase films & videos with public performance rights in order that they be used in public community settings.

_____ 091
TORONTO PUBLIC LIBRARY, FILM DEPARTMENT
40 Orchard View Blvd
TORONTO, ONTARIO
CANADA

Tel.: 1-416-393-7600
Fax.: 1-416-393-7782

Collections

Collections of Film, Video.

Animation, media literacy, health issues, business, children's, documentaries.
Films 2500, access to 25000
Video 300

Access

Catalogue on database.

Access to catalogue.

Access to materials.
Access by loan.

Fees – Copyright

Pricelist and conditions for use available.
Institution holds no copyright.
Films and video tapes may not be televised, edited or copied without written permission of the distributor or producer nor may they be shown at events where admission is charged.

_____ 092
UNIVERSITY OF TORONTO ARCHIVES
120 St. George Street
TORONTO, ONTARIO M5S 1A5
CANADA

Tel.: 1-416-978-5342
Fax.: 1-416-978-1667

Member of ICA.

Collections

Collections of Film, Video, Sound, other material from creators including records in the following forms : textual, graphic, architectural drawings, maps.

Material related to or created by the University of Toronto and individuals/organizations associated with the University. Includes films & videos (eg., unedited footage, home movies, instructionals), and audio tapes consisting mainly of Oral History interviews. Subjects include education, student activities, ceremonies, faculty, administration, and academic divisions and activities.

Films about 385 items (reels)
Video about 100 items (reels or cassettes)
Sound about 200 titles (oral history interviews)

Access

Catalogue on database.

Access to catalogue.

Access to materials: limited. Access to some films limited for conservation reasons. Some material (all media) restricted or closed for set time periods, to protect privacy of individuals.
Access on archives premises, by purchase.

Fees – Copyright

Fees for research for reuse and production purposes, reproduction.
The University owns copyright of material it created as well as some works it commissioned. The Archives may allow reproduction and broadcasting of these items. For material whose copyright is unknown or held by another body, the Archives require users to attempt to obtain permission before the Archives will reproduce material.

VICTORIA

_____ 093

BRITISH COLUMBIA ARCHIVES AND RECORDS SERVICE, SOUND AND MOVING IMAGE UNIT
655 Belleville Street
VICTORIA, B.C. V8V 1X4
CANADA

Tel.: 1-604-387-2963
Fax.: 1-604-387-2072

Member of IASA.

Collections

Collections of Film, Video, Sound, manuscript collections.

Video/films : primarily commercial, institutional and amateur films shot in British Columbia. Also television documentaries, drama, public affairs, newsclips. Sound recording oral history, radio broadcasts, miscellaneous actualities and music pertaining to British Columbia.
Films about 1950 titles (about 5000 cans)
Video about 200 titles
Sound about 17000 recordings

Access

Catalogue on database.

Access to catalogue: Access through Archives' Reference Room. Limited research by staff in response to telephone and written requests.

Access to materials: limited. Some copyright and restrictions.
Access on archives premises.

Fees – Copyright

Fees for copying equivalent to recovery costs.
Pricelist and conditions for use available.
Institution holds no copyright.
B.C. Archives holds many items which are under copyright and permission must be obtained from copyright holders before copies are provided.

_____ 094

UNIVERSITY OF VICTORIA ARCHIVES
McPherson Library, University of Victoria
P.O. Box 1800
VICTORIA, B.C. V8W 3H5
CANADA

Tel.: 1-604-721-8258
Fax.: 1-604-721-8215
Electronic mail: LARCHIVE @UVVM.CA

Member of IFLA.

Collections

Collections of Film, Video, Sound.

Relating to University of Victoria, B.C. : oral history interviews, some B.C. Material-interviews, films. Relating to post secondary education. Relating to Canadian Military.
Films 100 reels
Video 100
Sound 500 tapes

Access

Catalogue on database.

Access to catalogue: In Procite – not yet online.

Access to materials.
Access on archives premises, by purchase.

Fees – Copyright

Fees for research for reuse and production purposes.
Copyright holder is the institution.
Access by permission of copyright holder, mostly for research use only.

WINNIPEG

_____ 095

PROVINCIAL ARCHIVES OF MANITOBA
200 Vaughan Street
WINNIPEG, MANITOBA R3C 1T5
CANADA

Tel.: 1-204-945-3971
Fax.: 1-204-948-2008

Member of IASA, ICA.

Collections

Collections of Film, Video, Sound.

Films, videotapes, and sound recordings pertaining to the history of the Province of Manitoba acquired from private and Government sectors. Major themes include : ethnocultural history, broadcasting, industry and commerce, agriculture, aboriginal peoples, labour history.
Films about 5000 items (reels)
Video about 1000 items (cassettes and reels)
Sound about 4000 items (cassettes and reels)

Access

The catalogue is an unpublished list of items and fonds descriptions for use in the institution. Copies of descriptions and lists are available to clients.

Access to materials: As per restrictions (if any) stated in donor agreements or in the Freedom of Information Act.
Access on archives premises.

Fees – Copyright

Cost recovery fees are levied for copies of the catalogue entries. Audio and video reproductions are made free of charge if the client supplies blank tapes. Film to tape transfers are made at client's expense.
Access is provided in accordance with individual donor agreements, or Government Records Authority Schedules. Clients are responsible for obtaining copyrights where applicable. Access is normally provided on the premises. In special circumstances (requests from broadcast media) research copies are loaned.

CHILE

SANTIAGO

096
BIBLIOTECA NACIONAL DE CHILE
SECCION MUSICA Y MEDIOS MULTIPLES
Avenida Libertador Bernardo O'Higgins
Clasificador 1400
651 SANTIAGO
CHILE

Fax.: 56-2-381975

Member of IFLA.

Collections

Collections of Video, Sound
Sound collection includes the technics of engraving, notes about composers, collection of concert programmes, auditions, photographs, posters, books, magazines.

Collection includes the Archive of the Word. Original voices of authors, mostly literature, writers. Classic music. Chilean folklore. Latinamerican music. History of music and instruments.
Films 281
Video 35
Sound cassettes 1150, discs 290

Access

Catalogue on database.

Access to catalogue.

Access to materials: limited. Not authorized is rerecording of registered sound. As a general rule photocopying of scores for reasons of conservation is not permitted.
Access on archives premises.

097
CINETECA DE LA UNIVERSIDAD DE CHILE
Pedro de Valdivia 2454
SANTIAGO
CHILE

Tel.: 56-2-496895
Fax.: 56-2-2225116

Collections

Collections of Film, posters, clippings, photographs, specialised library.

Collection consists of 162 films 16mm, 108 films 35mm, 2 films 9mm.
Films 272

Access

Catalogue published.

Acces to catalogue: limited. Only at request of filmarchives.

Access to materials.

Fees – Copyright

Pricelist and conditions for use available.
Copyright holder is the institution.
Exchange between archives. Some copies on video for public use. Video copies in general not for public exhibition.

098
CORPORACION DE TELEVISION DE LA UNIVERSIDAD CATOLICA DE CHILE
ARCHIVE FROM CHANNEL 13
Ines Matte Urrejola 0848
Casilla 14600
SANTIAGO
CHILE

Tel.: 56-2-2519242
Fax.: 56-2-302146

Telex: 440182 UCTRECE
Member of IFTA.

Collections
Collections of Video.

All the programs produced by Channel 13 from 1978 to 1991.

Access
Catalogue on database.

Acces to catalogue: limited. Only for the staff of archive.

Access to materials: Every personal of Channel 13. Access on archives premises.

Fees – Copyright
Fees for research for reuse and production purposes.
Copyright holder is the institution.

_____ **099**

MINISTERIO DE EDUCACION – DIVISION DE CULTURA, CENTRO AUDIOVISUAL
Avenida Bernardo O'Higgins 1371 Oficina 302 Piso 3
768496 Correo 21
SANTIAGO
CHILE

Tel.: 56-2-6983351
Fax.: 56-2-6963252
Telex: 034-240567 MEDUC-CL

Collections
Collections of Film, Video, Sound.
Production : National and foreign ; distribution in open and closed circuits.

Arts, astronomy, biology, botanics, sciences, spanish language, ethnography, physics, geography, social science, orientation, music, health, education, chemistry, natural science, training, ecology, mathematics, a-v media, culture, history, theatre.
Films 2559
Video 381
Sound 1010

Access
Catalogue published.

Acces to catalogue: limited. Reserved for usage in Chile only.

Access to materials: limited. Some a-v materials are available.

CHINA, PEOPLE'S REPUBLIC

BEIJING

_____ **100**

CHINA RECORD CORPORATION
2 Fuxingmewai St.
100866 BEIJING
PEOPLE'S REPUBLIC OF CHINA

Tel.: 86-1-6092867
Fax.: 86-1-3262693
Telex: 222309CRC CN

Member of IASA.

Collections
Collections of Video, Sound.

Video 70000 copies
Sound 200000 pieces

Access
Catalogue on cards.

Access to catalogue.

Fees – Copyright
Fees for research for reuse and production purposes, research by archive staff.
Pricelist and conditions for use available.
Copyright holder is the institution.

_____ **101**

LIBRARY OF TSINGHUA UNIVERSITY
100084 BEIJING
PEOPLE'S REPUBLIC OF CHINA

Fax.: 86-1-2562768
Telex: 22617 QHTSC CN

Member of IFLA.

Collections
Collections of Video, Sound.

Teaching materials for English learning.
Video 100 items
Sound 3000 items

Access
Catalogue on cards.

Access to catalogue.

Access to materials.
Access on archives premises.

Fees – Copyright
Fees for facilities and handling.
Pricelist and conditions for use available.
Institution holds no copyright.
Access on archives premises.

102
ZHONGGUO DIANYING ZILIAOGUAN
CHINA FILM ARCHIVE
Xin Wai Dajie 25B
100088 BEIJING
PEOPLE'S REPUBLIC OF CHINA

Tel.: 86-1-201.4422
Fax.: 86-1-201.4752
Telex: 22195 FILM CN
Member of FIAF.

Collections
Collections of Film, Video, posters, stills, newspaper clippings, periodicals, books.

Positives, original negatives, dupe negatives, videos.

Access
Catalogue indexed on cards.

Acces to catalogue: limited.

Access to materials: limited.
Access on archives premises.

Fees – Copyright
Fees for research for reuse and production purposes, facilities and handling.
Pricelist and conditions for use available.
Institution holds no copyright.
Copyright belongs to State. Certificate must be shown when materials are consulted.

NANJING

103
NANJING UNIVERSITY, MAIN LIBRARY
Han-Kou Road 22
210008 NANJING, JIANGSU PROVINCE
PEOPLE'S REPUBLIC OF CHINA

Tel.: 86-25-634651-2943
Fax.: 86-25-307965
Telex: 86-25-634151 PRCNU CN
Member of IFLA.

Collections
Collections of Film, Video, Sound, microproducts, etc.

History, geography, biography, ecology, chemistry, language teaching.
Films 52
Video 98
Sound 1202

Access
Catalogue on cards.

Access to catalogue.

Access to materials.
Access by loan.

Fees – Copyright
Institution holds no copyright.
All of moving image and sound archives are offered to reading, listening borrow for free according to the International Copyright Law.

104
NANJING LIBRARY
66 Chengxian St.
P.O. Box 210018
210000 NANJING
PEOPLE'S REPUBLIC OF CHINA

Tel.: 86-25-637619
Member of IFLA.

Collections
Collections of Film, Video, Sound.

Our collection contains sports, classical music, folk music, classical literature and so on.
Films 1200
Video 1100
Sound 10760

Access
Catalogue on cards.

Access to catalogue.

Access to materials: limited.

Fees – Copyright
Fees for research by archive staff.
Pricelist and conditions for use available.
Copyright holder is the institution.

SHANGHAI

105
EAST CHINA NORMAL UNIVERSITY, DEPT. OF LIBRARY AND INFORMATION SCIENCE
3663 North Zhong-shan Road
200062 SHANGHAI
PEOPLE'S REPUBLIC OF CHINA

Tel.: 86-21-2577577-2511
Member of IFLA.

Collections
Collections of Video, Sound.

Optical discs, records, moving pictures, video tapes, and others.
Video 200
Sound 300

Access
Catalogue on cards.

Access to catalogue.

Access to materials.
Access by loan.

Fees – Copyright

Fees for research for reuse and production purposes.
Copyright holder is the institution.

SHANGHAI JIAO TONG UNIVERSITY LIBRARY 106
1954 Hua Shan Road
200030 SHANGHAI
PEOPLE'S REPUBLIC OF CHINA

Tel.: 86-21-4374062
Fax.: 86-21-4330892
Telex: 33262 JIASH CN

Member of IFLA.

Collections

Collections of Video, Sound.

AV collection subjects are as follows : English language training, history and culture, literature and art. Most of our collection is from the exchange services with other univeristy library in Shanghai.
Video 20000 items of microform and AV materials

Access

Catalogue on cards.

Access to catalogue.

Access to materials.
Access by loan.

Fees – Copyright

Fees for facilities and handling.
Pricelist and conditions for use available.
Institution holds no copyright.

COLOMBIA

MEDELLIN

UNIVERSIDAD DE ANTIOQUIA, ESCUELA INTERAMERICANAN DE BIBLIOTECOLOGIA – BIBLIOTECA 107
Clle 67 No 53-108
A.A. 1307
MEDELLIN
COLOMBIA

Tel.: 57-4-263.00.11 (ext.358), 57-4-263.44.36
Fax.: 57-4-263.82.82

Member of IFLA.

Collections

Collections of Video, Sound.

Specialized collection on librarianship and information science (3062 entries).
Video 7
Sound 25

Access

Catalogue on database.

Access to catalogue.

Access to materials.

SANTA FE DE BOGOTA

FUNDACION PATRIMONIO FILMICO COLOMBIANO 108
Carrera 13 # 13-24, piso 9, auditorio
SANTA FE DE BOGOTA
COLOMBIA

Tel.: 57-1-2815241, 57-1-2836496, 57-1-3425182/
Fax.: 57-1-2821665

Member of FIAF.

Collections

Collections of Film, Video, Sound, production files, scripts, stills, posters, books, magazines, censorship files, musical scores, all related materials (Colombian national production, priority).

Colombian newsreels, documentaries, commercial spots, fiction features, television production.
Films 50000 items (film + video + sound)

Access

Catalogue on database.

Acces to catalogue: limited. Staff and researchers.

Access to materials: limited, due to preservation and legal considerations ; also lack of equipment.
Access on archives premises, by loan, by hire, by purchase.

Fees – Copyright

Fees for research for reuse and production purposes, research by archive staff, facilities and handling, loan, copyright.
Pricelist and conditions for use available.
Institution holds no copyright.
Reuse and production purposes require copyright holder agreement.

CONGO

BRAZZAVILLE

_____ **109**
BIBLIOTHEQUE NATIONALE DU CONGO
B.P. 1489
BRAZZAVILLE
CONGO

Member of IFLA.

Collections
Collections of Film, Sound.

Collection consists of about 100 documentaries and nearly 1600 discs which are used for cultural animation at the library. Films are on several subjects.
Films 4 shelf metres
Sound 2 shelf meters

Access
Catalogue on cards.

Access to catalogue: no. The collections are just catalogued.

Access to materials: limited. For internal use only.
Access on archives premises.

Fees – Copyright
Fees for Membership, for cultural animations (projections, hearings) at the library. Free of charge at rural areas.
Library has no copyright.

COSTA RICA

SAN JOSE

_____ **110**
DIRECCION GENERAL DEL ARCHIVO NACIONAL DE COSTA RICA
Calle 7, avdas 4 y 6
P.O. Box 10217 – 1000
SAN JOSE
COSTA RICA

Tel.: 506-335754
Fax.: 506-219129

Member of ICA.

Collections
Collections of Film, Video, Sound.

Two recording projects "The year 48 in the spirit of Costaricans" (oral history) and "To conserve the voice is to project the present" (collection of national voices with life history). In video we keep records on contemporary events. In film mostly material of documentary type.

Films 31 films
Video 16 cassettes
Sound 310 tapes, 150 cassettes

Access
Catalogue indexed on cards.
Access to catalogue.
Access to materials.
Access on archives premises.

Fees – Copyright
Copyright holder is the institution.
The material can be reproduced on the request of users who have to respect and indicate clearly the copyright credits of the National Archive of Costa Rica.

CROATIA

ZAGREB

_____ **111**
HRVATSKE TELEVIZIJE
CROATIAN TELEVISION, INDOC CENTRE
Setaliste K. Marxa BB
41000 ZAGREB
CROATIA

Tel.: 38-41-519227
Fax.: 38-41-510093
Telex: 21477 or 21568

Member of IFTA.

Collections
Collections of Film, Video, stills, books.

The archive holdings include all documents dated from beginning of the Croatian Television (Televizija Zagreb) in 1956 (news, drama, educational programme, entertainment, etc...).
Films 36650 cans with 352764 items (titles)
Video 6000 AVR, 7000 VPR, 8000 U-Matic, 6000 Betacam, 600 VHS

Access
Catalogue on database.

Access to catalogue. The cards review (survey), database and the AV documents are free of charge.

Access to materials.
Access on archives premises.

Fees – Copyright
Fees for facilities and handling.
Pricelist and conditions for use available.
Copyright holder is the institution.
No charges for the license (copyright), only copying service and shipment are charged.

CUBA

HABANA

112
CENTRO DE DOCUMENTACION DE LA RADIO Y LA TELEVISION
DISCOTECA CENTRAL
23 y P
10400 LA HABANA
CUBA
Tel.: 53-7-72994, 53-7-328935

Collections
Collections of Sound.

Popular and classical music, national and foreign.
Sound 60000 discs

Access
Catalogue indexed on cards.

Access to catalogue.

Access to materials: limited for reasons of preservation.
Access by loan.

Fees – Copyright
Fees for research for reuse and production purposes.
Copyright holder is the institution.

113
CENTRO NACIONAL DE INFORMACION EN CIENCIAS MEDICAS
BIBLIOTECA MEDICA NACIONAL
23 y N
10400 LA HABANA
CUBA
Tel.: 53-7-324317

Collections
Collections of Video.

Collection on medical science.
Video 1087 programs

Access
Catalogue on database.

Acces to catalogue: limited for reasons of preservation.

Access to materials: limited for reasons of preservation.
Access on archives premises.

Fees – Copyright
Institution holds no copyright.

114
CINEMATECA DE CUBA
Calle 23 No 155
10300 LA HABANA 4
CUBA
Tel.: 53-7-3-4719, 53-7-30-5041 to 45
Cable : Cinemateca-Habana
Member of FIAF.

Collections
Collections of Film, Video, posters, photos, scripts, dialogue lists, press clippings, etc.

Accidents, arts, literature, science fiction, phantasy, social science, technology, sports, economy, history, etc.
Films 100000 reels
Video 120 cassettes

Access
Catalogue on database.

Acces to catalogue: limited. Access to catalogue and collection only for specialized persons like researchers, professors, students and approved researchers.

Access to materials: limited.
Access on archives premises.

Fees – Copyright
Pricelist and conditions for use available.
Institution holds no copyright.
Consultation of the archive on the premises, loans, rental.

115
CINEMATOGRAFIA EDUCATIVA
Ave 7° #2807 e/ 28 y 30
11300 LA HABANA
CUBA
Tel.: 53-7-27742, 53-7-27887

Collections
Collections of Film, Video, scripts.

Collection of educational films.
Films 100 hours
Video 150 hours

Access
Catalogue on database.

Access to catalogue.

Access to materials.
Access by hire, by purchase.

Fees – Copyright
Fees for research for reuse and production purposes, research by archive staff, facilities and handling.
Pricelist and conditions for use available.
Copyright holder is the institution.

116
EMISORA RADIAL "CMBF"
Infanta #105 e/ 25 y San Francisco
P.O. Box 3042
10300 LA HABANA
CUBA

Tel.: 53-7-704561

Collections
Collections of Sound.

Classical music, national and foreign opera.
Sound 8000 tapes, 10000 records, 10 CD's

Access
Catalogue indexed on cards.

Access to catalogue.

Access to materials: limited for reasons of preservation for staff only.
Access on archives premises.

Fees – Copyright
Institution holds no copyright.

117
EMISORA RADIAL COCO
15 #210 esq. J
10400 LA HABANA
CUBA

Tel.: 53-7-320095, 53-7-320494

Collections
Collections of Sound.

Popular and classical music, national and foreign.
Sound 4700 tapes, 3000 discs

Access
Catalogue indexed on cards.

Acces to catalogue: limited to specialists for reasons of preservation.

Access to materials: limited for reasons of preservation.
Access on archives premises.

Fees – Copyright
Institution holds no copyright.

118
EMISORA "RADIO PROGRESO"
Infanta #105 e/ 25 y San Francisco
P.O. Box 3042
10300 LA HABANA
CUBA

Tel.: 53-7-704561

Collections
Collections of Sound, scripts.

Classical music, popular and instrumental national and foreign music, dramas.
Sound 7000 music tapes, 12000 tapes with drama, 8500 discs

Access
Catalogue indexed on cards.

Access to catalogue.

Access to materials: limited for reasons of preservation.
Access on archives premises.

Fees – Copyright
Institution holds no copyright.
Possibility is offered to copy programs of the station.

119
EMISORA "RADIO REBELDE"
23 y M
6277
10400 LA HABANA
CUBA

Tel.: 53-7-327600, 53-7-320435

Collections
Collections of Sound.

Popular and classical music, national and international.
Sound 4225 tapes with 90000 music items, 1890 records with 18880 pieces of music

Access
Catalogue on database.

Access to catalogue.

Access to materials: limited to specialists for reasons of preservation.
Access on archives premises.

Fees – Copyright
Fees for research for reuse and production purposes.

120
EMPRESA "RADIO ARTE"
M y 23
10400 LA HABANA
CUBA

Tel.: 53-7-327511

Collections
Collections of Sound.

Popular and classical music, national and international. All kinds of sound effects.
Sound 20000 records, 500 tapes

Access

Catalogue indexed on cards.

Access to catalogue.

Access to materials: limited to specialists only for reasons of preservation.
Access on archives premises.

Fees – Copyright

Fees for research for reuse and production purposes.
Copyright holder is the institution.

121
ESTUDIOS CINEMATOGRAFICOS ICAIC, ARCHIVA DE SONIDO
Calle 23 #1256 e/ 14 y 16
10400 LA HABANA
CUBA

Tel.: 53-7-309336

Collections

Collections of Sound.

National and foreign music, sound effects, voices of national and foreign political and cultural personalities.
Sound 12000 hours

Access

Catalogue indexed on cards.

Acces to catalogue: limited to specialists due to conservation.

Access to materials: limited reproduction only in the archive.

Fees – Copyright

Fees for research for reuse and production purposes, research by archive staff, facilities and handling.
Pricelist and conditions for use available.
Institution holds no copyright.

122
HOSPITAL "HERMANOS AMEJJEIRAS" (BIBLIOTECA)
San Lazaro N° 701 e/Belascoain y Marques Gonzalez
10300 LA HABANA
CUBA

Tel.: 53-7-709935

Collections

Collections of Video.

Collection of videos on medicine.
Video 70 themes on 30 videocassettes

Access

Catalogue on database.

Acces to catalogue: limited to specialists for reasons of conservation.

Access to materials: limited to specialists for reasons of conservation.
Access on archives premises, by purchase.

Fees – Copyright

Videos are occasionally sold.

123
INSTITUTO CUBANO DE RADIO Y TELEVISION
M N°258
10400 LA HABANA
CUBA

Tel.: 53-7-327511 ext. 164

Collections

Collections of Sound.

Popular and classical music, national and foreign.
Sound 6000 tapes, 300 records

Access

Catalogue published.

Acces to catalogue: limited.

Access to materials: limited for reasons of conservation.

124
INSTITUTO CUBANO DE RADIO Y TELEVISION (ICRT)
CINEMATECO DEL ICRT
23 y M #258
10400 LA HABANA
CUBA

Tel.: 53-7-321219

Collections

Collections of Film, description of content.

Dramas, crime, history.
Films 70000 reels, 8000 titles

Access

Catalogue indexed on cards.

Access to catalogue.

Access to materials: limited for reasons of conservation.
Access by hire, by purchase.

Fees – Copyright

Fees for research for reuse and production purposes, research by archive staff, facilities and handling.
Pricelist and conditions for use available.

125
RADIO HABANA-CUBA
Infanta 105 e/25 y San Francisco
P.O. Box 6240
10300 LA HABANA
CUBA

Tel.: 53-7-75341, 53-7-74954
Telex: t x 0511344

Collections

Collections of Sound, scripts.

Popular music, classical music, speeches of political personalities, national and foreign, interviews, speeches of writers.
Sound 5740 music tapes, 4540 tapes spoken word, 2900 music records

Access

Catalogue indexed on cards.

Acces to catalogue: limited for reasons of preservation.

Access to materials: limited for reasons of preservation.
Access on archives premises.

Fees – Copyright

In case of programs the station owns the copyright.

126
UNIVERSIDAD DE LA HABANA
FILMOTECA UNIVERSITARIA
10400 LA HABANA
CUBA

Tel.: 53-7-329844

Collections

Collections of Film, press clippings, documents, photos, scripts, etc. related to film.

Contains features of different themes and origins and documentaries of various types. History, arts, science, etc. Mostly before 1966.
Films 500

Access

Catalogue indexed on cards.

Access to catalogue.

Access to materials limited, only unique copies. For reasons of preservation, usage on archive premises only.
Access on archives premises.

Fees – Copyright

Institution holds no copyright.
Most materials donated to the archive. No copyright problems.

127
UNIVERSIDAD DE LA HABANA
BIBLIOTECA CENTRAL "RUBEN MARTINEZ VILLENA"
San Lazaro y L
10400 LA HABANA
CUBA

Tel.: 53-7-75573
Telex: 512210 DICT-UH
Electronic mail: UNIVHAB%CENIAI HURACAN.CR

Collections

Collections of Video.

Social science, natural science and other university studies.
Video 111 video cassettes

Access

Catalogue published.

Access to catalogue.

Access to materials: limited for reasons of preservation.
Access on archives premises.

Fees – Copyright

Service if free for Cuban citizens.
Copyright holder is the institution.
Consultation of archive on the premises. Loan, rent and sales with permission from the copyright holder.

CZECH REPUBLIC

BRNO

128
ARCHIV MESTA BRNA
ARCHIVES OF THE TOWN OF BRNO
Dominikanske namesti 1
601 67 BRNO
CZECH REPUBLIC

Tel.: 42-5-2196

Collections

Collections of Film.

About history of Brno, about historic buildings and other monuments, the traffic in Brno and other. The films are produced from 1924 to 1991.
Films 124 films

Access

Acces to catalogue: limited. We have only the inventory.

Access to materials.
Access on archives premises.

PLZEN

129

ARCHIV MESTA PLZNE
ARCHIVES OF CITY PLZEN
Veleslavineva 19
P.O. Box 277
305 77 PLZEN
CZECH REPUBLIC
Tel.: 42-19-333 82

Collections

Collections of Film, Sound.

Film – News of City Plzen (politics, economy, culture, health service, sport) 60.-80.years 20.century (fund PKO). Sounds – of estates prof.Josef Skupa (Czech marionetteer) – Spejbl a Hurvinek, speach (Frantisek Josef I., K. Kramar, K. Gottwald, V.I.Lenin, J.V.Stalin, K. von Hätzendorf), hymns, music (B. Smetana, A. Dvorak, L. Janacek...), national songs, popular music, oriental music, sound effects.
Films 110
Sound 200 album of sounds

Access

Catalogue published, on cards.

Access to catalogue.

Access to materials.
Access on archives premises.

Fees – Copyright

Fees for research for reuse and production purposes.
Pricelist and conditions for use available.
Copyright holder is the institution.

PRAGUE

130

CESKA TELEVIZE
CZECH TELEVISION
ARCHIVE OF CZECHOSLOVAK TELEVISION
Jindrisska 16
111 50 PRAHA 1
CZECH REPUBLIC
Tel.: 42-2-235 18 38
Fax.: 42-2-692 31 94

Collections

Collections of Film, Video, Sound, photos.

Documentaries and acted programm : produced or transmitted by czech tv.
Films 150000 titles
Video 50000 titles
Sound 21000 titles

Access

Catalogue on database.
Access to catalogue.

Access to materials: limited. Originals can be seen in our tv projection, all materials everyone can buy as a copy.
Access on archives premises, by purchase.

Fees – Copyright

Fees for research for reuse and production purposes, research by archive staff.
Pricelist and conditions for use available.
Copyright holder is the institution.
The conditions for using records of our programmes depend on kind of using number of rewrited minutes and on type and age of the record. The exact conditions are necessary to negociate with czech telexport, department which has the pricelist.

131

NÁRODNÍ FILMOVÝ ARCHIV
NATIONAL FILM ARCHIVE
Národní 40
P.O. B. 1001
110 00 PRAGUE 1
CZECH REPUBLIC
Tel.: 42-2-260558, 42-2-260087
Fax.: 42-2-261618
Member of FIAF.

Collections

Collections of Film, Video, stills, posters, documents, publicity material, left estates, Archive of Czech Cinema.

Fiction and non-fiction, documentary-, popular-science, newsreels, animated- and other ; films made during the whole period from the beginning of Czech cinema (1898) up to the present time (i.e. positive and negative material). Foreign film production is being archived selectively. A collection of the so-called primitives, a collection of slapstick comedies.
Films 25000 titles
Video 1000 titles

Access

Catalogue on database.
Acces to catalogue: limited.

Access to materials: limited.
Access on archives premises.

Fees – Copyright

Fees for research for reuse and production purposes, research by archive staff, facilities and handling.
Copyright holder is the institution.

STATNI USTREDNI ARCHIV V PRAZE
STATE CENTRAL ARCHIVES IN PRAGUE
Karmelitska 2
118 01 PRAHA 1
CZECH REPUBLIC

Tel.: 42-2-531551

Member of ICA.

Collections

Collections of Film, Sound, archival collections.

Documents relating to history of Czek nation : political, economical, cultural events.
Films 211966 (mostly microfilms, microfiches, still negatives)
Sound 2593 (collection of records)

Access

Catalogue on cards.

Access to catalogue.

Access to materials. No apparatus for projection of films.
Access on archives premises, by loan.

Fees – Copyright

Fees for research for reuse and production purposes.
Pricelist and conditions for use available.
Copyright holder is the institution.
Consent from director of archives necessary.

PREROV NAD LABEM

CESKY ROZHLAS
CZECH RADIO
Castle 17
289 16 PREROV NAD LABEM
CZECH REPUBLIC

Tel.: 42-325-97811, 42-325-97812, 42-325-97862
Fax.: 42-325-97862

Collections

Collections of Sound, photos, production papers, scripts, scores, books.

Recordings of various domains.
Sound about 15000 hours

Access

Catalogue published, on cards.

Acces to catalogue: limited. By archive staff only.

Access to materials: limited. By archive staff only.
Access on archives premises, by loan, by purchase.

Fees – Copyright

Fees for research for reuse and production purposes, facilities and handling, copyright.
Pricelist and conditions for use available.
Copyright various.

USTI NAD LABEM

ARCHIV MESTA USTI NAD LABEM
ARCHIVE OF CITY USTI NAD LABEM
Hrncirska 2/65
P.O. Box 100
401 00 USTI NAD LABEM
CZECH REPUBLIC

Tel.: 42-47-24703

Collections

Collections of Sound.

78 RPM Records Collection (1901-1960) : classic, opera, talking, political, jazz & dance music, entertainer (poss. 50% records from The Gramophone Co, Ltd. Usti n.L., Czechoslovakia).
Sound poss. 12000 78' records

Access

Catalogue published, on cards.

Access to catalogue.

Access to materials.
Access on archives premises.

Fees – Copyright

Fees for research for reuse and production purposes.
Institution holds no copyright.

DENMARK

AALBORG

AALBORG UNIVERSITETSBIBLIOTEK
AALBORG UNIVERSITY LIBRARY
Langagervej 4
POB 8200
DK – 9220 AALBORG EAST
DENMARK

Tel.: 45-98-158522
Fax.: 45-98-156859
Telex: 69790 aub dk

Member of IASA, IFLA, IAML.

Collections

Collections of Sound, scores, books, magazines.

20th century composers : live concert recordings; private recordings from contemporary concerts and festivals. Contemporary music.
Sound about 600 titles/items (records and cassettes)

Access

Catalogue on database.

Access to catalogue. Online database : AUBOLINE (see Nordic databasguide).

Access to materials: Restricted access.
Access by loan.

Fees – Copyright

Fees for loan.
Institution holds no copyright.

AARHUS

136

ÅRHUS KOMMUNES BIBLIOTEKER
MUNICIPAL LIBRARIES OF ARHUS
Molleparken
DK – 8000 ÅRHUS C
DENMARK

Tel.: 45-86-136622
Fax.: 45-86-195076

Member of IFLA.

Collections

Collections of Film, Video, Sound.

Videos and films on several subjects – fiction as well as non fiction, including documentaries. LP, CM, MCs on classical, jazz, folk, avantgarde themes. Also talking books and none musical records.
Films 33 in collection of Local history
Video 469 in titles
Sound 8790 in titles, included talking books and nonce musical records

Access

Catalogue on database.

Access to catalogue.

Access to materials.
Access by loan.

137

STATSBILIOTEKET
STATE AND UNIVERSITY LIBRARY
STATE MEDIA ARCHIVE
Universitetsparken
DK – 8000 AARHUS C.
DENMARK

Tel.: 45-86-122022
Fax.: 45-86-132704
Telex: 645 15 (STABIB)

Member of IASA, IFLA.

Collections

Collections of Video, Sound. Being a legal deposit and research library the State and University Library contains as well all kinds of books, magazines, posters, scores, etc. related to the av-materials.

1. Danish national archive for radio and television (sound tapes, video/VHS) covering all subjects 2. Danish national archive for commercially produced sound recordings (cylinders, 78', vinyl records, MC, CD, etc.) covering all genres.
Video 13000 videotapes (items)
Sound 42000 radiotapes (items), 450000 sound recordings (discs) (items)

Access

Catalogue on database.

Access to catalogue.

Access to materials: limited. Radio/tv : for copyright reasons only access for research pruposes in the library. Sound recordings : can for preservation reasons only be used in the library's listening room.
Access on archives premises.

Fees – Copyright

Institution holds no copyright.
Generally, all kinds of access to the av-materials requires the permission of the copyright holders.

COPENHAGEN

138

DANMARKS BLINDEBIBLIOTEK
DANISH NATIONAL LIBRARY FOR THE BLIND
Teglvaerksgade 37
DK – 2100 KOBENHAVN 0
DENMARK

Tel.: 45-31-294822
Fax.: 45-31-291021

Member of IASA, IFLA.

Collections

Collections of Sound.

Talking books (mainly fiction in danish), talking magazines a.o. periodical, talking brochures, etc.
Sound Talking books : 7000 titles, talking magazines : 52 different

DENMARK – COPENHAGEN / 138

Access

Catalogue on database.

Acces to catalogue: limited. Catalogue (printed version and audio tape). Database : BC-BASIS requires password for access.

Access to materials: limited. Blind people (directly) and people with other reading dissabilities (via public libraries).
Access by loan.

Fees – Copyright

Pricelist and conditions for use available.
Institution holds no copyright.
No permission needed by loan.

139

DANMARKS RADIO
RADIO DENMARK, RADIO ARCHIVE
Islands Bruegge 81
DK – 2300 COPENHAGEN S
DENMARK

Tel.: 45-31-671233 ext. 5633
Telex: 22695 DANRAD DK

Member of IASA.

Collections

Collections of Sound.

"Permanent" collection : reel tapes, carefully selected high quality broadcasts of Radio Denmark – dating back to 1931. "Working" collection : DAT-tapes from oct. 1988. Total recording of all three nationwide programmes.
Sound Reel : 75000, DAT : 30000 (120 min's tapes)

Access

Catalogue on database.

Access to catalogue.

Access to materials: limited due to limited facilities and legal problems.
Access by loan, by purchase.

Fees – Copyright

Fees for facilities and handling.

140

DET DANSKE FILMMUSEUM
Store Sondervoldstraede 4
DK – 1419 COPENHAGEN K
DENMARK

Tel.: 45-31-576500
Fax.: 45-31-541312
Telex: 45-31-465 D-FILM DK

Member of FIAF, IAMHIST.

Collections

Collections of Film, Video, books, periodicals, stills, posters, programmes, press cuttings, apparatus.

A film archive with collections of films in all formats, a library and a stills collection and documentation department. An international collection, but specialized in Danish cinema.
Films 14500 prints and negatives
Video about 200

Access

Catalogue on cards.

Access to catalogue.

Access to materials.
Access on archives premises, by loan, by hire.

Fees – Copyright

Fees for hire of films, making of photos and photocopies.
Pricelist and conditions for use available.
Institution holds no copyright.
For use of films written authorizations from copyright holders are needed.

141

DET KONGELIGE BIBLIOTEK
THE ROYAL LIBRARY – KBA-FILMARCHIVE
Christians Brygge 8
P.O. Box 1219
DK – 1016 COPENHAGEN K
DENMARK

Tel.: 45-33-930111 ext. 338
Fax.: 45-33-932218
Telex: 15009

Member of IASA, IFLA.

Collections

Collections of Film.

Film portraits of danish authors.
Films 40

Access

Access to materials.
Access on archives premises.

Fees – Copyright

Copyright holder is the institution.

142

DET KONGELIGE BIBLIOTEK
THE ROYAL LIBRARY – MANISCRIPT DEPT
SOUND ARCHIVE
Christians Brygge 8
P.O. Box 1219
DK – 1016 COPENHAGEN K

DENMARK
Tel.: 45-33-930111 ext. 415
Fax.: 45-33-932218
Telex: 15009

Member of IASA, IFLA.

Collections

Collections of Sound.

Recordings of : Danish authors' reading of own works ; memoirs of Danish cultural personalities ; Danish participants in the Spanish Civil War ; Danish participants in the Resistance Movement during the German occupation 1940-1945 ; Circus artists.
Sound about 2500 tapes (1700 spool tapes, 800 cassette tapes)

Access

Catalogue on cards.

Acces to catalogue: limited. Only for use in the Reading Room.

Access to materials: limited. Only by prior appointment with the Manuscript Dept.
Access on archives premises.

Fees – Copyright

Copyright holder is the institution.
Permission of use should be obtained from living persons. Otherwise the Manuscript Dept gives permission.

ROSKILDE

143
ROSKILDE UNIVERSITETSBIBLIOTEK
ROSKILDE UNIVERSITY LIBRARY
Marbjergvej 35
P.O. Box 258
DK – 4000 ROSKILDE
DENMARK

Tel.: 45-46-757711
Fax.: 45-46-756102

Member of IFLA.

Collections

Collections of Video, Sound, books and magazines on av-materiels.

Universal collection – radio & TV broadcasts from Denmark & Sweden 1977ff.
Video 6000 (titles)
Sound 8000 (titles)

Access

Catalogue on database.

Access to catalogue.

Access to materials: limited. Not for private use, only research and education.
Access by loan.

Fees – Copyright

Institution holds no copyright.
According to an agreement with the organisation of copyright holders access is limited to research and education.

SOBORG

144
DANMARKS RADIO, TV- ARKIVET
DENMARKS RADIO, TELEVISION ARCHIVES
Morkhojvej
DK – 2860 – SOBORG
DENMARK

Tel.: 45-31-671233
Fax.: 45-39-661233 5528

Member of IFTA.

Collections

Collections of Film, Video.

Film collection as broadcast since 1951, part of VB collection as broadcast since 1959.
Films not calculated
Video not calculated

Access

Catalogue on database.

Acces to catalogue: limited. Inhouse users in co-operation with archive staff.

Access to materials for inhouse users and sales.
Access on archives premises, by loan, by purchase.

Fees – Copyright

Fees for research for reuse and production purposes, research by archive staff, free of charge for DR-production.
Copyright holder is the institution.
For copyright questions, please contact head of Sales Section, DR.

ECUADOR

QUITO

145
CINEMATECA NACIONAL DEL ECUADOR
Av. 6 Diciembre 794 y Patria
P.O. Box 17-01-3520
QUITO
ECUADOR

Tel.: 593-2-230-505

Member of FIAF.

Collections

Collections of Film, Video, advertising material on exhibition (1906-1990), co-production contracts (1980-1983). testimonies, reviews, posters, clipping, manuscripts, photos.

History, newsreels, folklore, ethnology, restored and blown up films from 9.5 to 16mm. Sound films of various gauges. National production in video.
Films 161 titles
Video 73 titles

Access

Catalogue on cards.

Acces to catalogue: limited due to legal problems.

Access to materials: limited to researchers for reasons of preservation and limited equipment. Access on archives premises.

Fees – Copyright

Fees for research by archive staff, Only video copies can be seen at the archive.
Institution holds no copyright.

ESTONIA

TALLIN

_____ 146

EESTI TELEVISIOON
ESTONIAN TELEVISION, TELEVISION ARCHIVES
12 Faehlmanni Street
200 100 TALLINN
ESTONIA

Tel.: 7-0142-434 650
Fax.: 7-0142-434 155
Telex: 7-0142-173 869 ETV SU

Collections

Collections of Film, Video, Sound.

Economy, agriculture, sports, transport, culture, music, history.
Films 250 hours
Video 3907 hours
Sound 400 hours

Access

Catalogue on database.

Access to catalogue.

Access to materials.
Access on archives premises, by loan, by hire, by purchase.

Fees – Copyright

Fees for facilities and handling.
Pricelist and conditions for use available.
Copyright holder is the institution.
The right holders permission is needed.

FIJI

SUVA

_____ 147

LIBRARY SERVICE OF FIJI
162 Ratu Sukuna road
P.O. Box 2526
SUVA
FIJI

Tel.: 679-315344, 679-315303
Fax.: 679-303511

Member of IFLA.

Collections

Collections of Film, Video, Sound.
Films 5
Video 20
Sound 30

Access

Catalogue on cards.

Access to catalogue.

Access to materials.
Access on archives premises, by loan.

Fees – Copyright

Free service.
Institution holds no copyright.
No copyright conditions yet.

FINLAND

HELSINKI

_____ 148

HELSINGIN KAUPPAKORKEAKOULUN KIRJASTO
HELSINKI SCHOOL OF ECONOMICS LIBRARY
Runeberginkatu 22-24
SF – 00100 HELSINKI
FINLAND

Tel.: 358-0-43131
Fax.: 358-0-4313539
Telex: 122220 econ sf

Member of IFLA.

Collections

Collections of Video.

Subject area : economics, management.
Video 1,5 shelf meters

Access

Catalogue on database.

Access to catalogue.

Access to materials.
Access by loan.

Fees – Copyright

Institution holds no copyright.

149
HELSINGIN KAUPUNGINKIRJASTO
HELSINKI CITY LIBRARY
Rautatieläisenkatu 8
P.O. Box 128, 00521 HELSINKI
SF – 00520 HELSINKI
FINLAND

Tel.: 358-0-15971
Fax.: 358-0-1597517
Telex: 124 794 hkk sf

Member of IFLA.

Collections

Collections of Video, Sound.

Videos : documentary videos, music, opera, ballet, feature films. Programmes of Finnish Broadcasting Company on video. Sounds : all kinds of music, talking books, language courses, documentary sounds.
Video 2500
Sound 90000

Access

Catalogue on database.

Access to catalogue.

Access to materials.
Access by loan.

Fees – Copyright

No fees.
The library pays for lending rights to copyright holders.

150
HELSINGIN YLIOPISTON KIRJASTO
HELSINKI UNIVERSITY LIBRARY
Unioninkatu 36
P.O. Box 312
SF – 00171 HELSINKI
FINLAND

Tel.: 358-90-1911
Fax.: 358-90-1912719
Telex: 121538 hyk sf

Member of IASA, IFLA.

Collections

Collections of Sound.

Legal deposit collection ; all sound recordings issued in Finland since 1981. Annual growth ca 4500 items.
Sound records and compact discs : 10000, cassettes/reel tapes : 12000, talking news papers : 18000

Access

Catalogue on database.

Access to catalogue.

Access to materials: limited. Materials can be used only in the library for research purposes, no home loans or interlending.
Access on archives premises, by loan.

Fees – Copyright

Institution holds no copyright.
Library is not allowed to make copies of sound recordings which are still controlled by copyright regulations.

151
OY. YLEISRADIO AB./RADIOARKISTO
FINNISH BROADCASTING COMPANY LTD (YLE)/RADIOARCHIVE
Radiokatu 5
P.O. Box 10
SF – 00241 HELSINKI
FINLAND

Tel.: 358-0-14801
Fax.: 358-0-1485570

Member of IASA.

Collections

Collections of Sound.

Radioprogrammes of YLE from year 1935 -.
Sound 240000 tapes

Access

Catalogue on database.

Acces to catalogue: limited. Archive has card catalogues and adb-system (IBM/stairs) on premises. Catalogues are not open for general access. Researchers require a special permission.

Access to materials: limited, as above. Recordings are exchanged with other collections on a mutual exchange basis.
Access on archives premises.

Fees – Copyright

Archive makes copies for researchers only with special agreement and then we make also an agreement for compensation.
Institution holds no copyright.
YLE has not all the copyrights for all the programmes. The copyright-question is very complicated in many cases.

152

OY. YLEISRADIO AB./TV 1
FINNISH BROADCASTING COMPANY/TV 1, TV ARCHIVES
Radiokatu 5 (JA.65)
P.O. Box 10
SF – 00241 HELSINKI
FINLAND

Tel.: 358-0-14802696
Fax.: 358-0-1483862
Telex: 121270 yletv sf
Member of IFTA.

Collections

Collections of Film, Video, programme contents reports, weekly radio and TV magazines, stills.

TV programme materials of all types including news since 1957. Historic Finnish film materials since 1906 (newsreels, documentaries and feature films).
Films 16mm : 17500 hours (68000 reels), 35mm : 2700 hours (9600 reels)
Video 2 inch : 17200 tapes, 1 inch : 45700 tapes, cassettes : 12000 tapes

Access

Catalogue on database.

Access to catalogue.

Access to materials: limited for non-commercial broadcast usage.
Access on archives premises, by purchase.

Fees – Copyright

Fees for copyright (licence/royalty).
Copyright holder is the institution.
There is practically no limitations for non-commercial broadcast usage.

153

OY. YLEISRADIO AB./TV 2
FINNISH BROADCASTING COMPANY/TV 2, TV ARCHIVES
Tohlopinranta 31
P.O. Box 196
SF – 33270 HELSINKI
FINLAND

Tel.: 358-31-456460
Fax.: 358-31-456688
Telex: 22176 yletv sf
Member of IFTA.

Collections

Collections of Film, Video, Sound, programme contents reports, radio and TV magazines, stills, records, audio tapes.

TV programme materials since 1957.
Films 16mm : 3200 hours (11300 reels)
Video 2 inch : 3500 tapes, 1 inch : 20000 tapes, cassettes : 3500 (Beta SP, VHS)
Sound records : 3000, audio master tapes : 1000

Access

Catalogue on database.

Access to catalogue.

Access to materials: limited for non commercial usage.
Access on archives premises, by purchase.

Fees – Copyright

Fees for copyright (licence/royalty).
Copyright holder is the institution.
There is practically no limitations for non-commercial broadcast usage.

154

PUOLUSTUSVOIMIEN ELOKUVA-ARKISTO
FILM ARCHIVE OF THE DEFENCE FORCES OF FINLAND
Et. Makasiinikatu 8 C
P.O. Box 919 00101 HELSINKI 10
SF – 00130 HELSINKI 13
FINLAND

Tel.: 358-0-1611
Fax.: 358-0-1612459

Collections

Collections of Film, Video, photographs.

Film material from 1911 to 1991 ; mostly documentary film on the Second World War and military educational films.
Films 500000 film metres

Access

Catalogue on database.

Access to catalogue.

Access to materials: limited.
Access by loan, by hire.

Fees – Copyright

Fees for research for reuse and production purposes, facilities and handling.
Copyright holder is the institution.

155
SUOMALAISEN KIRJALLISUUDEN SEURA
THE FINNISH LITERATURE SOCIETY, LITERATURE ARCHIVES
Mariank. 19 E
P.O. Box 259
SF – 00171 HELSINKI
FINLAND
Tel.: 358-0-13123260
Fax.: 358-0-13123268
Member of ICA, ICOM.

Collections
Collections of Sound, books on material (biographies, research material, articles).

Interviews of Finnish authors and researchers, tape recordings of literary seminars and congresses, meetings, slide series with tape recordings on authors and exhibitions.
Sound 2600 hours in 1990

Access
Catalogue on database.

Access to collections by staff only, legal restrictions.

Access to materials: limited. Author's permission on intimate material requested.
Access on archives premises.

Fees – Copyright
Fees for facilities and handling, Copies can be made for certain restricted research problem on author's permission, for the press and radio, television nets as well.
Pricelist and conditions for use available.
Institution holds no copyright.
Copyright belongs to the author or the right holders. Permission and payment to the author, not to the archives. Permission to publish the material in all must be sought from the society.

156
SUOMALAISEN KIRJALLISUUDEN SEURA
FINNISH LITERATURE SOCIETY
FOLKLORE ARCHIVES
Hallituskatu 1
P.O. Box 259
SF – 00171 HELSINKI
FINLAND
Tel.: 358-0-131231, 358-0-13123245
Fax.: 358-0-13123220

Collections
Collections of Video, Sound, field notes, photographs.

Finnish and Finno-Ugric folklore, folk music, oral history, cultural history.

Video 400 hours (Umatic, VHS, S-VHS)
Sound 12000 hours (open reels)

Access
Catalogue on database.

Access to catalogue by staff only.

Access to materials: Most of the collections are freely available to scholars.
Access on archives premises.

Fees – Copyright
Fees for facilities and handling.
Pricelist and conditions for use available.
Copyright holder is the institution.
The permission of the Society must be sought for publication of any of its material.

157
SUOMEN ÄÄNITEARKISTO R.Y.
FINNISH INSTITUTE OF RECORDED SOUND
Lumikintie 3 D 137
SF – 00820 HELSINKI
FINLAND
Tel.: 358-0-7556126 (evenings only)
Member of IASA.

Collections
Collections of Sound, record catalogues, books and periodicals on the recording industry.

The Institute aims to collect all Finnish (commercial) recordings issued up to 1980. There is also a secondary collection of foreign 78's.
Sound 50000 discs and tapes

Access
Catalogue published.

Access to catalogue.

Access to materials: limited by appointment only.
Access on archives premises.

Fees – Copyright
Pricelist and conditions for use available.
Institution holds no copyright.

158
SUOMEN ELOKUVA-ARKISTO
FINNISH FILM ARCHIVE
Pursimiehenkatu 29-31 A
P.O. Box 177
SF – 00151 HELSINKI
FINLAND
Tel.: 358-0-171417
Fax.: 358-0-171544
Telex: 125960 suelo sf
Member of FIAF.

Collections

Collections of Film, Video, stills, posters, scripts.

Domestic feature films and documentaries (pre-print materials, archival prints, screening prints, video copies). Foreign films distributed in Finland (screening prints, video copies).
Films 60000 titles
Video 7000 titles in 9000 copies

Access

Catalogue on database.

Access to catalogue.

Access to materials: limited for researchers and university students. For reuse purposes (rights have to be cleared by the user).
Access on archives premises.

Fees – Copyright

Fees for research for reuse and production purposes, facilities and handling.
Pricelist and conditions for use available.
Institution holds no copyright.
Copyrights generally held by the depositor of the material.

159
SUOMEN KIELEN NAUHOITEARKISTO
FINNISH LANGUAGE TAPE ARCHIVES
Sörnäisten rantatie 25
SF – 00500 HELSINKI
FINLAND

Tel.: 358-0-7315249, 358-0-7315248, 358-0-7315247, 358-0-7315246
Fax.: 358-0-7019583

Collections

Collections of Sound.

Linguistic material on Finnish dialects and related languages. Dialect material consists of story-telling about agriculture and folklore.
Sound 21300 hours of tape recordings on open reels

Access

Catalogue on cards.

Access to catalogue.

Access to materials.
Access on archives premises, by loan.

Fees – Copyright

No fees; but it's only allowed to use material for research.
Copyright holder is mainly the institution, in a few cases the informant. The whole situation, though, is a little bit unclear, due to the dizziness of the legislation.

160
SVENSKA LITTERATURSÄLLSKAPET I FINLAND
SOCIETY OF SWEDISH LITERATURE IN FINLAND
FOLKKULTURSARKIVET (THE FOLK CULTURE ARCHIVES)
Störnäs strandväg 25
SF – 00500 HELSINKI
FINLAND

Tel.: 358-90-7731077
Fax.: 358-90-632820

Collections

Collections of Film, Video, Sound.

Ethnographic films, ethnographic video, tapes : Finland-Swedish dialects, folk music, tradition recordings.
Films 31
Video 1
Sound 3300 tapes

Access

Catalogue published, on cards.

Access to catalogue.

Access to materials: limited.
Access on archives premises.

Fees – Copyright

Fees for facilities and handling, On archives premises.
Pricelist and conditions for use available.
Copyright holder is the institution.

161
TYÖVÄEN MUISTIETOTOIMIKUNTA
THE COMMISSION OF FINNISH LABOUR TRADITION
Paasivuorenkatu 5B
SF – 00530 HELSINKI
FINLAND

Tel.: 358-0-736322

Collections

Collections of Video, Sound.

From the year 1960 the commission has gathered tapes, cassettes and videos, which one has interviewed veterans in labour movement, personal memoirs. (Our collection includes about 200000 pages of labour memoirs).
Video 7 videocassettes (arrived in 1990)
Sound 780 tapes and cassettes of veteran interviews

Access

Catalogue on database.

Acces to catalogue: limited. Most of those tapes has lettered and they are available to read.

Access to materials: limited. They are preserved in the Finnish Labour Archives.
Access on archives premises.

Fees – Copyright

Fees for research for reuse and production purposes.
Copyright holder is the institution.
Tapes can be used on archives premission, and some by lone.

162

TYÖVÄENPERINNE – ARBETARTRADITION RY.
LABOUR HERITAGE
Paasivuorenkatu 5 B
SF – 00530 HELSINKI
FINLAND

Tel.: 358-0-736322

Collections

Collections of Film, Video.

Mainly of Finnish Labour Movement from 1930s until the present : trade unions, Workers' Sports Association in Finland, Social Democratic and Communist Parties, youth associations, culture, news reels, etc.
Films about 450 (stored in the premises of the Finnish Film Archive)
Video 159 VHS-copies, 48 U-Matic low band, 18 super-VHS

Access

Catalogue on database.

Access to catalogue.

Access to materials: limited. There are materials in our collection on which we don't own copyrights. These videos can only be seen on our premises.
Access on archives premises, by hire, by purchase.

Fees – Copyright

Fees for research for reuse and production purposes.
Pricelist and conditions for use available.
We have clearly stated in our catalogue on which films we own the copyrights and on which films we don't. All the films of KANSAN ELOKUVA- and ALLOTRIA-FILMI-filmcompanies (1946-62), some old 1930s material and our own productions (videos of old working methods, interviews, etc.) can be either hired or bought from us.

JOENSUU

163

JOENSUUN YLIOPISTON KIRJASTO
JOENSUU UNIVERSITY LIBRARY
Yliopistokatu 2
P.O. Box 111
SF – 80101 JOENSUU 10
FINLAND

Tel.: 358-73-1511
Fax.: 358-73-1512691
Telex: 46183 joy sf

Member of IFLA.

Collections

Collections of Film, Video, Sound.

Instructional materials for the teacher training at the university.
Films 4
Video 115
Sound about 2000

Access

Catalogue on database.

Access to catalogue.

Access to materials: partly limited.
Access on archives premises, by loan.

Fees – Copyright

Pricelist and conditions for use available.

JYVÄSKYLÄ

164

JYVÄSKYLÄN YLIOPISTON KIRJASTO
JYVÄSKYLÄ UNIVERSITY LIBRARY
Seminaarinkatu 15
P.O. Box 35
SF – 40351 JYVÄSKYLÄ
FINLAND

Tel.: 358-41-603447
Fax.: 358-41-603371
Telex: 28219 jyk sf

Member of IASA, IFLA, IAML.

Collections

Collections of Sound.

Collection contains sound recordings and other AV-material the library has got according the legal deposit since the year 1981. Material has been published in Finland.
Sound 22300

Access

Catalogue on database.

Access to catalogue: Everybody who wants can use the database (called MUSA). Finnish national discography called The Catalogue of Finnish sound recordings is published annually.

Access to materials: limited. It's possible to use the AV-collection only in Kyväskylä University Library for research purposes. No interlibrary lending.

Fees – Copyright

Institution holds no copyright.

TAMPERE

_____ 165
TAMPEREEN YLIOPISTON KANSANPER-INTEEN LAITOS
DEPARTMENT OF FOLK TRADITION, UNIVERSITY OF TAMPERE
Hatanpään valtatie 2B
P.O. Box 607
SF – 33101 TAMPERE
FINLAND

Tel.: 358-31-156495
Fax.: 358-31-157081
Telex: 22263 tayk sf

Member of IASA.

Collections

Collections of Sound, photographs, music papers.

Folk music, folklore, ethnographic material, oral history.
Sound 15000 tape reels

Access

Catalogue on database.

Access to catalogue.

Access to materials: limited. Access to original materials staff only, some limitations by informants and collectors.
Access on archives premises, by loan, by purchase.

Fees – Copyright

Fees for facilities and handling.
Pricelist and conditions for use available.
Copyright holder is the institution.

FRANCE

AIX EN PROVENCE

_____ 166
CENTRE DES ARCHIVES D'OUTRE-MER
29, chemin du Moulin de Testas
F – 13090 AIX EN PROVENCE
FRANCE

Tel.: 33-42.26.43.21

Member of ICA.

Collections

Collections of Film.
History of Algeria 1945-1962.

Access

Catalogue on database.

Access to catalogue: no.

Access to materials: limited.
Access on archives premises.

Fees – Copyright

Pricelist and conditions for use available.
Conditions are not yet defined.

ALENÇON

_____ 167
ARCHIVES DEPARTEMENTALES DE L'ORNE
6-10, avenue de Basingstoke
F – 61017 ALENÇON
FRANCE

Tel.: 33-33.32.09.00 poste 1901

Member of ICA.

Collections

Collections of Video, Sound.

Collection consists of audio-cassettes of popular songs (rural fiests), interviews. Recordings of historical films and documentaries, amateur video productions mainly on historical topics. Reportages of FR3 Basse Normandie on the Archives de l'Orne. Collection of ethnographic subjects.
Video 30 cassettes

Access

Catalogue on cards.

Access to catalogue only for audio cassettes.

Access to materials.
Access on archives premises.

Fees – Copyright

Copyright holder is the institution.
Written commitment is required not to use the documents for commercial purposes.

AMIENS

_____ 168
VILLE D'AMIENS, SERVICE DES ARCHIVES MUNICIPALES
50, rue Riolan
F – 80000 AMIENS
FRANCE
Tel.: 33-22.91.12.94

Collections
Collections of Sound.

Meetings of the town council since 1983.
Sound 241 cassettes

Access
Catalogue published.

Access to catalogue.

Access to materials.
Access on archives premises.

ANGERS

_____ 169
ARCHIVES DEPARTEMENTALES DE MAINE-ET-LOIRE
rue de Frémur
P.O. Box n° 106
F – 49000 ANGERS
FRANCE
Tel.: 33-41.47.10.47

Collections
Collections of Video.

Video cassettes on Anjou, history and tourism (3 cassettes). History and archivism (4 cassettes).
Video 7 cassettes

Fees – Copyright
Fees for research by archive staff.

_____ 170
ARCHIVES MUNICIPALES D'ANGERS, MAIRIE D'ANGERS
Bd de la Résistance et de la Déportation
P.O. Box 3527
F – 49035 ANGERS Cédex 01
FRANCE
Tel.: 33-41.86.10.10
Fax.: 33-41.88.09.04

Member of ICA.

Collections
Collections of Sound.

1 magnetic tape on "History of the hotels of the city of Angers". Cassettes from the "Internal Communication Department" : interviews with town officials to prepare the internal communication bulletin.
Sound 24 cassettes, 1 tape

Access
Catalogue on database.

Acces to catalogue: limited to the depositing department, due to rules of confidentiality.

Access to materials: limited.
Access on archives premises.

Fees – Copyright
Fees for research by archive staff.
Copyright holder is the institution.

BAGNEUX

_____ 171
ARCHIVES COMMUNALES DE BAGNEUX
57, avenue H. Ravera
F – 92220 BAGNEUX
FRANCE
Tel.: 33-1-46.56.54.01
Fax.: 33-1-47.35.90.90

Collections
Collections of Film, Video, Sound.

Social history based on the life of the county since 1945 : political events, speeches, manifestations, leisure – childrens holiday camps, fiests, sports, parties ; urbanism, architecture, public works.

Access
Access to materials.
Access on archives premises.

Fees – Copyright
Copyright holder is the institution.

BASTIA

_____ 172
ARCHIVES DEPARTEMENTALES DE LA HAUTE-CORSE, HOTEL DU DEPARTEMENT
F – 20405 BASTIA Cédex
FRANCE
Tel.: 33-95.32.06.45
Telex: 33-95.32.21.00

Collections
Collections of Video, Sound.

Video recordings : television TF1, A2, La 5, RAI, mainly FR3 with daily recording of news and the TV program "Corsica sera". Audio recordings : cassettes with traditional music, political debates, interviews with important personalities, records with songs.
Video 202 cassettes, 3 hours
Sound 10 cassettes of 90 minutes : traditional music. 40 cassettes of 90 minutes : interviews and political debates

Access

Acces to catalogue: limited. Access only to private sound collection of François Flori.

Access to materials: limited. On premises only.

BELFORT

_____ 173
SERVICE DES ARCHIVES ET DE L'ACTION CULTURELLE – BELFORT
4, rue de l'Ancien Théâtre
F – 90000 BELFORT
FRANCE
Tel.: 33-86.22.03.01

Collections

Collections of Video, Sound.

Collection of Radio-France-Belfort : audiotapes of broadcasts 1983-1984. Collection of the cultural centre (CEDAC) : video cassettes of lectures of various activities between 1976 and 1980 and of the strike at Alsthom-Belfort in 1979.
Video 80
Sound 126

Access

Catalogue on cards.
Access to catalogue.
Access to materials.
Access on archives premises.

BESANÇON

_____ 174
ATELIER AUDIOVISUEL DE LA VILLE DE BESANÇON
27, rue de la République
F – 25000 BESANÇON
FRANCE
Tel.: 33-81.81.37.44

Collections

Collections of Video.

Health, art brut, art history, botanics, jails, archeology, handicaps, regional architecture.
Video 17 video tapes

Access

Catalogue on cards.
Access to catalogue.
Access to materials.

Fees – Copyright

Pricelist and conditions for use available.
Copyright holder is the institution.
Access by lending, renting, selling.

BLOIS

_____ 175
CONSEIL GENERAL DE LOIR-ET-CHER
SERVICES DES ARCHIVES DE LOIR-ET-CHER
rue Louis Bodin
F – 41011 BLOIS Cédex
FRANCE
Tel.: 33-54.74.62.22

Collections

Collections of Film, Video, Sound.

Rural traditions, opening of the archive in 1965.
Films 2
Video 1
Sound 5

Access

Access to catalogue.
Access to materials: limited.
Access on archives premises.

Fees – Copyright

Institution holds no copyright.

BOBIGNY

_____ 176
ARCHIVES DEPARTEMENTALES DE LA SEINE-SAINT-DENIS
18, rue Salvador Allende
F – 93000 BOBIGNY
FRANCE
Tel.: 33-1-48.30.71.71

Collections

Collections of Film, Video, Sound, private production files and administrative papers.

Collection consists of recordings on sociology, history, culture and industry of the region Seine-Saint-Denis.
Films 566 titles
Video 3129 cassettes
Sound 1223 tapes and cassettes

Access

Catalogue published.

Access to catalogue.

Access to materials: limited due to legal and preservation problems.

Fees – Copyright

Communication free of charge within the archive.
Institution holds no copyright.
Access by lending and copying.

BOIS D'ARCY

_____ 177
SERVICE DES ARCHIVES DU FILM
7 bis, rue Alexandre Turpault
F – 78390 BOIS D'ARCY
FRANCE

Tel.: 33-1-34.60.20.50
Fax.: 33-1-34.60.52.25
Member of FIAF.

Collections

Collections of Film, posters, photos, scripts, books, periodicals, censorship documents, publicity materials, slides.

Fiction and non fiction feature and short films mainly french from early cinema up to now.
Films 106000 titles (about 1 million reels)

Access

Catalogue on database.

Acces to catalogue: limited. Some documents are secretly deposited.

Access to materials: limited. Only access to positive material. Limited access to material secretly deposited.
Access on archives premises, by loan.

Fees – Copyright

Fees for research for reuse and production purposes, research by archive staff, projection, consultation.
Pricelist and conditions for use available.
Institution holds no copyright.
Access depends on written agreement of right holders and depositors.

BORDEAUX

_____ 178
BIBLIOTHEQUE DE BORDEAUX
85, cours du Maréchal Juin
F – 33075 BORDEAUX Cédex
FRANCE

Tel.: 33-56.24.32.51
Fax.: 33-56.24.94.08

Collections

Collections of Video.

Documentaries or testimonies on current social, cultural, political, sports events. Animation films for children.
Video 1000 titles on 3/4", U-Matic, 600 titles on 8mm HB

Access

Catalogue on database.

Acces to catalogue: limited.

Access to materials: limited.

_____ 179
MEMOIRE DE BORDEAUX
Esplanade Charles de Gaulle
F – 33076 BORDEAUX Cédex
FRANCE

Tel.: 33-56.99.84.84 postes 2330/2335
Fax.: 33-56.96.19.40

Collections

Collections of Film, Video.

Population and society, culture, teaching, economics, health and social actions, sports and leisure, urbanism, architecture and equipment, testimonies and actors.
Films 253 titles
Video 422 titles

Access

Catalogue on cards.

Acces to catalogue: limited. By staff only.

Access on archives premises.

BOULOGNE BILLANCOURT

_____ 180
MUSEE DEPARTEMENTAL ALBERT KAHN
14, rue du Port
F – 92100 BOULOGNE BILLANCOURT
FRANCE

Tel.: 33-1-46.04.52.80
Fax.: 33-1-46.03.86.59

Member of ICOM.

Collections

Collections of Film, slides (72000).

Animated images (170000 metres) covering more than 48 countries between 1909 and 1931. It's part of the global work of Albert Kahn. Daily life, politics, geo-ethnology, personalities.

Access

Catalogue on database.

Access to catalogue.

Access to materials: no.
Access on archives premises, by loan, by hire.

Fees – Copyright

Fees for research for reuse and production purposes.
Pricelist and conditions for use available.
Copyright holder is the institution.
For consultation in view of lending and rent.

BRY SUR MARNE

_____ 181

INSTITUT NATIONAL DE L'AUDIO-VISUEL – INA
4, avenue de l'Europe
F – 94360 BRY SUR MARNE
FRANCE

Tel.: 33-1-49.83.22.01
Fax.: 33-1-49.83.25.85
Telex: INA PROD 261395

Member of IFTA, IASA.

Collections

Collections of Film, Video, Sound.

French radio and television archive since 1933.
Films 1850000 entries, 850000 hours of programme

Access

Catalogue on database.

Access to catalogue.

Access to materials.

Fees – Copyright

Fees for research for reuse and production purposes, research by archive staff, facilities and handling.
Pricelist and conditions for use available.
For copyright inquiry necessary.

CASTRES

_____ 182

ARCHIVES MUNICIPALES DE CASTRES
2, avenue du Sidobre
F – 81100 CASTRES
FRANCE

Tel.: 33-63.35.59.84

Collections

Collections of Video.

Videos shot during local manifestations and testimonies relevant to local history.
Video 35 cassettes

Access

Catalogue on cards.

Access to catalogue.

Access on archives premises.

Fees – Copyright

Fees for research for reuse and production purposes.
Copyright holder is the institution.

CRETEIL

_____ 183

ARCHIVES DEPARTEMENTALES DU VAL-DE-MARNE
8-10, rue des Archives
F – 94006 CRETEIL Cédex
FRANCE

Tel.: 33-1-45.13.80.50

Collections

Collections of Film, Video, Sound, slides, transcription of certain cassettes.

Collection of AV-materials on history and present life of the region of Val-de-Marne.
Films 20 titles
Video 1600 cassettes
Sound 300 cassettes and tapes

Access

Catalogue on cards.

Acces to catalogue: limited due to legal problems.

Access to materials: limited, only on appointment due to preservation problems.
Access on archives premises.

Fees – Copyright

No fees for research and consultation.
The Archive gives access to researchers on the premises to material for which the archive is authorized. For materials which can not be communicated freely, reproduction must be negotiated upon a written request with the institution or individual which has deposited the material or is the right holder.

DAINVILLE

_____ **184**
ARCHIVES DEPARTEMENTALES DU PAS-DE-CALAIS
1, rue du 19 mars 1962
F - 62020 DAINVILLE
FRANCE
Tel.: 33-21.71.10.90, 33-21.71.32.66

Collections
Collections of Video, Sound, books.

Administration, ethnology, history, art history, folk music, tourism.
Sound 21 items

Access
Catalogue indexed on cards.

Access to catalogue.

Access to materials. Free access.
Access on archives premises.

Fees - Copyright
No fees.

FOUGERES

_____ **185**
ARCHIVES MUNICIPALES DE FOUGERES
5, rue Porte Saint-Léonard
B.P. 111
F - 35301 FOUGERES Cédex
FRANCE
Tel.: 33-99.94.88.09
Fax.: 33-99.94.88.08
Member of ICA.

Collections
Collections of Video, Sound.

Sound : meetings of town council, speeches on the inauguration of the Place Jean Guehenno, testimonies of resistance fighters of World War II. Video : copies from the Institut National de l'Audiovisuel : TV broadcasts showing Jean Guehenno, Europe, Archives in France.
Video 5 cassettes
Sound 187 cassettes (245 hours)

Access
Catalogue published.

Access to catalogue.

Access to materials.
Access on archives premises.

Fees - Copyright
Institution holds no copyright.

IVRY SUR SEINE

_____ **186**
ETABLISSEMENT CINEMATOGRAPHIQUE ET PHOTOGRAPHIQUE DES ARMEES
E.C.P.A. Fort d'Ivry
F - 94205 IVRY SUR SEINE Cédex
FRANCE
Tel.: 33-1-49.60.52.00
Fax.: 33-1-49.60.52.06
Telex: ECPAIVR 263059 F
Member of FIAF.

Collections
Collections of Film, Video, autochrome photographies (3000000), slides.

Main events concerning the French army, ground, air, sea : missions, people, materials.
Films 80000 reels
Video about 500 hours

Access
Catalogue published, on cards.

Access to catalogue. Catalogue does not include all the collection.

Access to materials: limited due to reasons of preservation and censorship.
Access on archives premises, by loan, by purchase.

Fees - Copyright
Fees for research by archive staff.
Pricelist and conditions for use available.
Copyright holder is the institution.
No rights for loans, but rights for commercial exploitation.

LA ROCHE SUR YON

_____ **187**
ARCHIVES DEPARTEMENTALES DE LA VENDEE
14, rue Haxo
F - 85000 LA ROCHE SUR YON
FRANCE
Tel.: 33-51.37.71.33

Collections
Collections of Film, Video, Sound.

Subjects : wars of Vendée, monuments (abbey of la Grainetière, chapell of Mont des Alouettes), folklore, military music, religious songs (hymns of Père Grignion de Montfort), important personalities from Vendée (Jean Yole, Georges Clémenceau), trip of Charles De Gaulle in Vendée (1965), local animation.
Films 201
Video 2 cassettes
Sound 33 records, 7 cassettes, 2 tapes

Access

Access to catalogue: no. Catalogue unpublished, access is reserved to students and researchers preparing thesis or publications.

Access to materials: limited.
Access on archives premises, by loan.

188
CINEMATHEQUE DE VENDEE
16, rue Olivier de Clisson
F - 85000 LA ROCHE SUR YON
FRANCE

Tel.: 33-51.37.71.33
Fax.: 33-51.62.72.17

Collections

Collections of Film, Video, magazines, posters.

About 150 feature films, about 120 amateur films.

Access

Catalogue on cards.

Access on request.

Access on archives premises.

Fees – Copyright

Fees for research for reuse and production purposes.

LAVAL

189
ARCHIVES DEPARTEMENTALES DE LA MAYENNE
5, rue Ernest Laurain
F - 53000 LAVAL
FRANCE

Member of ICA.

Collections

Collections of Film, Video, Sound.

Sonotheque : collection of music, traditional songs and dances from Mayenne.
Films 1
Video 6 cassettes
Sound 36 cassettes, 15 tapes

Access

Catalogue on cards.

Acces to catalogue: limited.

Access to materials: limited.
Access on archives premises.

Fees – Copyright

Institution holds no copyright.

LORIENT

190
ARCHIVES MUNICIPALES DE LORIENT
2, boulevard du Général Leclerc
B.P. 2145
F - 56321 LORIENT Cédex
FRANCE

Tel.: 33-97.02.22.42
Fax.: 33-97.02.22.35
Telex: 950615

Collections

Collections of Film, Sound.

Official trips since 1960, cultural events since 1962, meetings of the town council since 1983.
Films 3
Sound 20 records

Access

Access to materials.
Access on archives premises.

Fees – Copyright

Copyright holder is the institution.

MONT DE MARSAN

191
ARCHIVES DEPARTEMENTALES DES LANDES
Impasse Montravel
F - 40000 MONT DE MARSAN
FRANCE

Tel.: 33-58.46.40.40
Fax.: 33-58.46.47.57

Collections

Collections of Sound.

Sound archives deposits regional radio, Radio-France-Landes : documents concern local life and events and ethnographic topics (life stories, costums, biographies).
Sound 993 hours

Access

Catalogue on database.

Access to catalogue.

Access to materials: limited.

Fees – Copyright

Copyright holder is the institution.
Consultation of documents only with agreement from regional radio station.

MONTPELLIER

_____ 192
ASSOCIATION POUR LA RECHERCHE, L'IMAGE ET LE SON – A.R.I.S.
31, rue Saint Guilhem
F – 34000 MONTPELLIER
FRANCE

Tel.: 33-67.66.02.09

Collections

Collections of Film, Video, sound tapes describing sequences of silent films.

Collection consists of Memoire du Languedoc, documentaries on cultural and environmental subjects, amateur films and professional documentaries.
Films 100
Video 50

Access

Catalogue on database.

Acces to catalogue: limited to programs using archive material.

Access to materials: limited for professionals.
Access on archives premises.

Fees – Copyright

Fees for research for reuse and production purposes.
Pricelist and conditions for use available.
Copyright holder is the institution.
For usage right holders permission needed.

MORHANGE

_____ 193
ARCHIVES CINEMATOGRPAHIQUES DE L'EST
Dalhain
F – 57430 MORHANGE
FRANCE

Tel.: 33-87.86.63.37

Collections

Collections of Film, photos, archives from distributors, posters, programs.

Features films : French cinema 1930-1945, occasionally German cinema 1945-1960, English cinema. Short films : animation films, slapstick comedies. Documentaries : on railways, geography, history.
Films 500 feature films, 550 short films

Access

Catalogue on cards.

Access to catalogue only for persons researching on history of cinema.

Access on archives premises.

Fees – Copyright

Fees for facilities and handling.
Pricelist and conditions for use available.
Institution holds no copyright.
Films are only shown on the premises for researchers on film history. Loans for occasional events provided that copyright problems have been solved in advance.

NANCY

_____ 194
CINEMATHEQUE DE LORRAINE
9, rue Michel Ney
F – 54000 NANCY
FRANCE

Tel.: 33-83.37.43.55, 33-83.32.77.63
Fax.: 33-83.32.78.12

Collections

Collections of Film, Video, photos, posters, production papers, apparatus.

Amateur films on regional subjects. Feature films and documentaries.
Films 900 titles, 100 hours amateur films
Video 120 hours video

Access

Catalogue on cards.

Access to catalogue.

Access to materials: limited. Projections only with agreement of rightholders.

Access on archives premises, by loan.

Fees – Copyright

Fees for research by archive staff, for using documentation material.
Pricelist and conditions for use available.
Copyright holder is the institution.
For consultation of material outside the Cinémathèque, the authorization of right holders is needed.

NANTES

_____ 195
ARCHIVES MUNICIPALES DE NANTES
1, rue d'Enfer
F – 44036 NANTES Cédex
FRANCE

Tel.: 33-40.41.91.34
Fax.: 33-40.41.92.39

Member of ICA.

Collections

Collections of Video.

Nantes from 1912 to 1990, "Archives – memory for the future".
Video 5

Access

Catalogue on database.

Access to catalogue through research database GESBIB in the reading room.

Access to materials: limited.

Fees – Copyright

Institution holds no copyright.

NICE

_____ 196

CINEMATHEQUE DE NICE – ACTION CULTURELLE MUNICIPALE
Acropolis – 3, Esplanade Kennedy
F – 06300 NICE
FRANCE

Tel.: 33-93.92.81.81
Fax.: 33-93.92.80.04

Collections

Collections of Film.

Fiction films.
Films 1310

Access

Acces to catalogue: limited to professional institutions (CNC or other cinematheques) on request.

Access to materials: limited.
Access on archives premises.

Fees – Copyright

Institution holds no copyright.
Limited number of films are accessible to students upon written request.

NIORT

_____ 197

ARCHIVES DEPARTEMENTALES DES DEUX-SEVRES
26, rue de la Blauderie
B.P. 505
F – 79000 NIORT
FRANCE

Tel.: 33-49.24.38.78

Member of ICA.

Collections

Collections of Film, Video, Sound.

Nature catastrophies, tourism, sports, folklore of Poitevin, industry, history.
Films 6
Video 3
Sound 11

Access

Access to materials: no.
Access on archives premises.

Fees – Copyright

Fees for research by archive staff.
Institution holds no copyright.

PALAISEAU

_____ 198

ECOLE POLYTECHNIQUE, BIBLIOTHEQUE
F – 91128 PALAISEAU Cédex
FRANCE

Tel.: 33-1-69.33.40.42
Fax.: 33-1-69.33.30.01

Member of IFLA.

Collections

Collections of Video, Sound.

Teaching materials in video, on scientific subjects produced or bought by the school. Sound : tapes for language learning, recordings of lectures in human and social sciences.
Video 400
Sound 1500

Access

Catalogue on database.

Acces to catalogue: limited to students and researchers of the school.

Access to materials: limited to students and researchers of the school.

Fees – Copyright

Copyright holder is the institution.
School requires copyright for reproducing audio and video cassettes.

PARIS

_____ 199

ARCHIVES NATIONALES, SECTION CONTEMPORAINE
60, rue des Francs-Bourgeois
F – 75141 PARIS Cédex 03
FRANCE

Tel.: 33-1-40.27.60.00 poste 6712
Member of ICA.

Collections
Collections of Video, Sound.

Speeches of presidents of the Republic, interviews about or with ministers from 3rd to 5th Republic, or high officials and various personalities, prisoners of World War II, resistance fighters. Audiovisual archives of the Ministry of Justice (trial of Klaus Barbie). Events on the archive (congress, inauguration, press conferences).
Video 591 videocassettes
Sound 278 cassettes, 1409 tapes

Access
Catalogue on cards.

Access to catalogue.

Access to materials: limited, depends on authorization of depositor or Direction of the Archive.
Access on archives premises.

Fees – Copyright
No fees. Legislation for fees still to be passed.
AV archive of Ministry of Justice : Ministry is the producer. Events on Archive : rights belong to TV.

___

200
BIBLIOTHEQUE DE L'UNIVERSITE PARIS 7
Tour centrale, 7e étage – 2, place Jussieu
F – 75251 PARIS Cédex 05
FRANCE

Tel.: 33-1-44.27.60.86
Fax.: 33-1-44.27.69.64
Member of IFLA.

Collections
Collections of Film, Video.
Medicine.
Films about 2000 (film and video)

Access
Access to catalogue: no.
Access to materials: Library users.
Access by loan.

___

201
BIBLIOTHEQUE NATIONALE
PHONOTHEQUE NATIONALE ET AUDIOVISUEL
2, rue Louvois
F – 75002 PARIS
FRANCE

Tel.: 33-1-47.03.88.20
Fax.: 33-1-42.96.84.47
Member of IASA, ICA, IFLA.

Collections
Collections of Film, Video, Sound, multi media documents and print collection on the history of sound recording, video and the different genres of music.

Universal collection in all fields of knowledge. Sound : published production distributed in France since 1889, legal deposit of phonogrammes since 1938. Linguistic and ethnomusicological sound archive since 1911. Video-film-multimedia : published production distributed in France. In the library on legal deposit since 1975 (video) and 1977 (film).
Films 14000 titles
Video 20000 titles video
Sound 1100000 phonogrammes, 600 phonographes

Access
Catalogue on database.

Database accessible within the library.

Access to materials: limited, bound on certain criteria. It is necessary to apply for permission in advance.
Access on archives premises, by purchase.

Fees – Copyright
Published documents : rights belong to right holders. Individual consultation on the premises free of charge if certain access criteria are met. For unpublished fond library may have the rights, access criteria remain as above. Reproductions are to be paid for and require right holders permission.

___

202
CENTRE GEORGES POMPIDOU – MUSEE NATIONAL D'ART MODERNE
F – 75191 PARIS Cédex 04
FRANCE

Tel.: 33-1-42.77.12.33
Fax.: 33-1-42.77.02.72
Telex: 212024

Collections
Collections of Film, Video.

Experimental films, films made by artists, films on art, documentaries on art.
Films 750 films, about 1000 reels
Video 300

Access
Catalogue on database.

Access to materials: limited to researchers due to conservation.
Access on archives premises.

Fees – Copyright
Institution holds no copyright.

Loans need agreement of copyright holder. Rights for diffusion are held for a few titles.

203
CENTRE GEORGES POMPIDOU – SERVICE AUDIOVISUEL
F – 75191 PARIS Cédex 04
FRANCE

Collections
Collections of Film, Video, Sound, slides.

Plastic arts, architecture, design, fashion, dance, music, theatre, history, society, literature, creative video, childrens programs, inhouse production, exhibition productions, co-productions with TV.
Films 80 titles
Video 640 tltles
Sound 1500 titles

Access
Catalogue on database.

Acces to catalogue: limited. Internal use only.

Access to materials: no.
Access by loan, by hire, by purchase.

Fees – Copyright
Fees for copying, possibly rights.
Pricelist and conditions for use available.
Copyright holder is the institution.

204
CENTRE NATIONAL DES ARCHIVES DE LA PUBLICITE – CNAP
113, rue des Moines
F – 75017 PARIS
FRANCE

Tel.: 33-1-42.28.89.89
Fax.: 33-1-46.27.35.52

Collections
Collections of Film, Video, Sound, photos, posters, press.

Advertising films (commercials) starting in 1900 till present days. Beauty, car, clothing, drink, financial, food, furniture, household cleaner, insurance, leisure, public information, toiletrie, white goods.
Films 120000 titles
Video 40000 titles
Sound 2000 radio spots

Access
Catalogue on database.

Acces to catalogue: limited to staff only. From 92 on, catalogue can be consulted by minitel.

Access to materials: limited to staff only.
Access on archives premises, by loan, by hire.

Fees – Copyright
Fees for research for reuse and production purposes, research by archive staff, facilities and handling.
Pricelist and conditions for use available.
Institution holds no copyright.

205
CINEMATHEQUE FRANCAISE
Palais de Chaillot, avenue Albert de Mun
F – 75116 PARIS
FRANCE

Tel.: 33-1-45.53.21.86
Fax.: 33-1-47.04.79.34

Member of FIAF.

Collections
Collections of Film, library, manuscripts, posters, photos, museum collection, costumes, apparatusses.

Films of all kinds from 1894.
Films 150000 reels, about 35000 titles

Access
Catalogue indexed on cards.

Access to catalogue: no.

Access to materials: limited, very strict rules followed.
Access on archives premises.

Fees – Copyright
Fees for viewing, handling.
Pricelist and conditions for use available.
Institution holds no copyright.
Films and other objects are deposited with the Cinematheque which is rarely own. Collection is neither for loan nor for sale.

206
INSTITUT DU MONDE ARABE
1, rue des Fossés Saint Bernard
F – 75005 PARIS
FRANCE

Tel.: 33-1-40.51.39.15
Fax.: 33-1-43.54.76.45
Telex: IMARABE 203 832 F

Collections
Collections of Film, Video, Sound.

In the AV Department : Videotheque : 400 documentaries on Arab civilization Phototheque : 15000 photos Music : 600 hours of Arab music.
Films about 60films
Video 350 titles
Sound 600 hours

Access

Catalogue on database.

Acces to catalogue: limited. Only from database.

Access on archives premises.

Fees – Copyright

Fees for facilities and handling, Actually free. AV-Department only holds rights for internal cultural diffusion. However for about 20 titles Department holds partly selling rights as co-producer of these films.

207
SERVICE HISTORIQUE DE L'ARMEE DE L'AIR

Château de Vincennes
B.P. 110
F – 00481 PARIS ARMEES
FRANCE

Tel.: 33-1-49.57.32.00 poste 2377
Fax.: 33-1-49.57.33.39

Member of IASA.

Collections

Collections of Sound.

Interviews with personalities, civilians and officiers which have participated in the history of military aviation since 1910.

Sound 650 interviews, about 1500 tapes

Access

Catalogue indexed on cards.

Access to catalogue: Inventory 1 to 145 is published. Rest is to be published.

Access to materials.

Access on archives premises.

Fees – Copyright

Fees for research by archive staff, Free for students and historians.

Copyright holder is the institution.

Conditions of interviewed persons on access have to be respected.

208
UNITED NATIONS EDUCATIONAL, SCIENTIFIC AND CULTURAL ORGANIZATION (UNESCO)

UNESCO AUDIO-VISUAL ARCHIVES
7, place de Fontenoy
P.O. 3.07 PARIS
F – 75700 PARIS
FRANCE

Tel.: 33-1-45.68.16.59 (video distribution), 33-1-45.68.10.00 (UNESCO switchboard)
Fax.: 33-1-45.67.30.72
Telex: 204461 PARIS, 270602 PARIS

Collections

Collections of Film, Video, Sound, photographs and slides (Photo Library).

Production on 16mm film has been transferred to Betacam SP video on themes related to UNESCO's programme : education, culture (particularly world heritage sites), science (mainly on environmental themes), communication and coverage of UNESCO conferences, projects, etc., as well as some Social Science themes.

Films minimum 5000 cans (originals, positives, sound)

Video 415 originals and 381 masters

Sound about 23500 recordings (accessible to professional radio stations)

Access

Catalogue indexed on cards.

Access to catalogue: Free of charge to published catalogue in English and French.

VHS video programmes available for non-commercial use from depositories worldwide listed in catalogue on loan. VHS programmes can be purchased from Headquarters. TV standards also available.

Access on archives premises, by loan, by purchase.

Fees – Copyright

Fees for facilities and handling.

As a rule, UNESCO holds the copyright to its PRODUCTIONS (for footage sales, TV broadcast) : however, it does not usually hold TV or footage rights to its CO-PRODUCTIONS.

209
VIDEOTHEQUE DE PARIS

Porte Saint Eustache
F – 75001 PARIS
FRANCE

Tel.: 33-1-40.26.30.40
Fax.: 33-1-40.26.40.96
Telex: 213 791 F

Member of IFTA.

Collections

Collections of Film, Video, posters.

Films and videos on Paris. Documentaries, features, newsreels, commercials from 1897 onwards.

Films 3000 titles
Video 4000 titles

Access

Catalogue on database.

Access to catalogue.

Access to materials: Permanent consultation of video collection (on 40 monitors) plus 4 daily showings.

Access on archives premises.

Fees – Copyright

Fees for research for reuse and production purposes, research by archive staff.
Pricelist and conditions for use available.
Institution holds no copyright.
Videotheque holds updated list of right holder of each film. It may link the demander with the right holder and facilitate all reproductions with the agreement of the right holder.

PAU

_____ 210
ARCHIVES DEPARTEMENTALES DES PYRENEES-ATLANTIQUES
boulevard Tourasse
F – 64000 PAU
FRANCE
Tel.: 33-59.02.67.06

Collections

Collections of Video, Sound.

Mainly recordings of oral testimonies collected by Association Mémoire Collective en Béarn and deposited with the archive. Recordings are about ethnographic inquiries and various radio broadcast, mainly on Béarn (agriculture, good, biographies, trade, teaching, fiests, history, popular medicine, jobs, fashion).
Sound about 300 hours

Access

Catalogue published.

Catalogue is published in the annual bulletin of the Association Mémoire Collective en Béarn.

Access to materials: limited. Justification of research and authorization of Director of Archive needed.
Access on archives premises.

Fees – Copyright

Copyright holder is the institution.

PERIGUEUX

_____ 211
ARCHIVES DEPARTEMENTALES DE LA DORDOGNE
9, rue Littré
F – 24000 PERIGUEUX
FRANCE

Collections

Collections of Sound.

Collection of recordings on regional events and traditions ; music editions from Ribéracois.

Sound Edition Ribéracois : 12h. Radio Périgueux : 8h

Access

Catalogue on cards.
Access to catalogue.
Access to materials.
Access on archives premises.

Fees – Copyright

Institution holds no copyright.

ROUEN

_____ 212
ARCHIVES DEPARTEMENTALES DE LA SEINE-MARITIME
Cours Clémenceau
F – 76101 ROUEN Cédex
FRANCE
Tel.: 33-35.03.54.95

Collections

Collections of Film, Video, Sound.

Magazines and actualities on regional events 1964-1983 (FR3 Haute-Normandie). Ethnology. Popular songs. Colleu fond.
Films 4524 reels and tapes (film and video)
Sound 40 hours

Access

Acces to catalogue: limited.
Access to materials: limited.

Fees – Copyright

Fees for research for reuse and production purposes, research by archive staff, facilities and handling.
Institution holds no copyright.
Colleu fond accessible on premises without any limitation. Commercial use depends on authorization of Mr Colleu.

SAINT BARTHELEMY D'ANJOU

_____ 213
CINEMATHEQUE REGIONALE DES PAYS DE LOIRE
20, rue des Cordelles
F – 49124 SAINT BARTHELEMY D'ANJOU
FRANCE
Tel.: 33-41.93.39.13

Collections

Collections of Film.

Collection of regional character on Loire themes : wine and vineyards, mechanical sports.
Films 500

Access

Catalogue on cards.

Access to catalogue: no, foreseen.

Access to materials: limited, copies accessible on video.

Access by hire, by purchase.

Fees – Copyright

Tarifs and conditions are estimated according the researchers.

Institution holds no copyright.

Right holder is the depositor. Each request is subject to negotiation.

SAINT BRIEUC

_____ 214

ARCHIVES DEPARTEMENTALES DES COTES-D'ARMOR
7, rue François Merlet
F – 22000 SAINT BRIEUC
FRANCE

Tel.: 33-96.78.78.77
Fax.: 33-96.78.67.29

Member of ICA.

Collections

Collections of Sound.

History of French Revolution in the regions Côtes d'Armor and Bretagne.
Sound 32 cassettes

Access

Catalogue on cards.

Access to catalogue.

Access to materials.
Access on archives premises.

Fees – Copyright

Copyright holder is the institution.

SAINT OUEN

_____ 215

CENTRE AUDIOVISUEL SNCF
9, quai de Seine
F – 93584 SAINT OUEN Cédex
FRANCE

Tel.: 33-1-40.10.58.00
Fax.: 33-1-40.10.58.05
Telex: 234067 SNCF CAV

Collections

Collections of Film, Video, Sound.

All subjects related to railway activities in France.
Two types of collection : edited films and stock shots.
Films 1200 titles
Video 400 titles
Sound 50 tapes

Access

Catalogue published.

Access to catalogue.

Access to materials: limited. Films lent free of charge. Stock shots to be consulted on the premises.
Access on archives premises, by loan, by purchase.

Fees – Copyright

Fees for research by archive staff, for films not published in catalogue.
Pricelist and conditions for use available.
Copyright holder is the institution.

SETE

_____ 216

GOULAMASTUDIO
6, rue Raymond Lefèbvre
F – 34200 SETE
FRANCE

Collections

Collections of Sound.

Rock'n'roll music, folkloric music, several interviews.
Sound 100 hours

Access

Catalogue published.

Access to catalogue.

Access to materials.
Access on archives premises, by purchase.

Fees – Copyright

Institution holds no copyright.

STRASBOURG

_____ 217

ARCHIVES DEPARTEMENTALES DU BAS-RHIN
5, rue Fischart
F – 67000 STRASBOURG
FRANCE

Tel.: 33-88.61.39.00

Member of ICA.

Collections

Collections of Film.

AV-documents disseminated by cultural department of the provincial government : documentaries (trips of the presidents, trips of schools, tourism, art). European fair, entry of French troops in Strasbourg 1918.
Films 7 reels

Access

Access to catalogue.

Access to materials: limited. Consultation without any limitations, but no projection of documents in the archive.
Access by loan.

Fees – Copyright

Copyright holder is the institution.
Written authorization of depositor needed.

THIONVILLE

___ 218
ARCHIVES MUNICIPALES DE THIONVILLE
Mairie de Thionville
B.P. 352
F – 57311 THIONVILLE
FRANCE

Tel.: 33-82.53.35.36
Fax.: 33-82.53.91.27

Member of ICA.

Collections

Collections of Film, Video, Sound.

Thionville, documentaries for school teaching 1935-1937 : crafts, industry, fishing, agriculture, animals, anatomy.
Films 140 reels
Video 30 reels
Sound 10 discs, 5 tapes

Access

Catalogue on cards.

Access to catalogue.

Access to materials: no. No equipment.
Access on archives premises.

Fees – Copyright

No rights.
Consultation on premises. For film agreement of Gaumont required.

TOULON

___ 219
CINEMATHEQUE MONDIALE DE LA MER ET DE L'EXPLORATION
La Nouvelle Espérance, chemin de la Batterie basse du Cap-Brun
F – 83000 TOULON
FRANCE

Tel.: 33-94.92.99.22
Fax.: 33-94.91.35.65

Collections

Collections of Film, Video.

Maritime and exploration themes (expeditions, diving, underwater archeology, pole missions) from 1896/1913 to present. All originals.
Films 250 films 16mm, 80 films 35mm
Video 200

Access

Catalogue published.

Access to catalogue.

Access to materials: limited.
Access on archives premises.

TOULOUSE

___ 220
ARCHIVES DEPARTEMENTALES DE LA HAUTE-GARONNE
11, boulevard Griffoul-Dorval
Toulouse-Rangueil
F – 31400 TOULOUSE
FRANCE

Tel.: 33-61.52.41.64
Fax.: 33-61.25.01.60

Member of ICA.

Collections

Collections of Video, Sound, texts of video presentations.

Traditions of region d'Oc, television reportages (local history and photography).
Video 74 cassettes
Sound 3 tapes

Access

Catalogue on database.

Acces to catalogue: limited. Only with agreement of producers (TV : FR3 and TLT).

No limitations for material which belongs to the archive.
Access on archives premises, by loan.

Fees – Copyright

Fees for renting rights, copyrights.
Pricelist and conditions for use available.
Copyright holder is the institution for educational use (for schools or general public) and for scientific research.

_____ 221
CINEMATHEQUE DE TOULOUSE
12, rue du Faubourg Bonnefoy
F – 31500 TOULOUSE
FRANCE

Tel.: 33-61.48.90.75
Fax.: 33-61.58.19.79

Member of FIAF.

Collections

Collections of Film, 700 scripts, 550000 stills, 41200 film posters, 12000 film books, 4000 indexes, 700 film magazine collections, 40000 files on films and cinema personalities.

Long and short films : fiction, documentaries, animation.
Films 16503 titles

Access

Catalogue on cards.

Acces to catalogue: limited. Staff only.

Access to materials: limited due to conservation, staff.
Access on archives premises.

Fees – Copyright

Fees for research by archive staff, facilities and handling.
Pricelist and conditions for use available.
Institution holds no copyright.

TULLE

_____ 222
ARCHIVES DEPARTEMENTALES DE LA CORREZE
Le Touron
F – 19000 TULLE
FRANCE

Tel.: 33-55.20.11.91

Collections

Collections of Video, Sound.
General life, local history, ethnology.
Films 1
Video 22 cassettes
Sound 98 tapes and discs

Access

Catalogue indexed on cards.
Access to catalogue. Catalogue is typed.
Access to materials: limited, limited equipment.

Fees – Copyright

Fees for research by archive staff.
Consultation only on archive premises.

VERSAILLES

_____ 223
ARCHIVES MUNICIPALES DE VERSAILLES
Mairie de Versailles, 4, avenue de Paris
R.P. 1144
F – 78011 VERSAILLES Cédex
FRANCE

Tel.: 33-1-30.97.81.60
Fax.: 33-1-30.97.80.01

Collections

Collections of Video, Sound.
Versailles, history.
Video 61 cassettes
Sound 165 cassettes

Access

Catalogue on cards.
Access to materials.

YVETOT

_____ 224
BIBLIOTHEQUE – MEDIATHEQUE
4, rue Pierre de Coubertin
B.P. 219
F – 76196 YVETOT Cédex
FRANCE

Tel.: 33-35.95.01.13
Fax.: 33-35.95.09.85

Collections

Collections of Video, Sound.
1000 video films (international and French fiction), 300 video documentaries, 11000 discs, cassettes, CD's.
Video 1300
Sound 11000 documents

Access

Catalogue published, on cards.
Access to catalogue.
Access by loan.

Fees – Copyright

Pricelist and conditions for use available.
Institution holds no copyright.

GERMANY

BADEN-BADEN

_____ 225

SÜDWESTFUNK
FERNSEH-ARCHIV DES SÜDWESTFUNK
Hans-Bredow-Straße
D – 76530 BADEN-BADEN
GERMANY
Tel.: 7221-920
Fax.: 7221-922062
Telex: 7221-7878195
Member of IASA.

Collections

Collections of Film, Video, covering material (manuscripts, production/transmission documents, etc.).

Films 16mm and 35mm, magnetic video tapes (2", 1", VHS, Betamax, etc.) : mainly own productions since 1955.

Access

Catalogue on database.

Acces to catalogue: limited. Both the Sound and the TV Archives are programme archives ; therefore no public access. Exceptions are made on request for scientific research, regard to regular operation.

Access to materials: limited. Both the Sound and the TV Archives are programme archives ; therefore no public access. Exceptions are made on request for scientific research, regard to regular operation.

Access on archives premises, by purchase.

Fees – Copyright

Fees for research for reuse and production purposes, facilities and handling, Both the Sound and the TV Archives are programme archives ; therefore no public access. Exceptions are made on request for scientific research, regard to regular operation.
Only in case of own production, the copyrights holders are the SWF and the author(s). Prices on request.

_____ 226

SÜDWESTFUNK
HOERFUNK-ARCHIV DES SÜDWESTFUNK
Hans-Bredow-Straße
D – 76530 BADEN-BADEN
GERMANY
Tel.: 7221-920
Fax.: 7221-922033

Telex: 7221-787810
Member of IASA.

Collections

Collections of Sound, covering material (manuscripts, production/transmission documents, etc.).

Magnetic tapes and discs (both analogue and digital), few shellacs ; own productions as well as industrial records since 1946.
Sound 500000 tapes, 60000 singles, 150000 LP's, 30000 CD's, 1000 shellacs

Access

Catalogue on database.

Acces to catalogue: limited. Both the Sound and the TV Archives are programme archives ; therefore no public access. Exceptions are made on request for scientific research, regard to regular operation.

Access to materials: limited. Both the Sound and the TV Archives are programme archives ; therefore no public access. Exceptions are made on request for scientific research, regard to regular operation.

Access on archives premises, by purchase.

Fees – Copyright

Fees for research for reuse and production purposes, facilities and handling, Both the Sound and the TV Archives are programme archives ; therefore no public access. Exceptions are made on request for scientific research, regard to regular operation.
Only in case of own production, the copyrights holders are the SWF and the author(s). Prices on request.

BERLIN

_____ 227

BERLINER STADTBIBLIOTHEK, PHONOTHEK
Breite Str. 32-34
D – 10178 BERLIN
GERMANY
Tel.: 30-2442366
Telex: 114513
Member of IASA.

Collections

Collections of Sound.

Discs, CD's, tapes, audiocassettes, historical formats.
Sound 67500 discs including historical formats, 450 CD, 7500 tapes

Access

Catalogue on database.

Access to catalogue.

Access to materials.

Access on archives premises, by loan.

Fees – Copyright

Institution holds no copyright.

228

BUNDESARCHIV – FILMARCHIV

Fehrbelliner Platz 3
D – 10707 BERLIN
GERMANY

Tel.: 30-86811
Fax.: 30-8681310

Member of FIAF, ICA, IAMHIST.

Collections

Collections of Film, Video. For films only : scripts, stills, posters, advertising material, newspaper clips, censorship documents, partly production files.

Fiction and non-fiction films mainly of German origin ranging from 1895 to present production.
Films 110000 titles

Access

Catalogue indexed on cards.

Access to catalogue.

Access to materials: limited. Depends on status of preservation and legal conditions in relation to request.

Access on archives premises, by loan.

Fees – Copyright

Fees for research for reuse and production purposes, facilities and handling.
Pricelist and conditions for use available.
Institution holds no copyright.
Access for commercial purposes only with agreement of right holder. Access to German feature films for non-commercial use only with agreement of right holders. Archive holds rights for viewing on archive premises and non-commercial showing of German non-fiction films.

229

DIE DEUTSCHE BIBLIOTHEK

DEUTSCHES MUSIKARCHIV
Gärtnerstraße 25-32
45 02 29
D – 12207 BERLIN
GERMANY

Tel.: 30-771 00 20
Fax.: 30-771 60 28

Member of IASA, IFLA, IAML.

Collections

Collections of Video, Sound, sheet music, machines, books, old catalogues, discographies.

700000 items, sheet music, LP's, 78s, CD's, cassettes, 45's, CD-Video/Laser-Discs, videotape/film, reel-to-reel tapes, cylinders, piano rolls.
Project : cataloging and documentation of historical sound recordings. Deutsches Musikarchiv is the German national archive for legal deposit of printed and recorded music and publisher of the parts of the German national bibliography : Musikalien-Verzeichnis, Musiktonträger-Verzeichnis.
Video 1000
Sound 450000

Access

Catalogue on database.

Access to catalogue.

Access to materials.

Access on archives premises.

Fees – Copyright

Fees only for copies under copyright conditions. Research only. No copies from sheet music. Copies from recorded music under copyright conditions.

230

LANDESBILDSTELLE BERLIN. ZENTRUM FÜR AUDIO-VISUELLE MEDIEN

LANDESBILDSTELLE BERLIN. CENTRE FOR AUDIO-VISUAL MEDIA
LANDESFILM- UND -TONARCHIV BERLIN
Wikingerufer 7
D – 10555 BERLIN
GERMANY

Tel.: 30-390 92 220
Fax.: 30-390 92 349

Member of IAMHIST.

Collections

Collections of Film, Video, Sound.

Archive footage, documentary films and sound recordings on the development and history of Berlin (among the stock film portraits and taped interviews of important Berliners) ; sound recordings of the sessions of Berlin parliament ; collection of films produced by/for the Press and Information Office of Land Berlin ; collection of pedagogical sound and video recordings.
Films about 2258000 m (negatives, positives ; 35 and 16mm)
Video about 7000 min.
Sound about 542600 min.

Access

Catalogue indexed on cards.

Access to catalogue: no. Catalogue only for use by staff.

Access to materials: Materials can be used according to arrangement with the archives. Access on archives premises.

Fees – Copyright

Fees for research for reuse and production purposes, research by archive staff, facilities and handling, Costs for copying materials at external printing labs to be paid by the user.
Pricelist and conditions for use available.
The institution is copyright-holder of most of the archives stock. But there are also materials the copyright of which is owned by other holders. Special arrangements for various forms of commercial use.

_____ 231

MUSEUM FÜR VÖLKERKUNDE BERLIN – ABTEILUNG MUSIKETHNOLOGIE
DEPARTMENT OF ETHNOMUSICOLOGY, ETHNOGRAPHICAL MUSEUM BERLIN
Arnimallee 23/27
D – 14195 BERLIN
GERMANY

Tel.: 30-8301.240
Fax.: 30-83 15 972
Telex: 18 31 60 staab

Member of IASA.

Collections

Collections of Video, Sound.

Archives of traditional music of all cultures of the world.
Sound more than 100000 recordings

Access

Catalogue on database.

Access to catalogue.

Access to materials by appointment.
Access on archives premises.

Fees – Copyright

Copyright depends on the specific collection, holder is in many cases the collector, copyright for traditional music is under discussion, the right holders permission is needed.

_____ 232

SENDER FREIES BERLIN, SCHALL- UND NOTENARCHIV
Masurenallee 8-14
D – 14057 BERLIN
GERMANY

Tel.: 30-313241

Fax.: 30-3015062
Telex: 182813

Member of IASA.

Collections

Collections of Sound, scores.

Music, spoken word, all kinds.
Sound 260000 tapes, 60000 records, 10000 CDs

Access

Catalogue on database.

Acces to catalogue: limited.

Access to materials: no.

_____ 233

STAATSBIBLIOTHEK ZU BERLIN, PREUßISCHER KULTURBESITZ
Unter den Linden 8
D – 10102 BERLIN
GERMANY

Tel.: 30-20378 257
Telex: 112 757

Member of IFLA.

Collections

Collections of Sound.

Classical music.
Sound 34000 discs

Access

Catalogue on cards.

Access to catalogue.

Access to materials.
Access on archives premises.

_____ 234

STIFTUNG DEUTSCHE KINEMATHEK
Pommernallee 1
D – 14052 BERLIN
GERMANY

Tel.: 30-30 307 234
Fax.: 30-302 92 94

Member of FIAF.

Collections

Collections of Film, Video, Sound, stills, posters, scripts, filmprogramms, advertising material, censorshipcards, set- and costume designs, musical scores, costumes, props.

Films and all related material from the national and international film history, from the beginning until today.
Films about 8000 titles
Video about 500
Sound about 500

Access

Catalogue on cards

Access to catalogue: no. For internal use only. It does exist a film catalogue for the non-commercial distribution.

Access to materials: Film distribution and internal use of the related material.
Access on archives premises, by loan.

Fees – Copyright

Fees for research for reuse and production purposes, research by archive staff, facilities and handling, There is no charge if the research is for scientific purposes.
Pricelist and conditions for use available.
Institution holds no copyright.
For research on the premises no copyright permission is asked. For the different forms of uses outside the permission by the copyright holder must be submitted in writing before the material can be used.

COLOGNE

_____ 235
DEUTSCHE WELLE, TONARCHIV
VOICE OF GERMANY, SOUND ARCHIVES
Raderberggürtel 50
D – 50968 KÖLN
GERMANY

Tel.: 221-3894321
Fax.: 221-3893000
Telex: 88 84 85

Member of IASA.

Collections

Collections of Sound, manuscripts, production papers.

Radio productions of Deutsche Welle on tapes, discs, compact discs, music cassettes (classical music, light music, non european and european folk music).
Sound 200000 tapes, 100000 discs, 10000 compact discs

Access

Catalogue indexed on cards.

Acces to catalogue: limited.

Access to materials: limited due to legal problems.
Access on archives premises.

Fees – Copyright

Fees for facilities and handling.
Copyright conditions have to be checked by the fees and licenses department in any single case.

_____ 236
WESTDEUTSCHER RUNDFUNK, BIBLIOTHEK UND ARCHIVE
Appellhofplatz 1
D – 50600 KÖLN
GERMANY

Tel.: 221-2201
Fax.: 221-2204800
Telex: 8 882 575

Member of IASA.

Collections

Collections of Film, Video, Sound, pictures.

Radio & television productions.
Films 150000
Video 153000
Sound 600000

Access

Catalogue on database.

Access to catalogue: no.

Access to materials: limited due to limited facilities, legal problems.
Access by purchase.

Fees – Copyright

Fees for facilities and handling, copyright.
Right holders permission is needed.

_____ 237
ZENTRALBIBLIOTHEK DER SPORTWISSENSCHAFTEN (DEUTSCHE SPORTHOCHSCHULE)
CENTRAL LIBRARY OF THE SPORT SCIENCES (GERMAN SPORTS ACADEMY)
Carl-Diem-Weg 6
D – 50927 KÖLN
GERMANY

Tel.: 221-4982214
Fax.: 221-4971782

Collections

Collections of Film, Video.

Sport sciences and practice.
Films 2423
Video 581

Access

Catalogue on database.

Acces to catalogue: limited, only for members of the institution.

Access to materials: limited, only for members of the institution.
Access on archives premises.

Fees – Copyright

Institution holds no copyright.

DRESDEN

238

SÄCHSISCHE LANDESBIBLIOTHEK, ABTEILUNG PHONOTHEK
(Stauffenbergallee 9 g) Marienallee 12
D – 01099 DRESDEN
GERMANY

Tel.: 351-57 21 93
Fax.: 351-5 32 21

Member of IASA, IAML.

Collections

Collections of Video, Sound.

The "Phonothek" is one of the main departments of the Sächsische Landesbibliothek. Her parts are the Archive collection (50% of entire holding), the Non-Circulating collection (20% ; both under supervision of the own sound studio of the Phonothek) and the Lending Collection (30% ; available in open-access area). Speciality : Sächsisches Tonträgerarchiv (Saxon Sounds Archives).
Video 1900 V-CD and VHS-cassettes
Sound 127000 historical records, LP, CD, MC, tapes

Access

Catalogue on cards.
Access to catalogue.
Access to materials: limited.
Access by purchase.

Fees – Copyright

Fees for research by archive staff.
Institution holds no copyright.

DÜSSELDORF

239

MANNESMANN ARCHIV
ARCHIVES OF THE MANNESMANN AG
Mannesmannufer 2
D – 40213 DÜSSELDORF
GERMANY

Tel.: 211-820 2200
Fax.: 211-820 2554
Telex: 8581481

Collections

Collections of Film, Video, Sound.

The Mannesmann-Concern, its plants, processes and products since 1936.
Films 7000 rolls (decreasing)
Video 150 (increasing)
Sound 40

Access

Catalogue on cards.
Acces to catalogue: limited, by staff only.
Access to materials.
Access on archives premises.

240

NORDRHEIN-WESTFÄLISCHES HAUPTSTAATSARCHIV
Mauerstr. 51
D – 40476 DÜSSELDORF
GERMANY

Tel.: 211-9449 01

Member of ICA.

Collections

Collections of Film, Video, Sound.

History of the "Land Nordrhein-Westfalen" (only documentary films) ; subjects : political, social, cultural, economical development, main events as well as daily life, documents on politicians, V.I.P.'s, important institutions, etc.
Films 1625 film boxes
Video 40 cartridges of videotape
Sound 1900 tapes

Access

Catalogue on database.
Access to catalogue.
Access to materials: limited. Limited technical facilities.
Access on archives premises, by purchase.

Fees – Copyright

Fees for research for reuse and production purposes, research by archive staff, facilities and handling.
Institution holds no copyright.
As the case may be, copyright conditions must be verified by those who have transferred the film (Administration, depositary, donor).

FRANKFURT

241

DEUTSCHES RUNDFUNKARCHIV
Bertramstraße 8
D – 60320 FRANKFURT/MAIN
GERMANY

Tel.: 69-156870
Fax.: 69-15687100

Member of IASA, IFLA.

Collections

Collections of Sound, printed matters.

Historic records and historic recordings on tape.
Sound gigantic

Access

Catalogue on database.

Access to catalogue.

Access to materials: limited for broadcasting companies and research.
Access on archives premises, by hire.

Fees – Copyright

Fees for research for reuse and production purposes, research by archive staff, facilities and handling.
Pricelist and conditions for use available.
Rightholder is the institution for reuse within the ARD Broadcasting Companies plus purposes of research.

242

STADT- UNE UNIVERSITÄTSBIBLIOTHEK FRANKFURT a.M.
FRANKFURT MUNICIPAL AND UNIVERSITY LIBRARY
Bockenheimer Landstrasse 134-138
D – 60325 FRANKFURT/MAIN
GERMANY

Tel.: 69-212 39244, 69-212 39230
Fax.: 69-212 39404

Member of IFLA.

Collections

Collections of Film, Video, Sound, books, periodicals.

German literature, German theatre ; Ethnomusicology (small quantity of material concerning Frankfurt).
Films 62 items (film and video)
Sound 3600 items

Access

Catalogue on database.

Access to catalogue.

Access to materials: limited for study purposes only.
Access on archives premises.

Fees – Copyright

No fees.
Institution holds no copyright.

GÖTTINGEN

243

INSTITUT FÜR DEN WISSENSCHAFTLICHEN FILM, ABT. DOKUMENTATION UND PUBLIKATIONEN
INSTITUTE FOR SCIENTIFIC FILMS, DEPT OF DOCUMENTATION/PUBLICATIONS
Nonnenstieg 72
D – 37075 GÖTTINGEN
GERMANY

Tel.: 551-2020
Fax.: 551-202 200
Telex: 96691

Member of IAMHIST.

Collections

Collections of Film, Video.

Instructional films from the natural sciences, medicine, psychology, ethnology + history.
Films about 8000 (film and video)

Access

Catalogue on database.

Access to catalogue.

Access to materials.
Access on archives premises, by loan, by purchase.

Fees – Copyright

Penalty fee for failing to return loaned materials by due date.
Pricelist and conditions for use available.
Copyright is partially with the institution, partially with other right holders.

HAMBURG

244

HAMBURGER ÖFFENTLICHE BÜCHERHALLEN – MUSIKBIBLIOTHEK
Große Bleichen 23-27
D – 20354 HAMBURG
GERMANY

Tel.: 40-35 60 60
Fax.: 40-35 60 62 11

Member of IFLA.

Collections

Collections of Sound.

CD, discs, audio-cassettes.
Sound 12461 records, 8802 cassettes, 3000 CDs

Access

Catalogue on cards.

Access to catalogue.

Access to materials Subscription-, reservation-fees.
Access by loan.

Fees – Copyright
Pricelist and conditions for use available.
Copyright holder is the institution.

_____ 245
NORDDEUTSCHER RUNDFUNK – FERNSEHEN, FERNSEHARCHIV
Gazellenkamp 57
D – 22504 HAMBURG
GERMANY

Tel.: 40-41560
Fax.: 40-566745
Telex: 211 849

Collections
Collections of Film, Video, Sound.
All television programs.

Access
Catalogue on database.

Access to catalogue: no.

Access to materials: limited.
Access by hire, by purchase.

Fees – Copyright
Fees for facilities and handling, hire, copyright.
Inquiry by letter.

HEIDELBERG

_____ 246
UNIVERSITÄTSBIBLIOTHEK HEIDELBERG
UNIVERSITY LIBRARY OF HEIDELBERG
Plöck 107-109
D – 69117 HEIDELBERG
GERMANY

Tel.: 6221-542380
Fax.: 6221-542623

Member of IFLA.

Collections
Collections of Video, Sound.

Medicine, biology, art, history, literature, film-history, fiction-films.
Video 4000
Sound 2000

Access
Catalogue on database.

Access to catalogue.

Access to materials: limited.
Access on archives premises.

Fees – Copyright
Institution holds no copyright.

KOBLENZ

_____ 247
BUNDESARCHIV – FILMARCHIV
Potsdamer Str. 1
D – 56075 KOBLENZ
GERMANY

Tel.: 261-5050
Fax.: 261-505 226
Telex: 261 852 BArch Ko

Member of FIAF, ICA, IAMHIST.

Collections
Collections of Film, Video. For films only : scripts, stills, posters, advertising material, newspaper clips, censorship documents, partly production files.

Fiction and non-fiction films mainly of German origin ranging from 1895 to present production.
Films 110000 titles

Access
Catalogue indexed on cards.

Access to catalogue.

Access to materials: limited. Depends on status of preservation and legal conditions in relation to request.
Access on archives premises, by loan.

Fees – Copyright
Fees for research for reuse and production purposes, facilities and handling.
Pricelist and conditions for use available.
Institution holds no copyright.
Access for commercial purposes only with agreement of right holder. Access to German feature films for non-commercial use only with agreement of right holders. Archive holds rights for viewing on archive premises and non-commercial showing of German non-fiction films.

MANNHEIM

_____ 248
INSTITUT FÜR DEUTSCHE SPRACHE, DEUTSCHES SPRACHARCHIV
INSTITUTE FOR THE GERMAN LANGUAGE, GERMAN ARCHIVE OF SPOKEN LANGUAGE
Friedrich-Karl-Str. 12
D – 68861 MANNHEIM
GERMANY

Tel.: 621-15810
Fax.: 621-4401200

Member of IASA.

Collections

Collections of Sound, 30% of the recordings are transcribed.

16 different corpora, corpus one with more than 5600 signle recordings of different german dialects.
Sound more than 10000 recordings

Access

Catalogue published.

Access to catalogue.

Access to materials: limited. Recordings of corpora 1,3,4,16 can be copied on tape.
Access by purchase.

Fees – Copyright

Fees for research for reuse and production purposes.
Copyright holder is the institution.
Copies are only made for scientific use. Purchaser has to confirm that there isn't any commercial use after receiving the copies. All requests will be answered without cost.

249
UNIVERSITÄT MANNHEIM – INSTITUT FÜR KOMMUNIKATIONS- UND MEDIENFORSCHUNG
UNIVERSITY OF MANNHEIM – INSTITUTE OF COMMUNICATIONS AND MEDIA RESEARCH
Schloß
D – 68131 MANNHEIM
GERMANY

Tel.: 621-2925534
Fax.: 621-2922586

Collections

Collections of Video, Sound.

Fictional (mainly literature) and non-fictional films. Audiovisual materials for foreign language teaching (course materials).
Video 7000 titles
Sound 3000 tapes

Access

Catalogue on database.

Acces to catalogue: limited to members of the University.

Access to materials: limited for non-commercial academic research.
Access on archives premises.

Fees – Copyright

Institution holds no copyright.
Right to use on archives premises only.

MARBACH A.N.

250
SCHILLER-NATIONALMUSEUM/ DEUTSCHES LITERATURARCHIV
Schillerhöhe 8-10
D – 71672 MARBACH a.N.
GERMANY

Tel.: 7144-8480
Fax.: 7144-15976

Member of IASA.

Collections

Collections of Video, Sound.

Archive material on the history of German-language literature : readings by authors, lectures, interviews, radio essays, television features, radio plays, video- and TV recordings of theatrical events, songs and operas based on literary texts, films of literary texts.
Video 1895 TV-videos
Sound 2668 records, 721 tapes, 339 cassettes, 349 CDs

Access

Catalogue on cards.

Access to catalogue.

Access to materials: limited. TV-videos available only to members of the Deutsche Schillergesellschaft.
Access on archives premises.

Fees – Copyright

Institution holds no copyright.

MARBURG/LAHN

251
UNIVERSITÄTSBIBLIOTHEK MARBURG
UNIVERSITY LIBRARY OF MARBURG
Wilhelm-Röpke-Str. 4
D – 35039 MARBURG/LAHN
GERMANY

Tel.: 6421-285102
Telex: 04 82372 umr

Member of IFLA.

Collections

Collections of Sound.

In principle literature (especially textbooks) of all disciplines studied at university level. Practically stress is laid – according to the disciplines preferred by blind students – on jurisprudence, economic sciences and psychology. Cassettes are produced on demand of blind students. Production in 1990 : about 7500 cassettes.

Video 1
Sound 9346 cassettes

Access
Catalogue on database.

Access to catalogue.

Access to materials: limited. Access for handicapped (blind or almost blind) people only. Access by loan.

Fees – Copyright
Pricelist and conditions for use available. Copyright holder is the institution. The University Library of Marburg has acquired from the publishers the limited copyright to produce 20 copies. The user is not allowed to copy himself.

MUNICH

_____ 252

BAYERISCHE STAATSBIBLIOTHEK, MUSIKABTEILUNG
BAVARIAN STATE LIBRARY, MUSIC DEPARTMENT
Ludwigstraße 16
D – 80328 MÜNCHEN
GERMANY

Tel.: 89-286 38353
Fax.: 89-286 38293

Member of IASA, IFLA.

Collections
Collections of Sound.

Music : 98% ; Speech : 2% – Western classical music : 90% ; Ethnomusicology (European) : 3% ; Ethnomusicology (Non-European) : 5% ; History, Language, Literature and poetry : 2%.
Sound about 45000 items (discs, CD's, tapes)

Access
Catalogue on database.

Acces to catalogue: limited. Only by staff of the Music Department.

Access to materials: limited. Collection not open for general access. Access only for scientific purposes.
Access on archives premises.

Fees – Copyright
No fees.
Institution holds no copyright.

_____ 253

BAYERISCHER RUNDFUNK, SCHALLARCHIV
BAVARIAN BRAODCASTING CORPORATION, SOUNDARCHIVE
Rundfunkplatz 1-2
D – 80335 MÜNCHEN
GERMANY

Tel.: 89-59002257
Fax.: 89-59002733
Telex: 89-52 107-0 brm d

Member of IASA.

Collections
Collections of Sound.

Radio program ; canned music.
Sound 550000 cans

Access
Catalogue on database.

Acces to catalogue: limited. By staff only.

Access to materials: limited. By staff only.
Access on archives premises.

_____ 254

INTERNATIONAL YOUTH LIBRARY
Schloß Blutenburg
D – 81247 MÜNCHEN
GERMANY

Tel.: 89-8112028
Fax.: 89-8117553

Member of IFLA.

Collections
Collections of Video, Sound.

Children's literature, still being developed.
Video 15
Sound 100

Access
Catalogue on cards.

Access to catalogue.

Access to materials: limited.
Access on archives premises.

Fees – Copyright
Institution holds no copyright.

SAARBRÜCKEN

_____ 255
SAARLÄNDISCHER RUNDFUNK, HÖRFUNK-ARCHIV
Funkhaus Halberg
D – 66100 SAARBRÜCKEN
GERMANY

Tel.: 681-602 2450
Fax.: 681-602 2469
Telex: 4 428 977, 4 428 969

Member of IASA.

Collections
Collections of Sound.

Radio programs, radio plays, features, etc. (all subjects), serious and light music.
Sound 145000 open reel tapes (96000 music, 49000 world), 92000 records

Access
Catalogue on database.

Access to catalogue.

Access to materials: limited for staff only ; legal problems.
Access on archives premises.

Fees – Copyright
Copyright holder is the institution.

_____ 256
SAARLÄNDISCHER RUNDFUNK, FERNSEH-ARCHIV
Funkhaus Halberg
D – 66100 SAARBRÜCKEN
GERMANY

Tel.: 681-602 2830
Fax.: 681-602 2822
Telex: 4 428 977, 4 428 969

Collections
Collections of Film, Video.

TV programs, TV news, TV plays, features, etc. (all subjects).
Films 16000 film cans
Video 9500 video tapes

Access
Catalogue on database.

Acces to catalogue: limited for staff only.

Access to materials: limited for staff only ; legal problems.
Access on archives premises.

Fees – Copyright
Copyright holder is the institution.

SCHLESWIG

_____ 257
LANDESARCHIV SCHLESWIG-HOLSTEIN/ LANDESFILMARCHIV
ARCHIVES OF LAND SCHLESWIG-HOLSTEIN/ FILM ARCHIVES
Prinzenpalais, Gottorfstraße 6
D – 24837 SCHLESWIG
GERMANY

Tel.: 4621-861800
Fax.: 4621-861801

Member of ICA.

Collections
Collections of Film, Video, Sound, production papers, scripts, books.

Documentary films about Schleswig-Holstein since 1895 : political events, social life, agriculture, industrial production, shipbuilding, transport.
Films 300 titles in 1500 cans
Video 120 video-copies of the film stock for usage on archives premises
Sound 50 hours

Access
Catalogue on database.

Access to catalogue: Catalogue of 120 titles published (1992), 300 titles on database.

Access to materials: Access to 120 titles ; no access at present to 180 titles because of security problems.
Access on archives premises, by loan, by purchase.

Fees – Copyright
Fees for research for reuse and production purposes, research by archive staff, facilities and handling.
Institution holds no copyright.
Purchase only with the right holders' permission and only for defined purposes (usage of the films for new productions, etc.).

STUTTGART

_____ 258
HAUPTSTAATSARCHIV STUTTGART
STUTTGART CENTRAL STATE ARCHIVES – AUDIOVISUAL ARCHIVE
Gutenbergstraße 109
D – 70197 STUTTGART
GERMANY

Tel.: 711-66 85 77
Fax.: 711-2125360

Member of ICA.

Collections

Collections of Video, Sound.

Copies of Radio and TV-Reports by Süddeutscher Rundfunk Stuttgart on current State affairs.
Video 500 Nos.
Sound 2000 Nos.

Access

Catalogue on database.

Access to catalogue.

Access to materials: limited for students or researchers.
Access on archives premises.

Fees – Copyright

No fees for research. Reuse with special permission only.
Institution holds no copyright.
Copyright is held by Süddeutscher Rundfunk.

_____ 259
SÜDDEUTSCHER RUNDFUNK STUTTGART, ARCHIVWESEN UND DOKUMENTATION
Neckarstraße 230
D – 70190 STUTTGART
GERMANY

Tel.: 711-92 90 32 84
Fax.: 711-2687034

Member of IASA, IAML.

Collections

Collections of Film, Video, Sound.

Film/video : collection of all own productions of SDR-Television programme covering especially own regional reporting, news and features.
Sound/music : collection of commercial records and collection of all own productions covering especially serious music played in by our Radio-Symphony Orchestra. Sound/word : collection of SDR Broadcasting own productions covering political reporting of Baden-Württemberg, cultural features and radio drama.
Films 2100 films (16mm + 35mm), 34000 VT-recordings
Video 9500 video tapes
Sound music : 150000 tapes, 18000 discs, 20000 CD ; Word : 106000 tapes, 2000 other

Access

Catalogue on database.

Access to catalogue.

Access to materials: limited. The legal position especially of own productions allows access only in very exceptional cases.
Access on archives premises.

Fees – Copyright

Fees for research for reuse and production purposes.
Pricelist and conditions for use available.

TÜBINGEN

_____ 260
UNIVERSITÄTSBIBLIOTHEK, PHONOTHEK
UNIVERSITY LIBRARY, PHONOTHEK
Wilhelmstr. 32
D – 72016 TÜBINGEN
GERMANY

Tel.: 7071-29 2577
Fax.: 7071-29 3123

Member of IFLA.

Collections

Collections of Film, Video, Sound.

Collection of records covering all musical epocs as well as ethnographic sound documents. Film and video collection only started recently, in addition to scientific literature of our special collections such as Middle Eastern/South Asian Studies ; Theology/Religious Studies.
Films under 20
Video under 20
Sound more than 9000 records

Access

Catalogue on cards.

Access to catalogue: Separate card catalogue for records ; films and videos are catalogued in the general alphabetical catalogue.

Access on archives premises.

Fees – Copyright

No fees.
Copyright stays with author/producer ; material is to be used only in a context of scientific research (not commercial).

WIESBADEN

_____ 261
DEUTSCHES INSTITUT FÜR FILMKUNDE/ DEPARTMENT FILMARCHIVE
Kreuzberger Ring 56
D – 65205 WIESBADEN
GERMANY
Tel.: 611-723310
Fax.: 611-723318
Member of FIAF.

Collections
Collections of Film, Video. Related materials available at Deutsches Institut für Filmkunde, Schaumainkai 41, D – 6000 Frankfurt/M. 70, tel : 69-617045, fax : 69-620060.

German feature films 1896-1945, besides that international classic films, films from former East-Germany.
Films about 6000
Video 300 (just for internal use)

Access
Catalogue on cards.

Access to catalogue: no.

Access to materials.

Access on archives premises, by loan.

Fees – Copyright
Fees for research for reuse and production purposes, research by archive staff, facilities and handling.
Pricelist and conditions for use available.
Copyright holder is the institution.
DIF holds non-commercial rights to films by former German company UFA.

_____ 262
HESSISCHES HAUPTSTAATSARCHIV
HESSIAN MAIN PUBLIC RECORD
Mosbacher Straße 55
D – 65187 WIESBADEN
GERMANY
Tel.: 611-8810
Fax.: 611-881 145
Member of ICA.

Collections
Collections of Sound.
Interviews with German expellees and with members of the resistance and victims of the Nazis ; with members of the youth organization of the SPD before 1933. Speeches of Hessian Ministers and civil servants. Hearing of witnesses in the Auschwitz-case.
Sound about 200 tapes

Access
Catalogue on cards.
Acces to catalogue: limited.
Access to materials: limited.
Access on archives premises.

Fees – Copyright
Institution holds no copyright.
Access according to the law of the Public Archives of Hesse or to special arrangements with interviewees.

GREECE

ATHENS

_____ 263
TAINIOTHIKI TIS ELLADOS
GREEK FILM ARCHIVE
Kanari 1, Kolonaki
GR – 106-71 ATHENS
GREECE
Tel.: 30-1-3612046, 30-1-3609695
Fax.: 30-1-3628468
Member of FIAF.

Collections
Collections of Film.
National and international fiction films, documentaries, newsfilms.

Access
Catalogue on cards.
Access to catalogue.

Access to materials: limited. The access is limited because the material is not classified and indexed yet.
Access on archives premises.

Fees – Copyright
Fees for research by archive staff.
The archive has copyright of a part of the material.

GUINEA

CONAKRY

_____ 264
SERVICE DE DOCUMENTATION ET ARCHIVES DE LA RADIO TELEVISION GUINEENNE
BP 391
CONAKRY

GUINEA – CONAKRY

REPUBLIC OF GUINEA
Tel.: 210-224-44.22.01, 210-224-44.22.05, 210-224-44.22.06
Telex: 22341 RTG
Member of IFTA, ICA.

Collections

Collections of Video, Sound.

Collection consists of video and sound recordings. Sound recordings : news, radio programs, contemporary and traditional music from Guinea. Video recordings : TV news, cultural broadcasts, fiction films, documentaries, contemporary and traditional music.
Video 5500 tapes
Sound 11025

Access

Catalogue on database.

Access to catalogue.

Access to materials: limited. Outside use for cultural institutions and researchers envisaged.

Fees – Copyright

Fees for research for reuse and production purposes, research by archive staff.
Copyright holder is the institution.

GUINEA-BISSAU

BISSAU

_____ 265
INSTITUTO NACIONAL DE ESTUDOS E PESQUISAS (INEP)
INSTITUT NATIONAL DES ETUDES ET DES RECHERCHES (INER)
Complexo Escolar, 14 de Novembro Cobornel
P.O. Box 112
BISSAU
GUINEA-BISSAU

Tel.: 252-21 13 01
Fax.: 28 20

Member of ICA.

Collections

Collections of Sound, photographies.

History, lectures, congresses, seminars, folkloric music, classical music, copies from foreign study and research centers.
Sound 497 cassettes (713 hours), 180 tapes (270 hours)

Access

Acces to catalogue: limited. Only catalogue of photos existing.

Access to materials: limited for reasons of preservation and lack of equipment.

HONG KONG

KOWLOON

_____ 266
HONG KONG POLYTECHNIC LIBRARY
Hung Hom
KOWLOON
HONG KONG

Tel.: 852-766 6863
Fax.: 852-765 8274
Telex: 38964 POLYX HX

Member of IFLA, FID.

Collections

Collections of Video, Sound, slides, microforms, microcomputer programs.

Visual arts, management and technology.
Video 12000 items, video discs : 1300 items
Sound 3000 items

Access

Catalogue on database.

Access to catalogue for Polytechnic staff and students and valid library users.

Access to materials: limited. Cater for polytechnic staff and students. Not for loan outside the library. Access by loan.

Fees – Copyright

No fees charged.
Institution holds no copyright.
All materials purchased are restricted by copyright condition by supplier/producer. Hence all materials have to be used inside library and not for outside, nor for inter-library loans.

_____ 267
TELEVISION BROADCASTS LTD (TVB), VIDEOTAPE LIBRARY/ARCHIVE
Clearwater Bay Road
KOWLOON
HONG KONG

Tel.: 852-719 4828
Fax.: 852-358 1337

Member of IFTA.

Collections

Collections of Film, Video, Sound, dubbed tape, script.

Film : mainly local and foreign feature. Video : drama series, variety, children, sport, educational, youth, women programme, documentary, talk show & magazine, game show. Sound : classical, orchestra, instrumental, jazz, electronic, mode music, Chinese music, world music, dance music, film sound track, sound effect, vocal, Japanese.
Films 7449
Video 1" : 74545 + 13849 (cassette type)
Sound 22365 (LP + EP + CD + 1/4" DAT)

Access

Catalogue on database.

Acces to catalogue: limited.

Access to materials: limited.
Access on archives premises.

Fees – Copyright

This is a private archive. Fees by negotiation.
Copyright holder is the institution.

HUNGARY

BUDAPEST

_____ 268
HUNGARIAN RADIO, SOUND ARCHIVE
Bródy Sándor utca 5.-7.
H – 1800 BUDAPEST
HUNGARY
Tel.: 36-1-1388310
Fax.: 36-1-1387926
Member of IASA.

Collections

Collections of Sound, production papers.

Radio programmes, reports, interviews to the programmes.
Sound 440000 tapes, 40000 discs, 1000 CDs

Access

Catalogue on database.

Acces to catalogue: limited for radio purposes, and with special permission.

Access to materials: limited for radio purposes, and with special permission.
Access by loan, by purchase.

Fees – Copyright

Fees for copies for commercial purposes.
Pricelist and conditions for use available.
Copyright holder is the institution.
Access according to the prescriptions of the Hungarian Copyright Office.

_____ 269
MAGYAR FILMINTÉZET/FILMARCHIVUM
HUNGARIAN FILM INSTITUTE/FILMARCHIVE
Budakeszi út 51/b.
H – 1021 BUDAPEST
HUNGARY
Tel.: 36-1-1767106, 36-1-1429136
Fax.: 36-1-1429136
Member of FIAF.

Collections

Collections of Film, Video, scripts, stills, posters.

Hungarian feature and non-feature films, Easterneuropean cinema, some classics of the world cinema.
Films 20000 titles
Video 3300 cassettes (VHS, U-KCA)

Access

Catalogue on cards.

Access to catalogue.

Access to materials: limited.
Access on archives premises.

Fees – Copyright

Fees for research for reuse and production purposes.
Pricelist and conditions for use available.
Right to use on archive premises.

_____ 270
ORSZAGOS SZÉCHÉNYI KÖNYVTAR
NATIONAL SZÉCHÉNYI LIBRARY,
MANUSCRIPT DIVISION AND CONTEMPORARY DIVISION
Budavári Palota, F-épület
H – 1827 BUDAPEST
HUNGARY
Tel.: 36-1-1757533
Fax.: 36-1-2020804
Telex: 224226 bibln.h.
Member of IASA, IFLA.

Collections

Collections of Film, Video, Sound, transcripts.

Manuscript Division collects oral history materials and their transcripts, related to Hungarian literature, history and history of culture ; Contemporary Division collects video materials, related to the same topics.
Films 180
Video 242
Sound 3585 items

Access

Catalogue indexed on cards.

Acces to catalogue: limited with restrictions.

Access to materials: limited with restrictions.

Access on archives premises.

Fees – Copyright

Fees for facilities and handling.
Institution holds no copyright.
Copyrights holder is either the interviewmaker or the interviewed person, or both of them.

ICELAND

REYKJAVIK

_____ 271

KVIKMYNDASAFN ISLANDS
THE ICELANDIC FILM ARCHIVE
Laugavegur 24
P.O. Box 320
121 REYKJAVIK
ICELAND

Tel.: 354-1-10940
Fax.: 354-1-627171

Member of FIAF.

Collections

Collections of Film, Video, documents, still photos, posters, cinema equipment of historical interest.

Mostly Icelandic documentaries and feature films, also all kinds of raw footage and some foreign films, especially if they relate to Iceland.
Films about 500 original titles and about 400 titles for unpublished works
Video about 50 masters and 100 VHS
Sound about 40 mag.filmtracks + about 60 sound neg.

Access

Catalogue on database.

Access to catalogue.

Access to materials.
Access on archives premises.

Fees – Copyright

Institution holds no copyright.
The consent of copyright owners is needed if film material is to be taken from the premises. Yet filmmakers are allowed to borrow non-master copies such as VHS for selecting purposes without such permission. The Archive owns copyright to some of the films in the collection.

_____ 272

RIKISUTVARPID (RUV), SAFNADEILD
ICELANDIC NATIONAL BROADCASTING SERVICE, ARCHIVES
Efstaleiti 1
150 REYKJAVIK
ICELAND

Tel.: 354-1-693000
Fax.: 354-1-693010
Telex: 2066

Member of IFTA, IASA.

Collections

Collections of Film, Video, Sound.

Own production of television and radio programs, mainly news program, documentary, drama, music, etc. Published music material local and foreign on LP's and CD's.
Films 17000 titles
Video 7000 titles
Sound 70000 items

Access

Catalogue on database.

Access to catalogue.

Access to materials: limited.
Access by loan.

Fees – Copyright

Fees for transcript of material for private use.
Copyright holder is either the institution or others.
Access to the material (lease or sale) is dependent on agreement with the copyright holders.

INDIA

BOMBAY

_____ 273

NATIONAL CENTRE FOR THE PERFORMING ARTS
Dorabji Tata Road, Nariman Point
BOMBAY – 400 021
INDIA

Tel.: 91-22-231055
Fax.: 91-22-2048187
Telex: 011-82731 (TATA IN)

Collections

Collections of Film, Video, Sound.

Indian classical music, Indian folk music, western classical music, soliloquy play reading, poetry reading, interviews of drama/film personalities, feature & short films related to performing arts.

Films 37 titles (35/16mm)
Video 258 hours (U-Matic/VHS PAL)
Sound 2032 hours (6.3mm magnetic tape)

Access

Catalogue on database.

Access to catalogue.

Access to materials.
Access on archives premises.

Fees – Copyright

No fees.
Copyright holder is the institution.
Written application requesting for access (only for listening and viewing) within the premises. Application to be addressed to the Director or Deputy Director of the archives. No copying (dubbing) is permitted.

HYDERABAD

_____ 274

ANDHRA PRADESH STATE ARCHIVES, FILM ARCHIVES DIVISION

Abhilekha Nilayam, Tarnaka
HYDERABAD – 500007 A.P.
INDIA

Tel.: 91-842-868371, 91-842-868372

Collections

Collections of Film, Sound.

Films available on social themes. Music on Gramophone discs on Indian Classics.

Access

Acces to catalogue: limited. Catalogue under compilation.

Access to materials: Facilities and resources limited.
Access on archives premises, by loan.

Fees – Copyright

Fees not worked out yet.
Film Archives Division of the Andhra Pradesh State Archives has been set up very recently. Films and Music records are being added. Catalogues have to be worked out.

NEW DELHI

_____ 275

ALL INDIA RADIO, TRANSCRIPTION & PROGRAMME EXCHANGE SERVICE

Parliament Street, Akashvani Bhavan, IVth Floor
NEW DELHI – 110001
INDIA

Tel.: 91-31-3717927
Member of IASA.

Collections

Collections of Sound.

Collection of important broadcast material like classical, light, folk music & talks, plays, features, operas, interviews, etc. Collection recording of eminent old masters/musicians (tapes & discs).
Sound 38000 tapes

Access

Catalogue indexed on cards.

Acces to catalogue: limited for Archives staff only.

Access to materials: limited for Archives staff only.

Fees – Copyright

Fees for research by archive staff.
Material is meant for broadcast from AIR stations and for research by Archives/AIR staff only. Each case is examined by the competent authority before the material is made available.

_____ 276

MASS COMMUNICATION RESEARCH CENTRE, LIBRARY RESOURCE AND DOCUMENTATION UNIT

Jamia Milha Islamia
NEW DELHI – 110025
INDIA

Tel.: 91-31-6846811-13
Telex: 75210 MCRC IN

Collections

Collections of Film, Video, Sound, slide tape programmes & stock-shots.

Programs on education and social development.
Films 140 (16mm)
Video 813
Sound 285

Access

Catalogue on database.

Access to catalogue: On line information search by title, subject, producer, production year, production & key words.

Access to materials: limited for students of Mass Communication & staff of the Mass Communication Research Centre.
Access on archives premises, by purchase.

Fees – Copyright

Fees for research for reuse and production purposes.
Pricelist and conditions for use available.
Copyright holder is the institution.

PUNE

277

NATIONAL FILM ARCHIVE OF INDIA
Law College Road
PUNE – 411004
INDIA

Tel.: 91-212-331559, 91-212-338516, 91-212-333649, 91-212-336253
Telex: 145 7759 NFAI IN

Member of FIAF.

Collections

Collections of Film, Video, Sound, press clippings, still photographs, wall posters, slides, books, periodicals, post shooting scripts, glass negatives, glass slides.

Films : features, shorts (Indian & foreign), censor cuts, study extracts. Video : U-Matic & VHS cassettes of Indian & foreign films. Sound : audio cassettes, disc records and optical sounds of interviews of film personalities, songs, speeches and sound track of feature films.
Films 5690
Video 676
Sound audio cassettes : 151, discs : 1822

Access

Catalogue on database.

Acces to catalogue: limited.

Access to materials: limited.
Access on archives premises, by hire.

Fees – Copyright

Fees for facilities and handling.
Institution holds no copyright.

INDONESIA

JAKARTA

278

ARSIP NASIONAL REPUBLIK INDONESIA
NATIONAL ARCHIVES OF THE REPUBLIC OF INDONESIA
Jalan Ampera Raya
JAKARTA SELATAN 12560
INDONESIA

Tel.: 62-21-7805851
Fax.: 62-21-7805812

Member of ICA.

Collections

Collections of Film, Video, Sound, posters, slides.
Politics, economy, culture, military, sports, pictures, speeches, etc.

Access

Catalogue on database.

Access to catalogue.

Access to materials: limited for preservation & security.
Access on archives premises, by purchase.

Fees – Copyright

Fees for research for reuse and production purposes, research by archive staff, facilities and handling, copyright.
Pricelist and conditions for use available.
Copyright holder is the institution.
For purchase the right holders permission is needed.

IRAN

TEHRAN

279

FILM KHANE-YE MELLI-E
NATIONAL FILM ARCHIVE OF IRAN
Baharestan sq.
P.O. Box 5158
TEHRAN 11365
IRAN

Tel.: 98-21-311242
Fax.: 98-21-678155
Telex: 215642 RECU IR

Member of FIAF.

Collections

Collections of Film, Video, posters, stills, slides, books and other publications.

Iranian and foreign films & videos.
Films 10000 reels
Video 500 titles

Access

Catalogue indexed on cards.

Acces to catalogue: limited for researchers, filmmakers, televisionmakers, students, archivists, programmers.

Access to materials: limited for researchers, filmmakers, televisionmakers, students, archivists, programmers.
Access on archives premises, by loan.

Fees – Copyright

Fees for research for reuse and production purposes.
Copyright holder is the institution.
The National Film Archive of Iran is the holder of non-commercial and cultural rights of its collection.

___ 280
SEDA VA SIMA
THE MAIN OFFICE OF RADIO AND TELEVI-
SION'S ARCHIVES AND LIBRARIES
Valie Asr Ave, JameJam St
P.O. Box 15335-768
TEHRAN
IRAN
Tel.: 98-21-21962650, 98-21-21962679
Telex: 212505 IRIB

Collections
Collections of Film, Video, Sound, slides and photographs archives.
Films Video, Sound: 1166 square meter

Access
Catalogue published.
Acces to catalogue: limited.
Access to materials: limited.
Access by purchase.

Fees – Copyright
Fees for research for reuse and production purposes.
Pricelist and conditions for use available.
Copyright holder is the institution.
Each applicant must have a letter of introduction at first. The Archive charges the applicants according to the pricelist of the Radio and Television Organization.

IRELAND

DUBLIN

___ 281
IRISH FILM INSTITUTE
6, Eustace Street
DUBLIN 2
IRELAND
Tel.: 353-1-6795744
Fax.: 353-1-6799657
Member of FIAF.

Collections
Collections of Film, Video, cinema related stills, promotional literature, posters, scripts.

Irish and Irish related film – feature, documentary, newsreel, informational, amateur, professional film (35mm, 16mm, 8mm & 9.5mm). Reference copies on VHS; The collection is largely non-fiction. Earliest film 1910 – collection includes contemporary material.
Films about 7500 cans of film (about 3000 titles)
Video about 110 VHS

Access
Catalogue on database.

Acces to catalogue: limited. Catalogue is currently supervised by archive staff – access to database is restricted to archive staff.

Access to materials: limited. Access limited to one day per week – access only to viewing copies of films. Access preferably on video.
Access on archives premises.

Fees – Copyright
Fees for research for reuse and production purposes, facilities and handling, When the Archive provides prints, a handling fee is levied.
Pricelist and conditions for use available.
Receipt of copyright permission is the responsibility of the user. The Archive provides as much assistance as possible in locating copyright holders.

___ 282
RADIO TELEFIS EIREANN (RTE)
IRISH NATIONAL RADIO + TELEVISION
BROADCASTING SERVICE, SOUND LIBRARY
Donnybrook
DUBLIN 4
IRELAND
Tel.: 353-1-642399, 353-1-642430
Fax.: 353-1-643083
Telex: 93700

Collections
Collections of Sound, books, cuttings, information data bases.

Collection of full programmes & extracts from RTE Radio Programmes 1940- to date covering all facets of Irish life. Irish language, Irish art & traditional music, the arts, politics, sport, news. Also collection of discs covering all facets of music & spoken arts.
Sound 30000 hours 1/4" tape, 250000 vinyl, 50000 CD discs

Access
Catalogue on database.

Acces to catalogue: limited due to limited facilities.

Access to materials: limited due to limited facilities and legal problems.

Fees – Copyright
Fees for research for reuse and production purposes, research by archive staff, facilities and handling.
Pricelist and conditions for use available.
Copyright holder is the institution.

IRELAND – DUBLIN

283
RADIO TELEFIS EIREANN (RTE)
IRISH NATIONAL BROADCASTING ORGANISATION, PROGRAMME/VISUAL LIBRARY
Donnybrook
DUBLIN 4
IRELAND

Tel.: 353-1-643139
Fax.: 353-1-643096
Telex: 93700

Member of IFTA.

Collections
Collections of Film, Video, illustrations (stills and slides).

RTE programmes and news reports of national interest and importance some historical material of national importance, from external (non-RTE) sources.
Films Substantial RTE film & video broadcast holding since 1962

Access
Catalogue on database.

Acces to catalogue: limited. Mainly for broadcast purposes but limited access for research purposes.

Access to materials: limited. Dependent on purpose of request.
Access on archives premises, by loan, by purchase.

Fees – Copyright
Fees for research for reuse and production purposes, research by archive staff, facilities and handling.
Pricelist and conditions for use available.
Copyright holder is the institution.
Rate cards available on request.

284
TAISCE CHEOL DUCHAIS EIREANN
IRISH TRADITIONAL MUSIC ARCHIVE
63 Merrion square
DUBLIN 2
IRELAND

Tel.: 353-1-619699
Fax.: 353-1-686260

Member of IASA.

Collections
Collections of Video, Sound, printed materials, manuscript materials, photographs, ephemera.

Collection of all materials relating to Irish traditional music in Ireland and abroad, and representative collection of traditional music of other countries.
Video 200 items
Sound 5000 items

Access
Catalogue on database.

Acces to catalogue: limited, by staff availability only.

Access to materials.
Access on archives premises.

Fees – Copyright
Fees for research by archive staff, facilities and handling, copyright reproduction.
Institution holds no copyright.
To acquire copies of material in copyright, user must supply written permission from copyright holder.

285
UNIVERSITY COLLEGE DUBLIN
IRISH DIALECTS ARCHIVE
Belfield
DUBLIN 4
IRELAND

Tel.: 353-1-7068385
Fax.: 353-1-2694409
Telex: 32693 EI
Electronic mail: CLUNEKM@IRLEARN.BITNET

Collections
Collections of Sound.

Sound and card archive of Modern Irish dialects.
Video 100
Sound 2000 tapes

Access
Catalogue on cards.

Acces to catalogue: limited to students and scholars.

Access to materials: limited to students and scholars.
Access on archives premises.

ISRAEL

ASHRAT

286
BEIT LOHAMFI HAGHETAOT
GHETTO FIGHTERS' HOUSE
Kibbutz Lohamei Haghetaot
Post ASHRAT 25220
ISRAEL

Tel.: 972-4-820412, 972-4-825542
Fax.: 972-4-826455

Collections

Collections of Film, Video, Sound.

The Holocaust, World War II, History of European jewry, Resistance in occupied countries during World War II, Jewish emigration under the Nazis, Birth of the State of Israel, Several feature films.
Films 351
Video 540
Sound 985

Access

Catalogue on database.

Access to catalogue.

Access to materials: limited.
Access on archives premises, by hire.

Fees – Copyright

Fees for research for reuse and production purposes.
Copyright holder is the institution.
Only for research, education and producing new material.

HAIFA

_____ 287
TECHNION – MACHON TECHNOLOGY LEISRAEL
TECHNION – ISRAEL INSTITUTE OF TECHNOLOGY
TECHNION – AUDIO-VISUAL LIBRARY
Technion City
HAIFA 32000
ISRAEL

Tel.: 972-4-292019

Member of IFLA.

Collections

Collections of Video, Sound.

Video cassettes for 45 lectures of basic courses in science, engineering and medicine. Video cassettes in science and technology.
Video 800 video cassettes

Access

Catalogue published.

Access to catalogue: no.

Access to materials.
Access on archives premises.

Fees – Copyright

There is no possibility of reproduction.

JERUSALEM

_____ 288
JAD-VASHEM – THE HOLOCAUST MARTYRS' AND HEROES' REMEMBRANCE
Har Hazikuron Jerusalem
P.O.B. 3477
JERUSALEM 91034
ISRAEL

Tel.: 972-2-751611
Fax.: 972-2-433511
Telex: 26573

Member of ICA.

Collections

Collections of Film, Video, Sound.

Materials concerning the Holocaust, the life of the Jews between the two World Wars, and materials concerning World War II.
Films 150
Video 530
Sound 80

Access

Catalogue on cards.

Access to catalogue.

Access to materials.
Access on archives premises, by hire, by purchase.

Fees – Copyright

Fees for facilities and handling.
Pricelist and conditions for use available.
For some of the materials the copyright holder is the institution, but for other material not.

_____ 289
JEWISH NATIONAL AND UNIVERSITY LIBRARY
NATIONAL SOUND ARCHIVES
Givat Ram
P.O. Box 503
JERUSALEM
ISRAEL

Tel.: 972-2-666804
Fax.: 972-2-660351
Telex: 972-2-25367

Collections

Collections of Video, Sound.

Traditional Jewish music, Liturgical music of Eastern Churches and folk music of Muslims in Israel.
Video 90 cassettes
Sound 6785 tapes, 835 cassettes, 235 PCN cassettes, 3400 records

Access
Catalogue on database.
Access to catalogue.
Access to materials.
Access on archives premises.

Fees – Copyright
Fees for research for reuse and production purposes.
The individual researchers own the rights to the material.

290

STEVEN SPIELBERG JEWISH FILM ARCHIVE
Law Building, Hebrew University, Mt. Scopus
JERUSALEM
ISRAEL

Tel.: 972-2-812061
Fax.: 972-2-322545 Att : Film Archive
Electronic mail: BITNET:H7UWL AT HVJIVM1

Member of FIAF, IAMHIST.

Collections
Collections of Film, Video, library of print documentation.

Jewish/Israeli documentary film material.
Films 5000
Video 1500

Access
Catalogue on database.
Acces to catalogue: limited.
Access to materials: limited.
Access on archives premises.

Fees – Copyright
Fees for research for reuse and production purposes, research by archive staff, facilities and handling.
Pricelist and conditions for use available.
Copyright holder is the institution.

RAMAT GAN

291

UNIVERSITAT BAR ILAN
BAR ILAN UNIVERSITY
P.O. Box 90000
RAMAT GAN 52900
ISRAEL

Tel.: 972-3-5318486
Fax.: 972-3-349233
Electronic mail: T05614@BARILVM

Member of IFLA.

Collections
Collections of Film, Video, Sound.

American and English literature, psychology, education, the aged, social work, economics, communication, politics, music.
Films 100
Video 1000
Sound 10750

Access
Catalogue on database.
Acces to catalogue: limited.
Access to materials: limited.
Access on archives premises.

ITALY

GEMONA

292

LA CINETECA DEL FRIULI
THE FRIULI FILM ARCHIVE
via Osoppo 26
I – 33013 GEMONA (UDINE)
ITALY

Tel.: 39-432-980458
Fax.: 39-432-970542

Member of FIAF.

Collections
Collections of Film, books, magazines, posters, stills.

Silent and sound films from 1891 to 1989.
Films 4500 titles (16+35mm)

Access
Catalogue on database.
Access to catalogue.
Access to materials.
Access on archives premises, by loan.

Fees – Copyright
Fees for research for reuse and production purposes, research by archive staff, facilities and handling.
Pricelist and conditions for use available.
Institution holds no copyright.
The rights holders' permission is needed.

MILANO

_____ 293
BIBLIOTECA COMUNALE, SEZIONE FONOTECA
MILAN PUBLIC LIBRARY, SOUND RECORDING DEPARTMENT
Corso di Porta Vittoria, 6
I – 20122 MILANO
ITALY
Tel.: 39-2-62083638
Fax.: 39-2-76006588
Member of IASA, IFLA.

Collections
Collections of Video, Sound, musical scores and librettos.

The collection includes records & video of classical, popular, folk music, jazz, foreign languages for self instruction, theatre and literature in Italian and foreign languages.
Video 2500
Sound 32000

Access
Catalogue on cards.

Access to catalogue.

Access to materials.
Access on archives premises.

Fees – Copyright
Institution holds no copyright.

_____ 294
CINETECA ITALIANA ARCHIVIO STORICO DEL FILM MUSEO DEL CINEMA
Villa comunale, via Palestro 16
MILANO
ITALY
Tel.: 39-2-799224
Member of FIAF, ICOM.

Collections
Collections of Film, Video.

Films from the film history since 1905 to present, international production. Silent Italian films. Short films, documentaries, newsreels, animation films, slapstick comedies.
Films about 10000 titles
Video about 1000 titles

Access
Catalogue on cards.

Acces to catalogue: limited due to legal problems.

Access to materials: limited due to preservation.
Access on archives premises.

Fees – Copyright
Fees for research by archive staff.
Institution holds no copyright.

PALERMO

_____ 295
CENTRO PER LE INIZIATIVE MUSICALI IN SICILIA – CIMS
CENTER FOR MUSICAL INITIATIVES IN SICILY
Piazza Sett'Angeli, 10
I – 90134 PALERMO
ITALY
Tel.: 39-91-589441, 39-91-6111253
Fax.: 39-91-6111293
Member of IASA.

Collections
Collections of Sound.

Sicilian folk music.
Sound about 1000 hours

Access
Catalogue on database.

Access to catalogue.

Access to materials: limited due to preservation.
Access on archives premises.

Fees – Copyright
Fees for research by archive staff.
Institution holds no copyright.

_____ 296
FOLKSTUDIO
Piazza Sett'Angeli, 10
I – 90134 PALERMO
ITALY
Tel.: 39-91-589441, 39-91-6111253
Fax.: 39-91-6111293
Member of IASA.

Collections
Collections of Sound.

Sicilian folk music.
Sound about 2000 hours

Access
Catalogue on database.

Access to catalogue.

Access to materials: limited due to preservation.
Access by purchase.

Fees – Copyright
Fees for facilities and handling

297

ISTITUTO DI SCIENZE ANTROPO-LOGICHE E GEOGRAFICHE – UNIVER-SITA DI PALERMO
INSTITUTE OF ANTHROPOLOGICAL AND GEOGRAPHIC SCIENCES – UNIVERSITY OF PALERMO
Piazza Ignazio Florio, 24
I – 90139 PALERMO
ITALY
Tel.: 39-91-589441, 39-91-6111253
Fax.: 39-91-6111293

Collections
Collections of Video, Sound.
Sicilian folkmusic.
Video 3 hours
Sound 500 hours of recording

Access
Catalogue on database.
Acces to catalogue: limited.
Access to materials: limited.
Access on archives premises.

Fees – Copyright
Fees for research by archive staff.
Institution holds no copyright.

ROME

298

ARCHIVIO AUDIOVISIVO DEL MOVIMENTO OPERAIO E DEMOCRATICO
via F.S. Sprovieri, 14
I – 00152 ROMA
ITALY
Tel.: 39-6-5896698, 39-6-5818442, 39-6-5896508
Fax.: 39-6-5896940
Member of IAMHIST.

Collections
Collections of Film, Video, Sound, photos, production papers, scripts, scores, censorship documents, stills, books, magazines.
Contemporary history, working class, sovietic cinema, political events, communist parties history.
Films 5000 hours (16 and 35mm)
Video 1000 hours (VHS, 3/4, 1 inch)
Sound 3000 hours (1/2 inch)

Access
Catalogue on cards.
Acces to catalogue: limited by staff only.
Access to materials: limited for preservation.
Access by purchase.

Fees – Copyright
Fees for research for reuse and production purposes, research by archive staff, copyright.
Copyright holder is the institution.

299

ARCHIVIO CENTRALE DELLO STATO
P.le degli Archivi, 27
I – 00144 ROMA
ITALY
Tel.: 39-6-5920371, 39-6-5920372, 39-6-5920373
Fax.: 39-6-5413620
Member of ICA.

Collections
Collections of Film.
Propaganda films produced after World War II.
Films 630 reels

Access
Catalogue on cards.
Access to catalogue: no. Cataloguing underway.
Access to materials: no.

300

DISCOTECA DI STATO
NATIONAL SOUND ARCHIVE
via Caetani, 32
I – 00186 ROMA
ITALY
Tel.: 39-6-6868364
Fax.: 39-6-6866812
Member of IASA.

Collections
Collections of Video, Sound, scripts (especially for field recordings), concert programmes, books, catalogues, journals.
Western art music, ethnic and folk culture (music, dialects, tales, etc.), oral history (mainly Italian), dramatic theater.
Video some hundreds (collection started in 1990)
Sound 170000 discs, about 10000 hours on tape

Access
Catalogue published, on cards.
Access to catalogue.
Access to materials.
Access on archives premises.

Fees – Copyright
We make copies for research, teaching and other non-commercial purposes, the requester must supply the tape or cassette for the copy.
We hold copyright for recordings produced by the Discoteca di Stato. For other materials we follow the Italian law on copyright.

301
ISTITUTO DI RICERCA PER IL TEATRO MUSICALE – I.R.TE.M.
INSTITUTE FOR RESEARCH ON MUSIC THEATRE
SOUND ARCHIVE OF CONTEMPORARY MUSIC
via Francesco Tamagno, 65
I – 00168 ROME
ITALY

Tel.: 39-6-6147277
Fax.: 39-6-6144371

Member of IASA.

Collections
Collections of Sound, general reference books, scores, biographies, magazines.

Archive collects tapes, LP's, and CD's of music written after 1900.
Sound about 3000 items

Access
Catalogue on cards.

Access to catalogue only in the presence of staff.

Access to materials only in the presence of staff.
Access on archives premises.

Fees – Copyright
No fees.
Institution holds no copyright.

TURIN

302
MUSEO NAZIONALE DEL CINEMA
Palazzo Chiablese, Piazza San Giovanni, 2
I – 10122 TORINO
ITALY

Tel.: 39-11-4361148, 39-11-4361387
Fax.: 39-11-5212341

Member of FIAF, IFTA, IFLA, IAMHIST, ICOM.

Collections
Collections of Film, Video, Sound, posters, photos, books, periodicals, museum objects, also pre-cinema.

Film collection includes mainly Italian silent films, in particular films from Turin.
Films 2000 (silent, sound, features, documentaries)
Video 200 titles
Sound 1500 discs

Access
Catalogue on cards.

Acces to catalogue: limited, cataloguing underway.

Access to materials: limited upon request for studies, researchers.
Access on archives premises, by loan.

Fees – Copyright
Fees for research for reuse and production purposes, research by archive staff, for lending, copyright and reproduction.
Copyright holder is the institution.

303
RADIOTELEVISIONE ITALIANA, RAI
via Cernaia, 33
I – 10121 TORINO
ITALY

Tel.: 39-11-8102626
Fax.: 39-11-8102586
Telex: 221035 RAI TO I

Member of IFTA.

Collections
Collections of Film, Video, Sound, photos, newspapers, records, tapes, music, etc.

All topics broadcasted by RAI.
Films 1000000
Video 250000
Sound 300000 tapes, 500000 records

Access
Catalogue on database.

Access to catalogue.

Access to materials for public with specific autorization.

Fees – Copyright
Fees according to the request.
Copyright situation has to be checked in each individual case. A RAI Department is in charge for commercial usage of archive material.

VENICE

304
ARCHIVIO STORICO DELLE ARTI CONTEMPORANEE – BIENNALE DI VENEZIA
HISTORICAL ARCHIVES OF CONTEMPORARY ARTS – BIENNALE OF VENICE
S. Croce 2214
I – 30125 VENEZIA
ITALY

Tel.: 39-41-521711
Fax.: 39-41-5240817
Telex: 410685 BLE VE

Member of IASA.

Collections

Collections of Film, Video, Sound, books, scores, reviews, photos, posters.

It begins from 1970.
Films 1200
Video 3850 tapes
Sound 2950 tapes, 3850 records

Access

Catalogue published, on cards.

Access to catalogue.

Access to materials: not directly but through laboratory.
Access on archives premises, by loan.

Fees – Copyright

Fees for facilities and handling, to lend the tapes. Pricelist and conditions for use available.
Copyright holder is the institution.
To ask permission for publication.

JAMAICA

KINGSTON

_____ 305
NATIONAL LIBRARY OF JAMAICA, AUDIO VISUAL ARCHIVE DEPARTMENT
12 East Street
Box 823
KINGSTON
JAMAICA

Tel.: 1-809-9220620
Fax.: 1-809-9225567
Telex: Cable NALIBJAM

Member of IFLA.

Collections

Collections of Film, Video, Sound, photographs & scripts.

Documentary films on Jamaica, covering all subjects. Black & white 16mm archival film from the Television Departments of the Jamaica Broadcasting Corporation and the Jamaica Information Service. Audio tape recordings from radio stations and oral history cassette tapes from the Jamaica Memory Bank Project – Video cassettes of a documentary cultural or historical nature are also included – also recordings of Jamaica music.
Films 8016 cans
Video 260 – 1 hour
Sound 1364 sound recordings

Access

Catalogue on cards.

Acces to catalogue: inhouse catalogue limited to staff only.

Access to materials: limited because of limited facilities.
Access on archives premises.

Fees – Copyright

No fees charged at present but a deposit copy of any production using material from the collection is requested in lieu of fees.
Institution holds no copyright.
Copyright is held by the institution responsible for the production of the material. Access to view is unrestricted but permission in writing must be obtained from the copyright holder if any portion is to be reproduced.

_____ 306
UNIVERSITY OF THE WEST INDIES, RADIO EDUCATION UNIT
LIBRARY OF THE SPOKEN WORD
UWI, Mona Campus
P.O. Box 37
KINGSTON 7
JAMAICA

Tel.: 1-809-9275730
Fax.: 1-809-9271920
Telex: UNIVERS

Collections

Collections of Sound, typewritten transcripts of audio programmes available on sheets or bound as books.

Comprises programmes prepared by REU/UWI for broadcast throughout the Region since 1954. Topics include Trade Unionism, Literature, WI Personalities, Government and Politics, Workers Education, Children's Stories, Caribbean History, Social Studies, Science and Technology, Drama and Poetry, Environmental Issues, Gender Studies, etc.
Sound about 2000 hours sound recording

Access

Catalogue published.

Acces to catalogue: limited, needs updating.

Access to materials: limited. Services of Librarian for search & to monitor collection generallly not in place.
Access on archives premises.

Fees – Copyright

Fees for facilities and handling.
Pricelist and conditions for use available.
Copyright holder is the institution.

Credits to author(s) or speaker(s), also to SOURCE i.e. REU/UWI are required in all or any forms of reproduction of the REU materials. Recordings dubbed (copied) for researchers/clients are for private or EDUCATIONAL use only, NOT FOR COMMERCIAL purposes e.g. broadcasting for profit or distribution on gramophone records or tapes which are sold inter alia.

JAPAN

AICHI-KEN

___ 307
NAGOYA SHOKA DAIGAKU, JOHO SENTA
NAGOYA UNIVERSITY OF COMMERCE, INFORMATION CENTER
4-4, Sagamine, Nisshin-Cho, Aichi-Gun
AICHI-KEN 470-01
JAPAN

Tel.: 81-5617-32111
Fax.: 81-5617-40341

Member of IFLA.

Collections
Collections of Film, Video, Sound.

Educational materials, primarily in the fields of business, economics and computer programming, in Japanese, and English language instruction.
Films 10 titles
Video 90 titles
Sound 50 titles

Access
Catalogue on cards.

Access to catalogue.

Access to materials: limited to faculty and students.
Access on archives premises.

Fees – Copyright
Institution holds no copyright.

KYOTO

___ 308
KYOTO SANGYO UNIVERSITY LIBRARY
Kamigamo, Kita-ku
KYOTO 603
JAPAN

Tel.: 81-075-7012151
Fax.: 81-075-7224306

Member of IFLA.

Collections
Collections of Film, Video, Sound.
General.
Films 232 (16mm) titles
Video 2762 and laser disk 521 titles
Sound 3847 titles

Access
Catalogue on database.

Acces to catalogue: limited only in library.

Access to materials: limited only in library.

Fees – Copyright
Fees for reproduction.
Institution holds no copyright.

TOKYO

___ 309
KOKURITSU KOKKAI TOSHOKAN
NATIONAL DIET LIBRARY
10-1, Nagatacho 1 chome, Chiyoda-ku
TOKYO 100
JAPAN

Tel.: 81-3-35812331
Fax.: 81-3-35979104
Telex: 2225393 NADLIB

Member of IFLA.

Collections
Collections of Sound, scores.

Western classical music, Japanese music, language, etc.
Sound LP 175000, EP 100000, SP 15000, CD 27000 discs, cassette tape 2200 volumes

Access
Catalogue on cards.

Access to catalogue.

Access to materials: limited for research study only. The duplication is not permitted.
Access on archives premises.

Fees – Copyright
Free of charge.
Institution holds no copyright.
The right holders permission is not needed on archives premises.

___ 310
TOKYO KOKURITSU KINDAI BIJUTSU-KAN FILM CENTER
THE NATIONAL FILM CENTER, THE NATIONAL MUSEUM OF MODERN ART, TOKYO
FILM CENTER-ARCHIVE

3-1-4 Takane
SAGAMIHARA-SHI, KANAGAWA-KEN 229
JAPAN
Tel.: 81-3-427580128
Fax.: 81-3-427574449
Member of FIAF.

Collections

Collections of Film, books, magazines, still photos, posters, press materials, scripts and machineries.

Japanese films including features, documentaries, animation and newsreels.
Films 12000 titles

Access

Catalogue published, on cards.

Acces to catalogue: limited.

Access to materials: limited.
Access on archives premises.

Fees – Copyright

Fees for facilities and handling.
Institution holds no copyright.
Only for archival use.

JORDAN

AMMAN

_____ 311
THE UNIVERSITY OF JORDAN LIBRARY
AMMAN
JORDAN

Tel.: 962-6-843555 ext 3135
Fax.: 962-6-832318
Telex: UNVJ. JO 21629

Member of IFLA.

Collections

Collections of Film, Video, Sound.

Arts, History, Engineering and technology, English language Teaching, Medical Education.
Films 23
Video 104
Sound 276

Access

Catalogue on cards.

Acces to catalogue: limited.

Access to materials: limited.
Access on archives premises.

Fees – Copyright

Fees for research for reuse and production purposes.

KENYA

NAIROBI

_____ 312
KENYA BROADCASTING CORPORATION – VOICE OF KENYA
Harry Thuku Road
P.O. Box 30456
NAIROBI
KENYA

Tel.: 254-2-334567
Fax.: 254-2-332797
Telex: 25361

Member of IASA, IFLA.

Collections

Collections of Film, Video, Sound, books.

Kenya Broadcasting Corporation archives and libraries has huge collection of programmes in the archives in form of music on Gramophone records and sound effects, mood music, folk music of Kenya and Africa.
Films with magnetic sound track : 10000 ft
Video U-Matic video cassettes : 3000 hours, video tapes : 4000 hours
Sound Gramophone records : 350000, audio tapes : 15000

Access

Catalogue indexed on cards.

Acces to catalogue: limited. Catalogue is restricted to KBC staff only.

Access to materials: limited. Limited to the use of KBC staff otherwise through URTNA – PEC.

Fees – Copyright

Fees only allowed if the materials is for training purposed.
Copyright is with KBC or producer.

_____ 313
KENYA NATIONAL ARCHIVES
Moi Avenue
P.O. Box 49210
NAIROBI
KENYA

Tel.: 254-2-228959

Member of IASA, ICA.

Collections

Collections of Film, Video, Sound, photographs.

Audio-visual material – Subjects : Agriculture, Transport, Folk-Music and Kenyan History.
Films 89
Video 13
Sound 819

Access

Catalogue published.

Access to catalogue.

Access to materials.
Access on archives premises.

Fees – Copyright

Fees for research for reuse and production purposes.
Pricelist and conditions for use available.
Copyright holder is the institution.
Access to the archives is through application to the Director of Kenya National Archives.

KIRIBATI

BAIRIKI

_____ 314
KIRIBATI NATIONAL ARCHIVES
P.O. Box 6
BAIRIKI, TARAWA
KIRIBATI

Tel.: 686-21337
Fax.: 686-28222

Member of ICA, IFLA.

Collections

Collections of Film, Video, Sound.

Mainly on full music and radio programs. Films and videos are on Kiribati only.
Films 15 items
Video 10 items
Sound about 500 tapes

Access

Catalogue indexed on cards.

Access to catalogue.

Access to materials.
Access by loan.

Fees – Copyright

No fees charged.
Institution holds no copyright.

KOREA, DEMOCRATIC PEOPLE'S REPUBLIC

PYONGYANG

_____ 315
CHOSON MINJUJUI INMINGONGH-WAGUK KUGGA YONGHWA MUHONGO
NATIONAL FILM ARCHIVE OF THE DEMOCRATIC PEOPLE'S REPUBLIC OF KOREA
15 Sochangdong, Central District
PYONGYANG
D.P.R. OF KOREA

Tel.: 850-2-3 45 51
Telex: 5345 nfa kp

Member of FIAF.

Collections

Collections of Film, Video, stills, posters, scripts.

Principally 35mm films, all national productions, foreign films of value.
Films 20000 feature films

Access

Catalogue on database.

Acces to catalogue: limited.

Access to materials: limited.
Access on archives premises, by loan, by hire.

Fees – Copyright

Institution holds no copyright.
Access according to given items.

KOREA, REPULIC OF

SEOUL

_____ 316
HANKUK YONGSANG CHARYOWON
KOREAN FILM ARCHIVE
700, Seocho-dong, Seocho-gu
Seocho P.O. Box 91
SEOUL 137-070
REPUBLIC OF KOREA

Tel.: 82-2-521-3147 to 9
Fax.: 82-2-582-6213
Telex: ARTCNTR K29150

Member of FIAF.

Collections

Collections of Film, Video, scripts, censorship documents, stills, posters, books, magazines.

Korean feature films.

Films feature films : 1932 titles of negative, 708 titles of prints, shorts : 529 titles
Video 820 titles in feature

Access

Catalogue published.

Acces to catalogue: limited.

Access to materials: limited.
Access on archives premises, by loan.

Fees – Copyright

Fees for facilities and handling.
Pricelist and conditions for use available.
Institution holds no copyright.
The right holders permission is needed.

317

SEOUL NATIONAL UNIVERSITY LIBRARY

San 56-1, Shillim-dong, Kwanak-gu
SEOUL 151-742
REPUBLIC OF KOREA

Tel.: 82-2-877-5690
Fax.: 82-2-871-2972
Telex: 82-2-29664

Member of IFLA.

Collections

Collections of Video, Sound, collections which contain additional data on production of our AV-materials : newspapers, books.

Natural sciences, Korean studies, Language, Classical music, Chinese history, etc.
Video 40 cartridge
Sound Compact Discs (140 sheets), Disc LP 33.3 rpm (1000 sheets), Cassette Tapes (191 cartridge)

Access

Catalogue on database.

Access to catalogue.

Access to materials: limited, due to preservation, limited facilities, legal problems.
Access on archives premises.

Fees – Copyright

Fees for facilities and handling.
Pricelist and conditions for use available.
Copyright holder is the institution.
The Library Director permission is needed in use of a number of subjects (only part of Korean Studies).

LESOTHO

MASERU

318

LESOTHO GOVERNMENT ARCHIVES

Ministry of Tourism, Sports & Culture
P.O. Box 52
MASERU
LESOTHO

Tel.: 266-323034

Member of ICA.

Collections

Collections of Sound.

Tapes, speeches of the Prime Minister and other government officials.
Sound 20 tapes

Access

Catalogue on cards.

Access to catalogue: no. There is no prepared catalogue for these collections. The tapes are labelled on boxes.

LIECHTENSTEIN

VADUZ

319

LIECHTENSTEINISCHES LANDESARCHIV

FL – 9490 VADUZ
LIECHTENSTEIN

Tel.: 41-75-6 61 11

Collections

Collections of Film, Video, Sound.

Only materials concerning the Principality of Liechtenstein.
Films 100 films
Video 150 videos
Sound 200 tapes

Access

Access to catalogue.

Access to materials.
Access on archives premises.

Fees – Copyright

Fees for research for reuse and production purposes.
Usually copyrights holder is the producer.

LUXEMBOURG

LUXEMBOURG

320

CINEMATHEQUE MUNICIPALE/VILLE DE LUXEMBOURG
rue de la Chapelle 19
L – 1325 LUXEMBOURG
LUXEMBOURG

Tel.: 352-4796 2644, 352-4796 3028
Fax.: 352-459375

Member of FIAF.

Collections

Collections of Film, posters, photos, books, magazines.

Feature films, documentaries, from USA, France, Italy, Germany and others.
Films 8000 titles

Access

Catalogue on database.

Access to catalogue: no.

Access to materials: limited to researchers upon request (and if accepted).
Access on archives premises.

Fees – Copyright

Under certain conditions access is free for researchers.
Institution holds no copyright.
Access depends on individual case.

MALAWI

ZOMBA

321

NATIONAL ARCHIVES OF MALAWI
McLeod Road
P.O. Box 62
0000 ZOMBA
MALAWI

Tel.: 265-522 922, 265-522 184

Member of ICA, IFLA.

Collections

Collections of Film, Sound, microfiches and tapes.

Poetry, folk music, culture, anthropology, tourism, works, treasury, agriculture, health, judicial, aviation, commerce and industry, transport, defence, economics, missionary, journals.
Films 1711
Sound 350

Access

Catalogue indexed on cards.

Access to catalogue: Library materials open to the public but consultation restricted to premises only while public archives, official authority must be obtained.

Access to materials.
Access on archives premises.

Fees – Copyright

Fees for research for reuse and production purposes.
Copyright holder is the institution.
All research is done at the premises and the researcher is obliged to deliver one copy of his/her work at his/her expense resulting from the use of materials in the National Archives.

MALAYSIA

BANGI

322

UNIVERSITI KEBANGSAAN MALAYSIA, PERPUSTAKAAN
NATIONAL UNIVERSITY OF MALAYSIA, LIBRARY
43600 BANGI, SELANGOR
MALAYSIA

Tel.: 60-3-8250199
Fax.: 60-3-8256067
Telex: UNIKEB MA 31496

Member of IFLA.

Collections

Collections of Film, Video, Sound.

The library has a growing collection of non-book materials which are kept separately from the books and journals. The collection is divided into 3 categories : audio visual materials, microfilms, maps. The total collection is about 184206 volumes, consisting of 12051 audio visual materials, 171512 microforms and 643 maps.
Films 750 titles
Video 920 titles
Sound 300 titles

Access

Catalogue on cards.
Access to catalogue.

Access to materials: limited.
Access on archives premises.

Fees – Copyright

Fees for copyright.
Institution holds no copyright.

JITRA

323
UNIVERSITI UTARA MALAYSIA, LIBRARY
Sintok
06010 JITRA, KEDAH
MALAYSIA

Tel.: 60-4-741801
Fax.: 60-4-741959
Telex: MA42050 UTAMAS

Member of IFLA.

Collections
Collections of Video, Sound.

Management and related subjects.
Video 800 items
Sound 500 itams

Access
Catalogue on database.

Access to catalogue.

Access to materials.
Access on archives premises, by loan.

Fees – Copyright
Pricelist and conditions for use available.
Copyright holder is the institution.
Duplication of material not permitted.

KUALA LUMPUR

324
NATIONAL ARCHIVES OF MALAYSIA
Jalan Duta
50568 KUALA LUMPUR
MALAYSIA

Tel.: 60-3-2562688
Fax.: 60-3-2555679

Collections
Collections of Film, Video, Sound, magazines, film scripts, film posters, still photographs.

Film : documentaries depicting historical, social, economic, political scenarios, entertainment, news, etc. Video : copies of documentaries and special events and seminars. Sound (tapes and disc) : recording of speeches, patriotic songs, popular songs, instrumentals, dating back to 1920s.
Films 1000 reels
Video 400 units
Sound 2500 units

Access
Acces to catalogue: limited. Reference to accession lists.

Access to materials.
Access on archives premises.

Fees – Copyright
Fees for research for reuse and production purposes, research by archive staff.
Institution holds no copyright.
Creating agencies hold the copyright.

325
PERPUSTAKAAN NEGARA MALAYSIA
NATIONAL LIBRARY OF MALAYSIA
1st Floor, Wisma Sachdev, Jalan Raja Laut
50572 KUALA LUMPUR
MALAYSIA

Tel.: 60-3-2923144
Fax.: 60-3-2917436
Telex: NATLIB MA 30092

Member of IFLA.

Collections
Collections of Film, Video, Sound, fiche, kit, cards, maps, posters, charts, photographs, CD-ROM, educational games.

Economics, managements, language, history.
Films microfilms, filmstrips, films & slides : 7090 units
Video 396 units
Sound cassettes, phonographs : 2154 units

Access
Catalogue on database.

Access to catalogue.

Access to materials.
Access on archives premises.

Fees – Copyright
Fees for research for reuse and production purposes.

MINDEN, PENANG

326
UNIVERSITI SAINS MALAYSIA LIBRARY
11800 MINDEN, PENANG
MALAYSIA

Tel.: 60-4-877888 ext. 3722
Fax.: 60-4-871526
Telex: USMLIB MA 40254

Member of IFLA.

Collections
Collections of Film, Video, Sound, slides, film-loops, kits.

The media collection is made up of the various media items like videotapes, 16mm film, slides, filmloops, models and maps. The collection is for the use of our University Students and staff only. The subject ranges from fine arts, education, history, management to physics, pharmacy, chemistry and applied science.
Films 562 titles
Video 9026 titles
Sound 3161 titles

Access

Catalogue on database.

Access to catalogue.

Access to materials: limited for staff and students of the University.
Access on archives premises.

Fees – Copyright

Institution holds no copyright.
The collection is subject to compliance under the Malaysian Copyright Act 1987.

MARSHALL ISLANDS

MAJURO

327
MUSEUM OF THE MARSHALL ISLAND (ALELE MUSEUM AT NATIONAL ARCHIVES)
P.O. Box 629
MAJURO
MARSHALL ISLANDS

Tel.: 6929-3550
Fax.: 6929-3386, 6929-3325

Member of ICA.

Collections

Collections of Film, Video, Sound.

Oral tradition, contemporary and traditional songs and dances.
Video 906
Sound 295

Access

Access to materials: Limited facilities for copying.

MAURITIUS

FOREST SIDE

328
THE MAURITIUS BROADCASTING CORPORATION
1, Louis Pasteur Street
B.P. 48
FOREST-SIDE
MAURITIUS

Tel.: 230-6755001, 230-6755002, 230-6755003, 230-6755004
Fax.: 230-6757332
Telex: MAUBROAD 4230

Collections

Collections of Film, Video, Sound.

Local : Events/Programmes : political, historical, national, conferences, folk, variety, sports, debates, documentaries. Foreign : important news items, sports.
Films 1500
Video 2000
Sound 1000

Access

Catalogue published.

Acces to catalogue: limited for MaBC staff.

Access to materials: limited for MaBC staff.

Fees – Copyright

Fees for loan.

PORT LOUIS

329
MINISTRY OF INFORMATION, MAURITIUS
New Government Centre
PORT-LOUIS
MAURITIUS

Tel.: 230-2011278
Fax.: 230-2088243
Telex: 4249 – EXTERN IW

Collections

Collections of Film.

Films covering official functions of the government.
Films limited number of film

Access

Acces to catalogue: limited in quantity of materials.

Access to materials: limited for preservation.
Access on archives premises.

Fees – Copyright

Copy of film can be released on VHS video cassette. Cassette has to be provided.
Copyright holder is the institution.
Covered by copyright laws in force in the country.
Request to be made in writing to the principal Assistant Secretary, Ministry of Information, Government House, Port Louis, Mauritius, Indian Ocean.

REDUIT

___ 330
MAURITIUS COLLEGE OF THE AIR
REDUIT
MAURITIUS

Tel.: 230-4647106, 230-4647108, 230-4647136
Fax.: 230-547675
Telex: 4739 MESYND IW

Collections

Collections of Film, Video, Sound.

Films 200
Video 4000
Sound 500

Access

Catalogue published.

Access to catalogue.

Access to materials: limited. On closed-access, but some materials are available for loan to members.

___ 331
UNIVERSITY OF MAURITIUS, LIBRARY
REDUIT
MAURITIUS

Tel.: 230-4541041
Fax.: 230-4549642
Telex: 4621 UNIM IW

Member of IFLA.

Collections

Collections of Sound.

Audio cassette tapes of recorded talks, conferences and seminars held on the University premises.
Sound 236 cassettes

MEXICO

MEXICO, D.F.

___ 332
ARCHIVO GENERAL DE LA NACION
Eduardo Molina y Albañiles, Col. Penitenciaría Ampliación
Apartado Postal 1999, México 1, D.F.
15350 MÉXICO, D.F.
MEXICO

Tel.: 52-5-7895915
Fax.: 52-5-7895915

Member of ICA.

Collections

Collections of Film, Video, Sound.

Filmarchive on Jose Lopez Portillo : 1976-1982. Activities of the president, election campaigns, political activities, press conferences. Television Rural Mexicana : 1979-1982. Medical training to farmers. La Hora Nacional 1960-1976. Sunday radio program.
Films 2000 items
Video 4422 items
Sound 1794 items

Access

Catalogue published.

Access to catalogue.

Access to materials: limited due to lack of equipment, especially for obsolete TV formats.
Access on archives premises.

Fees – Copyright

Fees for research for reuse and production purposes.
Copyright holder is the institution.

___ 333
BIBLIOTECA DEL CENTRO DE INFORMACION CIENTIFICA Y HUMANISTICA
Circuito exterior, Ciudad universitaria
P.O. Box 20-281
MEXICO, D.F.
MEXICO

Tel.: 52-5-5505215, 52-5-5505216, 52-5-5505217, 52-5-5505218, 52-5-5505219 ext. 4215
Fax.: 52-5-5480858
Telex: 1774523 UNAMME

Member of IFLA.

Collections

Collections of Video.

Technical science, information science, librarianship.
Video 25 cassettes (20 hours)

Access
Catalogue on cards.

Access to catalogue.

Access to materials: limited. On the premises only.
Access on archives premises.

Fees – Copyright
Fees for facilities and handling.
Pricelist and conditions for use available.
Copyright holder is the institution.

334
BIBLIOTECA NACIONAL – INSTITUTO DE INVESTIGACIONES BIBLIOGRAFICAS
CENTRO CULTURAL, CIUDAD UNIVERSITARIA
Delegacion Coyoacan
P.O. Box 29124
04510 MEXICO D.F.
MEXICO

Tel.: 52-91-6651344, 52-91-6656271 ext. 7025
Fax.: 52-91-6650951

Member of IFLA.

Collections
Collections of Video, Sound, posters, photographs, scores, books.

Video made by UNAM as teaching material.
Mexican and foreign music. Music history.
Video 20000 items (40000 hours)
Sound 3450 items (discs, records, CD's, cassettes)

Access
Catalogue on cards.

Access to catalogue.

Access to materials: limited. Material handled by library staff.
Access on archives premises.

Fees – Copyright
Fees for duplication.
Pricelist and conditions for use available.
Institution holds no copyright.
Copyright only of parts of the printed material and the UNAM videos.

335
CINETECA NACIONAL
av. México-Coyoacán 389
C.P. 03330 MEXICO, D.F.
MEXICO

Tel.: 52-5-6888814, 52-5-6888824
Fax.: 52-5-6884211
Telex: 1760050 RTCME

Member of FIAF.

Collections
Collections of Film, Video.

National and foreign 35mm and 16mm, black and white and color. Video national and foreign Beta, VHS and 3/4".
Films 4366
Video 10000

Access
Catalogue indexed on cards.

Acces to catalogue: limited. Lending catalogue available.

Access to materials: limited. Only for catalogued material.
Access on archives premises, by loan, by hire.

Fees – Copyright
Fees for research by archive staff.
For titles on which the Cineteca holds rights it is necessary to make a request and an agreement on loan.

336
CORPORACION MEXICANA DE RADIO Y TV. S.A. DE C.V. (IMEVISION)
CANAL 13 – IMEVISION
Periferico sur 4121, Col. Fuentes del Pedregal
MEXICO, D.F. 14141
MEXICO

Tel.: 52-5-6456579
Fax.: 52-5-6451585
Telex: 1777642 TVNTME

Collections
Collections of Film, Video.

On culture, information, entertainment, education, goods and services.

Access
Catalogue published.

Access to catalogue.

Access to materials.

Fees – Copyright
Fees for research for reuse and production purposes, research by archive staff.
Pricelist and conditions for use available.

337
UNIVERSIDAD NACIONAL AUTONOMA DE MEXICO, DIRECCION GENERAL DE ACTIVIDADES CINEMATOGRAFICAS
FILMOTECA DE LA UNAM
San Ildefonso # 43 Col. Centro Deleg. Cuauhtemoc
P.O. Box 45002
06020 MEXICO, D.F.

MEXICO
Tel.: 52-5-7024503, 52-5-7026432
Telex: UNAME FILMOTECA 1777429
Member of FIAF.

Collections
Collections of Film, Video, books, magazines, scripts, microfilm, photos, posters, programs, discs, records, apparatusses, documentation material.

Archive is specialized in cinematography, in the diffusion of film culture, conservation, preservation and restoration.
Films 11500 titles
Video 1500 titles

Access
Catalogue on database.

Acces to catalogue: limited to researchers and institutions working on specific projects.

Access to materials: limited to researchers and institutions working on specific projects.
Access by loan, by hire, by purchase.

Fees – Copyright
Pricelist and conditions for use available.
Copyright holder is the institution.
We don't have rights to all titles. In general all titles are available to be consulted or used for cultural activities.

338
UNIVERSIDAD NACIONAL AUTONOMA DE MEXICO, DIRECCION GENERAL DE BIBLIOTECAS
Edificio de la Biblioteca Central, Circuito interior, Ciudad Universitaria 70-408, Delegacion Coyoacan 04510 MEXICO, D.F.
MEXICO

Tel.: 52-5-505215
Fax.: 52-5-501398
Member of IFLA.

Collections
Collections of Film, Video, Sound.

General (eg. geographic, science and technology, library science, art, life sciences, etc.).
Films 863
Video 207
Sound 107

Access
Catalogue on database.
Access to catalogue.
Access to materials: limited.

NAMIBIA

WINDHOEK

339
NATIONAL ARCHIVES OF NAMIBIA
4 Lüderitz Street
Private Bag 13250
WINDHOEK 9000
NAMIBIA

Tel.: 264-61-293387
Member of ICA.

Collections
Collections of Film, Video, Sound.

Source of collection : Namibian Broadcasting Co. news cassettes, private filmmakers, archival films, newscutting from U.K., Germany and South Africa.
Films about 380 reels
Video about 40 masters, about 68 show videos, about 366 NBC news, 454 education videos
Sound about 2000 NBC radio cassette material, about 40 oral history cassettes

Access
Catalogue on database.

Access to catalogue.

Access to materials.
Access on archives premises, by purchase.

Fees – Copyright
No fees are charged.
No copyright restrictions for viewing. For duplication the copyright holder is the production company or the donor.

NETHERLANDS

AMSTERDAM

340
DONEMUS
Paulus Potterstraat 16
NL – AMSTERDAM
NETHERLANDS

Tel.: 31-20-6764436
Fax.: 31-20-6733588
Member of IASA.

Collections
Collections of Sound.

Sound library of Dutch contemporary music.
Sound 8000 recorded items

Access
Catalogue on cards.

Access to catalogue.

Access to materials.
Access on archives premises.

Fees – Copyright
Institution holds no copyright.
No copying.

341

GEMEENTE ARCHIEF AMSTERDAM
AMSTERDAM CITY ARCHIVES : LES
ARCHIVES MUNICIPALES D'AMSTERDAM
Amsteldijk 67
NL – 1074 HZ AMSTERDAM
NETHERLANDS

Tel.: 31-20-6646916
Fax.: 31-20-6750596

Member of IASA, IAMHIST.

Collections
Collections of Film, Video, Sound, slides. Also documents regarding the audiovisual material in the collection.

Audiovisual material regarding the city of Amsterdam and its history.
Films about 500 films
Video about 3000 video tapes
Sound about 1000 sound tapes and 2000 LP's, singles and CDs

Access
Catalogue on cards.

Acces to catalogue: limited. Catalogues have not been published yet but can be worked through on the premises.

Access to materials.
Access on archives premises.

Fees – Copyright
Fees for facilities and handling, duplicates. No fees for viewing and other kinds of research, only fees for duplication material.
In the case that the Amsterdam City Archives is not the copyright holder, copyrights must first be cleared.

342

NEDERLANDS FILMMUSEUM
Vondelpark 3
NL – 1071 AA AMSTERDAM
NETHERLANDS

Tel.: 31-20-5891400
Fax.: 31-20-6833401

Member of FIAF.

Collections
Collections of Film, posters, paper archives, stills, apparatus.

Access
Catalogue on database.

Acces to catalogue: limited for staff only.

Access to materials: limited for staff, scientists, professional filmmakers.
Access on archives premises.

Fees – Copyright
Fees for research for reuse and production purposes, facilities and handling.
Pricelist and conditions for use available.
Institution holds no copyright.

343

OPENBARE BIBLIOTHEEK AMSTERDAM
PUBLIC LIBRARY OF AMSTERDAM
Prinsengracht 587
NL – 1016 HT AMSTERDAM
NETHERLANDS

Tel.: 31-20-5230900
Fax.: 31-20-5230948

Member of IFLA.

Collections
Collections of Sound.

20th Century music, jazz, modern music.
Sound 15000 items

Access
Catalogue on cards.

Access to catalogue: Card catalogue on music department.

Access to materials: By intervenience of a music-librarian the customer can ask for the collection.
Access on archives premises.

Fees – Copyright
No fees at all.

344

STICHTING FILM EN WETENSCHAP – AUDIOVISUEEL ARCHIEF
FILM AND SCIENCE FOUNDATION, AUDIOVISUAL ARCHIVES
Zeeburgerkade 8
NL – 1019 HA AMSTERDAM
NETHERLANDS

Tel.: 31-20-6652966
Fax.: 31-20-6659086

Member of IFTA, IASA, IAMHIST.

NETHERLANDS – AMSTERDAM / 344

Collections

Collections of Film, Video, Sound.

Film : trade-unions, pol.parties, Roman Catholic organisations, a.o. Video : off-air recordings Dutch television 1979-1991, a.o. Sound : records Dutch Radio Union (1930-1960), off-air radio recordings 1970-1991, oral history recordings, sound collections of diverse (see film) organisations.
Films 2000 cans
Video 200000 hours
Sound 35000 titles, 15000 hours

Access

Catalogue on database.

Access to catalogue.

Access to materials: limited for preservation (listening to archival copy only).
Access on archives premises.

Fees – Copyright

Fees for research for reuse and production purposes, facilities and handling.
Institution holds no copyright.
Right holders permission is needed for all reuse and production purposes except for scientific research and education.

345

STUDENTS LIBRARY OF THE BLIND
Molenpad 2
NL – 1016 GM AMSTERDAM
NETHERLANDS

Tel.: 31-20-6266465
Fax.: 31-20-6208459

Member of IFLA.

Collections

Collections of Sound.
Lecture for students and profession.
Sound 15000

Access

Catalogue on database.

Access to materials: limited.
Access by loan.

Fees – Copyright

Institution holds no copyright.

ARNHEM

346

GEMEENTEARCHIEF ARNHEM
Westervoortsedijk 2
NL – 6827 AS ARNHEM
NETHERLANDS

Tel.: 31-85-574544

Member of IASA, IAMHIST.

Collections

Collections of Film, Video, Sound.

Local history.
Films 135 titles
Video 820 titles
Sound 1500 titles

Access

Catalogue on database.

Access to catalogue.

Access to materials: no.
Access on archives premises.

Fees – Copyright

Fees for research for reuse and production purposes.

ENSCHEDE

347

UNIVERSITEITSBIBLIOTHEEK TWENTE
P.O. Box 217
NL – 7500 AE ENSCHEDE
NETHERLANDS

Tel.: 31-53-892074
Fax.: 31-53-351805
Telex: 44200

Member of IFLA.

Collections

Collections of Film, Video, Sound.

A library collection for educational purposes + a historical collection of university related materials.
Films 140
Video 980
Sound 260

Access

Catalogue on database.

Acces to catalogue: limited for students and staff only.

Access to materials for students and staff ; others on special request.
Access on archives premises.

Fees – Copyright

Copyright holder is the institution.

GRONINGEN

_____ 348
UNIVERSITEITSBIBLIOTHEEK GRONINGEN
UNIVERSITY LIBRARY GRONINGEN
Broerstraat 4
P.O. Box 559
NL – 9700 AN GRONINGEN
NETHERLANDS

Tel.: 31-50-635000
Fax.: 31-50-634996

Member of IFLA.

Collections
Collections of Video, Sound, dia, microfilms, software.

Basic materials on History, Literature, movies.
Video 1200
Sound 500

Access
Catalogue on database.

Access to catalogue.

Access to materials in the library only.
Access by loan.

Fees – Copyright
Institution holds no copyright.
There is no copying possible.

HILVERSUM

_____ 349
N.O.B. – FONOTHEEK
RADIO SOUND ARCHIVES – DUTCH BROADCASTING CORPORATION
Insulindelaan 16
Postbox 10
NL – 1200 JB HILVERSUM
NETHERLANDS

Tel.: 31-35-772395
Fax.: 31-35-772375

Member of IASA.

Collections
Collections of Sound.

Radioprograms and records, CD's and so on.
Sound 30000 items (fragments of) radio programs, 1500000 titles of music

Access
Catalogue on database.

Acces to catalogue: limited. Broadcasting corporations only.

Access to materials: limited. Broadcasting corporations only.
Access on archives premises, by loan.

Fees – Copyright
No fees for broadcasting corporations.
Institution holds no copyright.
People should access to the broadcasting companies in the Netherlands.

ROTTERDAM

_____ 350
BIBLIOTHEEK ERASMUS UNIVERSITEIT
LIBRARY ERASMUS UNIVERSITY
Burgemeester Oudlaan 50
P.O. Box 1738
NL – 3000 DR ROTTERDAM
NETHERLANDS

Tel.: 31-10-4081201
Fax.: 31-10-4532311

Member of IFLA.

Collections
Collections of Video.

Instructional videos for students.
Video 1250

Access
Catalogue on database.

Access to catalogue.

Access to materials.
Access on archives premises.

Fees – Copyright
Copyright holder is the institution.

_____ 351
GEMEENTEBIBLIOTHEEK ROTTERDAM
CITY LIBRARY OF ROTTERDAM
Hoogstraat 110
P.O. Box 22140
NL – 3011 PV ROTTERDAM
NETHERLANDS

Tel.: 31-10-4338911
Fax.: 31-10-4338338

Member of IFLA.

Collections
Collections of Film, Video, Sound.

Films, video's and audio, mostly for educational use.
Films 1000
Video 5000
Sound 1000

Access

Catalogue on database.

Access to catalogue.

Access to materials.
Access by loan.

Fees – Copyright

Fees for loan.
Pricelist and conditions for use available.
Institution holds no copyright.

_____ 352

GEMEENTELIJKE ARCHIEFDIENST ROTTERDAM
MUNICIPAL RECORD OFFICE OF ROTTERDAM
Robert Fruinstraat 52
P.O. Box 25082
NL – 3001 HB ROTTERDAM
NETHERLANDS

Tel.: 31-10-4775166
Fax.: 31-10-4780721

Member of IASA.

Collections

Collections of Film, Video, Sound.

Film, video and sound recordings concerning Rotterdam.
Films 1200 items
Video 700 items
Sound 2750 items

Access

Catalogue on cards.

Acces to catalogue: limited. Catalogue is not yet completed, no subject entries.

Access to materials: limited. Professionals and students only, sound collection for everyone who is interested.

Fees – Copyright

Fees for research for reuse and production purposes, research by archive staff, copying requested items.

THE HAGUE

_____ 353

DIENST OPENBARE BIBLIOTHEEK DEN HAAG
MUNICIPAL PUBLIC LIBRARY THE HAGUE
Bilderdijkstraat 1-3
P.O. Box 30313
NL – 2513 CM DEN HAAG
NETHERLANDS

Tel.: 31-70-3469235
Fax.: 31-70-3649283

Member of IFLA.

Collections

Collections of Video, Sound.

Sound : classical music, popular music, jazz, sundries. Video : feature and documentary films.
Video 3000 volumes
Sound 32500 CDs and 12500 LP records

Access

Catalogue on database.

Access to catalogue.

Access to materials.
Access by loan.

Fees – Copyright

Pricelist and conditions for use available.
Institution holds no copyright.

_____ 354

FILM- EN FOTOARCHIEF VAN DE RIJKSVOORLICHTINGSDIENST
AUDIOVISUAL ARCHIVE OF THE NETHERLANDS GOVERNMENT INFORMATION SERVICE
Moordlinde 64
P.O. Box 20006
2500 EA THE HAGUE
NETHERLANDS

Tel.: 3170-3564105 (photographs archive),
3170-3564106/7/9 (film archive),
3170-3564108/10 (secretariat)
Fax.: 3170-3647756
Telex: 33159 ERVEDE

Member of FIAF, IFTA, IASA, ICA, IAMHIST.

Collections

Collections of Film, Video, photographs (about 1500000).

Documents produced by or in possession of Central Gov't related to history of Netherlands and former colonies.
Films about 45000000 ft (film and video)

Access

Catalogue on database. (IBM-based)

Access to catalogue: Catalogue only in Dutch. System used is adaptation of IBM (STAIRS). Information up to 1989 on test.

Access to materials: Service is a public archive. It is in principle open to all, on arrangement.
Access on archives premises, by loan, by purchase.

Fees – Copyright

Fees for facilities and handling. Licence fees depend on intended use and distribution area. Pricelist and conditions for use available. For most documents coyrights or ownership rights are with the archive itself. If not, rights may be cleared.

355

NEDERLANDSE LUISTER- EN BRAILLEBIBLIOTHEEK
DUTCH TALKING AND BRAILLE LIBRARY
Zichtenburglaan 260
NL – 2544 EB DEN HAAG
NETHERLANDS

Tel.: 31-70-3211211
Fax.: 31-70-329447

Member of IFLA.

Collections

Collections of Sound.

15000 novels (Dutch language 97%, English, German, French 3%). 11000 non fiction books. 4000 titles for the youth (fiction and non fiction). *Sound* totally 30000 titles (150000 copies)

Access

Catalogue published.

Access to catalogue.

Access to materials: Available for people that are unable to read printed books (reading handicap) : the blind and the partially sighted.

Fees – Copyright

No fees for loan.
Pricelist and conditions for use available.
Copyright holder is the institution.
For loan the library holds the copy rights. For selling permission is needed from the original publisher.

356

RIJKSARCHIEFDIENST
Prins Wilhelm Alexanderhof
P.O. Box 90520
NL – THE HAGUE
NETHERLANDS

Tel.: 31-70-38143
Fax.: 31-70-3473231

Member of ICA.

Collections

Collections of Film, Video, Sound.

Films 100 (film + video)
Sound 2400

TILBURG

357

OPENBARE BIBLIOTHEEK TILBURG
PUBLIC LIBRARY TILBURG
Koningsplein 1
Postbus 3195, NL – 5003 DD TILBURG
NL – 5038 WG TILBURG
NETHERLANDS

Tel.: 31-13-355055
Fax.: 31-13-368049

Member of IFLA.

Collections

Collections of Video, Sound.

Videos: feature films and informative movies.
Compact discs : popmusic and classical music.
Music-cassettes : popmusic.
Video 2200 items
Sound 6500 CD's and 4100 music-cassettes

Access

Catalogue on database.

Access to catalogue.

Access to materials.
Access by loan.

Fees – Copyright

Fees for loan.
Pricelist and conditions for use available.
Institution holds no copyright.
In the Netherlands a library pays "loanright" to the Ministry ; this is a sort of fee. From the total national purchase of this fees the Ministry pays an amount to the copyright holders.

UTRECHT

358

BIBLIOTHEEK RIJKSUNIVERSITEIT UTRECHT
UNIVERSITY LIBRARY OF UTRECHT
Wittevrouwenstraat 7-11
P.O. Box 16007
NL – 3500 DA UTRECHT
NETHERLANDS

Tel.: 31-30-392600
Fax.: 31-30-328198
Telex: 47103

Member of IFLA.

Collections

Collections of Video, Sound.

General, art history, music, sociological, theatre and veterinary.
Video 7600
Sound 7100 LP's, CD's, MC's

Access

Catalogue on database.

Access to cardcatalogue only in library; database via network.

Access to materials but limited facilities.
Access on archives premises.

Fees – Copyright

Institution holds no copyright.

NEW ZEALAND

AUCKLAND

_____ 359

ARCHIVE OF MAORI AND PACIFIC MUSIC

Anthropology Department, University of Auckland
Private Bag
AUCKLAND
NEW ZEALAND

Tel.: 64-9-737999
Fax.: 64-9-3023245

Member of IASA.

Collections

Collections of Video, Sound, documentation of field collections.

Ethno-music of New Zealand and the Pacific (Maori).
Video 527 tapes
Sound 4000 hours

Access

Catalogue on database.

Acces to catalogue: limited. On premises.

Access to materials.
Access on archives premises.

Fees – Copyright

Institution holds no copyright.
Copyright held by depositors. Contracts with depositors allow varying degrees of access.

CHRISTCHURCH

_____ 360

RADIO NEW ZEALAND SOUND ARCHIVES

Kent House, CNR Durham + Chester Sts.
P.O. Box 1484
CHRISTICHURCH
NEW ZEALAND

Tel.: 64-3-799600

Fax.: 64-3-793426
Telex: NZ 31031

Member of IASA.

Collections

Collections of Sound, documents & photographs.

Predominantly N.Z. Broadcasting material 1935 to present day.
Sound 80000 cylinders, 78's, LP's + 45's, 15000 lacques discs, 10000 reel to reel tapes, 12000 cassettes (analogue + digital)

Access

Catalogue on database.

Access to catalogue: Select listings available without charge.

Access to materials: Copies available to order.
Access on archives premises, by purchase.

Fees – Copyright

Fees for research for reuse and production purposes, research by archive staff, facilities and handling.
Pricelist and conditions for use available.
Copyright holder is the institution.

LOWER HUTT

_____ 361

TELEVISION NEW ZEALAND (TVNZ), PRODUCTION LIBRARY AND ARCHIVES

1 Fairway Drive
P.O. Box 30945
LOWER HUTT
NEW ZEALAND

Tel.: 64-4-6190600
Fax.: 64-4-693810

Member of IFTA.

Collections

Collections of Film, Video, documentation files, programme scripts, programme schedules.

New Zealand television programmes and news items dating from 1960 when television started in New Zealand. Stock footage on all subjects available. Also hold and have access to movie newsreels dating back to 1940.
Films 250000 plus programmes, news items
Video 10000 plus programmes

Access

Catalogue on database.

Access to catalogue via Library Research staff.

Access to materials subject to preservation and copyright restrictions.
Access on archives premises, by purchase.

Fees – Copyright

Fees for research for reuse and production purposes, research by archive staff, facilities and handling, Royalties charged for use in educational, commercial and television productions.
Pricelist and conditions for use available.
Copyright holder is the institution.
In most cases (95%), copyright is with TVNZ.

WELLINGTON

362

ALEXANDER TURNBULL LIBRARY
Molesworth St.
P.O. Box 12-349
WELLINGTON
NEW ZEALAND

Tel.: 64-4-743000
Fax.: 64-4-743035
Telex: 31525

Member of IASA, IFLA, IAML.

Collections

Collections of Video, Sound, music scores, books, magazines, some scripts & production papers, ephemera.

Published & unpublished sound & video recordings relating to New Zealand & New Zealanders. N.Z. music : contemporary classical, Maori, popular, folk, band, jazz, country & religious. Spoken word : oral histories.
Video published items : about 206 ; unpublished items : 30
Sound published items : about 4500 ; unpublished items : 5907 (including 4280 oral history tapes)

Access

Catalogue on database.

Access to catalogue.

Access to materials: Due to conservation requirements, prior notice may be required for access so a listening copy can be made for use within the Library.
Access on archives premises.

Fees – Copyright

Fees for tape dubbing.
Pricelist and conditions for use available.
Institution holds no copyright.
Access restricted to some unpublished items ; written permission of copyright owner required.

363

NATIONAL LIBRARY OF NEW ZEALAND, SOUND AND MUSIC CENTRE
Molesworth Street
P.O. Box 1467
WELLINGTON
NEW ZEALAND

Tel.: 64-4-743000
Fax.: 64-4-743035

Member of IASA.

Collections

Collections of Video, Sound, books, scores, gramophones, A/V equipment.

A general collection of world music covering all styles.
Video 400 items
Sound 29536 items

Access

Catalogue on database.

Acces to catalogue: limited. Staff retrieval only.

Access to materials.
Access on archives premises, by loan.

Fees – Copyright

No fees.
Institution holds no copyright.
Listening copies of N.Z. material for use within library only.

364

NEW ZEALAND FILM ARCHIVE/NGA KAITIAKI O NGA TAONGA WHITIAHYA
82 Tory St.
P.O. Box 9544
WELLINGTON
NEW ZEALAND

Tel.: 64-4-3847647
Fax.: 64-4-3829595

Member of FIAF.

Collections

Collections of Film, Video, Sound, books, periodicals, scripts, documentation, stills, posters, props, equipment, etc.

Mostly NZ content.
Films 10000
Video 500
Sound 100 items

Access

Catalogue on database.

Access to catalogue.

Access to materials subject to preservation requirements.

Access on archives premises.

Fees – Copyright

Fees for research for reuse and production purposes, research by archive staff, facilities and handling.
Pricelist and conditions for use available.
Institution holds no copyright.
Donor/copyright clearance essential for reuse.

NIGERIA

AKURE

365

FEDERAL UNIVERSITY OF TECHNOLOGY, AKURE LIBRARY
P.M.B. 704, AKURE
AKURE
NIGERIA

Member of IFLA.

Collections

Collections of Film, Video, Sound.
Microforms, slide films, filmstrip, cinefilms.
Films 11316
Video 65
Sound 15

Access

Catalogue published.
Acces to catalogue: limited.
Access to materials.
Access on archives premises, by loan.

Fees – Copyright

Fees for research for reuse and production purposes, facilities and handling.
Pricelist and conditions for use available.
Copyright holder is the institution.

366

FEDERAL UNIVERSITY OF TECHNOLOGY, UNIVERSITY LIBRARY EDUCATIONAL TECHNOLOGY CENTRE
P.M.B. 704
AKURE
NIGERIA

Tel.: 234-32-200090

Member of IFLA.

Collections

Collections of Film, Video, Sound.
Educational materials, research materials, teaching materials, information retrieval materials.
Films 11864
Video 54
Sound 20

Access

Catalogue on cards.
Acces to catalogue: limited.
Access to materials.
Access on archives premises, by loan.

Fees – Copyright

Fees for facilities and handling.
Pricelist and conditions for use available.

IBADAN

367

UNIVERSITY OF IBADAN, COLLEGE OF MEDICINE, E. LATUNDE ODEKU MEDICAL LIBRARY
IBADAN
NIGERIA

Member of IFLA.

Collections

Collections of Sound.
Medical Journal articles on tapes (audio) covering the broad areas of medicine and surgery, dentistry. The collection includes also slide/tape programmes.
Sound 642 audio tapes

Access

Catalogue indexed on cards.
Access to catalogue.
Access to materials: limited.
Access on archives premises.

Fees – Copyright

No fees charged.
Institution holds no copyright.

LAGOS

368

NIGERIAN INSTITUTE OF INTERNATIONAL AFFAIRS LIBRARY
13-15 Kofo Abayomi Rd. Victoria Island
GPO Box 1727
LAGOS
NIGERIA

Tel.: 234-1-615606, 234-1-615607, 234-1-615608, 234-1-615609, 234-1-615610
Telex: 22638

Member of IFLA, FID.

Collections

Collections of Film, Video, Sound, microfilms.

Phonotapes-recordings from seminars, lectures, briefings and conferences organised by NIIA, video-recording and cassette tapes are from Oral Documentation Project and Nigerian Television Newsweek Programme.
Films 80
Video 80
Sound 374

Access

Access to materials except oral documentation tapes and video.

Fees – Copyright

Copyright holder is the institution.

_____ 369
UNIVERSITY OF LAGOS LIBRARY
LAGOS
NIGERIA

Tel.: 234-1-821273

Member of IFLA.

Collections

Collections of Video, Sound.

Video 10
Sound 3653

Access

Catalogue indexed on cards.

Access to catalogue.

Access to materials.
Access on archives premises.

MAIDUGURI

_____ 370
UNIVERSITY OF MAIDUGURI, RAMAT LIBRARY
Bama Road
PMB 1069
MAIDUGURI
NIGERIA

Tel.: 234-76-231725
Telex: 82102 UNIMAI NG

Member of IFLA.

Collections

Collections of Video, Sound.

Video contains convocation ceremonies of the University of Maiduguri. Audio-cassette contains the University Library's In-house seminars.
Video 10
Sound 26 audio-cassette

Access

Catalogue on cards.

Access to catalogue.

Access to materials.
Access on archives premises, by loan.

Fees – Copyright

Fees for loss or damage of materials.
Pricelist and conditions for use available.
Institution holds no copyright.

NORWAY

BERGEN

_____ 371
BERGEN OFFENTLIGE BIBLIOTEK
BERGEN PUBLIC LIBRARY
GRIEG-SAMLINGEN/GRIEG COLLECTION
Strømgaten 6
N – 5015 BERGEN
NORWAY

Tel.: 47-5-97 85 82, 47-5-97 85 83
Fax.: 47-5-32 56 05

Member of IAML.

Collections

Collections of Sound, computerized data base with scanned and word processed original manuscripts from the composer Edvard Grieg (1843-1907).

Sound : recordings of music by Edvard Grieg. Data base : original score manuscripts, correspondance, articles, diaries, photos, etc. from the composer Edvard Grieg are in the process of being digitalized by means of scanning to be shown on screen together with word processed text as well as bibliographic descriptions. Main part of documents to be computerized by mid-1993, in connection with Grieg's 150th Anniversary.
Sound LPs : 557 ; CDs : 25

Access

Catalogue on database.

Access to catalogue.

Access to materials.
Access on archives premises, by purchase.

Fees – Copyright

Copyright holder is the institution.

HØVIKODDEN

_____ 372
HENIE-ONSTAD KUNSTSENTER
HENIE-ONSTAD ART CENTER
Sonja Henies v. 31
N – 1311 HØVIKODDEN
NORWAY

Tel.: 47-2-54 30 50
Fax.: 47-2-54 32 70

Member of IFLA.

Collections
Collections of Film, Video, Sound, Sonja Henie archive.

Contemporary music, interviews with artists, recordings of performances/concerts, etc. Documentation-videos/films. All of Sonja Henie's movies, film/video as visual art medium.
Films 206
Video 146
Sound tapes/cassettes : 1168, records/compact discs: 683

Access
Catalogue on cards.

Access to catalogue: Catalogues of the collection are not published – access to catalogues in the library.

Access to materials: limited. The material is not lent out. Cassettes, records and compact-discs can be listened to in the library.

KRISTIANSAND

_____ 373
STATSARKIVET I KRISTIANSAND
NATIONAL ARCHIVES OF NORWAY, KRISTIANSAND DEPARTMENT
Vesterveien 4
N – 4613 KRISTIANSAND
NORWAY

Tel.: 47-42-25511
Fax.: 47-42-20411

Member of ICA.

Collections
Collections of Sound.
Maritime culture.
Sound 320 cassettes (177 interviews)

Access
Catalogue on database.
Access to catalogue.
Access to materials.
Access on archives premises, by purchase.

Fees – Copyright
Fees for research for reuse and production purposes.
Pricelist and conditions for use available.
Copyright holder is the institution.

MO I RANA

_____ 374
NASJONALBIBLIOTEKAVDELINGA I RANA
NORWEGIAN NATIONAL LIBRARY, RANA BRANCH
NASJONATT AUDIOVISUETT ARKIV
Langneset 29
P.O. Box 278
N – 8601 MO
NORWAY

Tel.: 47-87-21111
Fax.: 47-87-55460

Member of IFLA.

Collections
Collections of Film, Video, Sound.

A national audio visual archive will be established by the end of 1991. It will receive a legal deposit of Norwegian radio and television programmes, initially from the state broadcasting (NRK), later from other selected broadcasting. A legal deposit of film and sound material will also be part of the archive.
Video NRK-TV on S-VHS starting from July 1st, 1990

Access
Acces to catalogue: limited. Catalogue system under discussion.

For research & documentation.

Fees – Copyright
Fees: Under discussion.
Institution holds no copyright.

OSLO

_____ 375
ARBEIDERBEVEGELSENS ARKIV OG BIBLIOTEK
THE NORWEGIAN LABOUR-MOVEMENT ARCHIVE & LIBRARY
Folkets Hus – Youngsgt. 11 C
N – 0181 OSLO 1
NORWAY

Tel.: 47-2-40 17 58
Fax.: 47-2-40 17 63

Member of IASA.

Collections

Collections of Sound.

Interviews of politicians and veterans from the Norvegian Labour-movement. Recordings from union-congresses, annual-meetings and political discussions from the 1950's until today. Most of the recordings appear on open reel tapes.
Sound about 3000 hours

Access

Access to materials: limited.
Access on archives premises.

Fees – Copyright

Copyright holder is the institution.

376

NORSK FILMINSTITUTT
Grev Wedels Plass 1
P.B. 482 – SENTRUM
N – 0105 OSLO 1
NORWAY

Tel.: 47-2-42 87 40
Fax.: 47-2-33 22 77

Member of FIAF.

Collections

Collections of Film, Video, stills, posters and documentation.

Norwegian short and feature films from the early years up to days productions on film and video. Norwegian Film Institute is the National filmmuseum and archive.
Films 578 Norwegian feature films and 5250 short films registered on data. Unfortunately the Institute still has a great number of non-registered films

Access

Catalogue on database.

Access to catalogue: Both card and database (SIFT).

Access to materials.
Access on archives premises.

Fees – Copyright

Fees for research for reuse and production purposes, facilities and handling.
Copyright holder is the institution.
In most of the cases it is the copyright owners material, but if the material is restored by Norwegian Film Institute and without any identification the owner of the material is NFI and we take a fee for commercial use.

377

NORSK JAZZARKIV
NORWEGIAN JAZZ ARCHIVES
Toftes gate 69
N – 0552 OSLO 5
NORWAY

Tel.: 47-2-37 09 09
Fax.: 47-2-35 69 38

Member of IASA.

Collections

Collections of Film, Video, Sound, photos, scrapbooks, concert programmes, posters, books, newspapers and periodicals.

Material from the history of jazz in Norway and Norwegian jazz life.
Films 3 items
Video 85 items
Sound LP/CD/taperecordings : 1020

Access

Catalogue on database.

Access to catalogue.

Access to materials: No copying.
Access on archives premises.

Fees – Copyright

No copying of sound material.

378

NORSK LYD- OG BLINDESKRIFTBIBLIOTEK
NORWEGIAN TALKING AND BRAILLE BOOK LIBRARY
Sporveisgt. 8-10
Box 5900 HEGDEHAUGEN
N – 0308 OSLO
NORWAY

Tel.: 47-2-46 69 90
Fax.: 47-2-60 70 54

Member of IFLA.

Collections

Collections of Sound.

10000 talking books, recorded special for the blind in our studios.
Sound 10000 (adding 300 titles each year)

Access

Catalogue on database.

Access to catalogue: Catalog of talking books is produced and distributed each year in printing and in sound.

Access to materials.
Access by loan.

Fees – Copyright

Copyright holder is the institution.
Need for talking books must be documented.

379
NORSK LYDARKIV UNIVERSITETSBIBLIOTEKET I OSLO
NATIONAL SOUND ARCHIVES, ROYAL UNIVERSITY LIBRARY
Observatoriegaten 1
N – 0254 OSLO
NORWAY

Tel.: 47-2-55 36 30
Fax.: 47-2-43 44 97
Telex: 76078 ub n

Member of IASA.

Collections
Collections of Sound.

Norwegian and Norwegian-related music or artists. Special : Bauer-Müller collection of operatic records 1896-1952. Beethoven collection : LP's, 78*, pianorolls and tapes. About 400 master-tapes of Norwegian music, 1000 wax cylinders folk music.
Sound 30000 units

Access
Catalogue on database.

Access to catalogue.

Access to materials.
Access on archives premises.

Fees – Copyright
Fees for research by archive staff, cassette copy. Right holders' permission is needed for copies.

380
NORSK RIKSKRINGKASTING, PLATESAMLINGEN
NORWEGIAN BROADCASTING CORPORATION, RECORD LIBRARY
Bj. Bjørnsons pl. 1
N – 0340 OSLO
NORWAY

Tel.: 47-2-45 86 03
Fax.: 47-2-45 95 59

Member of IASA, IFLA.

Collections
Collections of Sound.

Gramophone records (78-45-LP) and CDs.
Sound about 230000

Access
Catalogue on database.

Acces to catalogue: limited to institution staff only.

Access to materials: limited to institution staff only.
Access on archives premises, by loan.

381
NORSK RIKSKRINGKASTING, PROGRAMSAMLINGEN
NORWEGIAN BROADCASTING CORPORATION, PROGRAMME COLLECTION
N – 0340 OSLO
NORWAY

Tel.: 47-2-45 86 22
Fax.: 47-2-45 77 60

Member of IASA, IFLA.

Collections
Collections of Sound.

Radio broadcasts from 1934 – music, theatre, spoken word, news, etc.
Sound 24000 tapes

Access
Catalogue on database.

Acces to catalogue: limited. Institution staff only.

Access to materials: limited. Institution staff only.
Access on archives premises, by loan.

Fees – Copyright
Fees for research for reuse and production purposes.
Copyright holder is the institution.

382
RIKSARKIVET, PRIVATARKIVAVDELINGEN
NATIONAL ARCHIVES OF NORWAY, DEPARTMENT FOR PRIVATE ARCHIVES
Folke Bernadottes vei 21
PB 10 KRINGSJA
N – 0807 OSLO 8
NORWAY

Tel.: 47-2-23 74 80
Fax.: 47-2-23 74 89

Member of ICA.

Collections
Collections of Sound.

Our sound records are parts of private archives. Subjects are : the traditional farming community, temperance movements, religion, etc.
Sound about 2200 hours

Access
Acces to catalogue: limited. Catalogues not complete.

Access to materials: limited due to copyrights reserved, conditions of material.

STAVANGER

_____ 383
STATSARKIVET I STAVANGER
THE STATE ARCHIVES IN STAVANGER
Bergjelandsgt 30
N – 4012 STAVANGER
NORWAY

Tel.: 47-4-50 12 60
Fax.: 47-4-50 12 90

Collections
Collections of Film, Video.

Mostly local history from the city of Stavanger/County of Rogaland, some related to agriculture.
Films about 10 hours playing time (16mm/35mm)
Video aout 5 hours playing time (VHS/U-Matic)

Access
Access to materials: limited due to right holders' clause.
Access on archives premises.

Fees – Copyright
Institution holds no copyright.
Right holder's permission needed for use of some of the film material. Use outside archives premises very limited for other than right holder.

TROMSØ

_____ 384
STATSARKIVET I TROMSØ
NATIONAL ARCHIVES OF NORWAY, TROMSØ DEPARTMENT
Breivika
Box 622
N – 9001 TROMSØ
NORWAY

Tel.: 47-83-83820
Fax.: 47-83-87630

Member of ICA.

Collections
Collections of Sound.

Dialectal excerpts from northern Norway.
Sound 110 tapes, 165 hrs

Access
Access to materials: limited.
Access on archives premises.

Fees – Copyright
Institution holds no copyright.

TRONDHEIM

_____ 385
TRONDHEIM FOLKEBIBLIOTEK
TRONDHEIM PUBLIC LIBRARY
Peter Egges Plass 1
Postuttak
N – 7004 TRONDHEIM
NORWAY

Tel.: 47-7-54 75 00
Fax.: 47-7-52 75 75

Member of IFLA.

Collections
Collections of Video, Sound.

Professional/technical videos wide-range musical collection.
Video 1000 items
Sound 1500 CD's, 3500 LP's

Access
Catalogue on database.

Access to catalogue.

Access to materials: limited. LP's not for loan.
Access by loan.

Fees – Copyright
Pricelist and conditions for use available.
Institution holds no copyright.

PAPUA NEW GUINEA

BOROKO

_____ 386
INSTITUTE OF PAPUA NEW GUINEA STUDIES, MUSIC ARCHIVE
Angall Drive
Box 1432
BOROKO
PAPUA NEW GUINEA

Tel.: 675-25-4644
Fax.: 675-21-1445

Member of IASA.

Collections
Collections of Sound, and accompanying printed + visual material (e.g., slides, 8mm film, video).

Primarily Papua New Guinea traditional & popular musics. Commercial + field recordings. Copies of historic recordings of PNG musics from other archives (1898-present).
Films 9 reels
Video 33 tapes
Sound 6100 tapes, discs, CDs

Access

Catalogue on database.

Access to catalogue: Staff only.

Access to materials on-premises listening for unrestricted materials.
Access on archives premises, by purchase.

Fees – Copyright

Fees for copying materials.
For commercial recordings, companies hold rights. Outside collectors or institutions hold rights for their collections deposited with us. We have rights for recordings we have made ourselves. However, Papua New Guinea does not presently have any copyright laws.

___
387
NATIONAL LIBRARY OF PAPUA NEW GUINEA
P.O. Box 5770
BOROKO
PAPUA NEW GUINEA

Member of ICA.

Collections

Collections of Film, Video.

Papua New Guinea : history, geography, sport, politics.
Films 4000 16mm reels
Video 600 VHS-Pal video cassettes, 700 U-Matic tapes

Access

Catalogue published.

Access to catalogue.

Access to materials: no due to limited facilities.
Access by loan.

Fees – Copyright

No fees.
Conditions for use available.
Institution holds no copyright.
No copyright in PNG.

PERU

LIMA

___
388
ARCHIVO GENERAL DE LA NACIÓN
NATIONAL ARCHIVES OF PERU
DIREÇÇIÓN DE ARCHIVO AUDIOVISUAL
Manuel Cuadros s/n
P.O. Box 3124
LIMA 100
PERU
Tel.: 51-14-275930
Member of ICA.

Collections

Collections of Video, Sound, posters, photos.

Documents produced by Peruvian state institutions no longer in existance.
Video 192 items
Sound 280 items

Access

Catalogue indexed on cards.

Access to catalogue.

Access to materials: limited due to lack of equipment.

Fees – Copyright

Fees for research by archive staff. Services provided for serious research.
Consultation on the premises.

___
389
UNIVERSIDAD CATOLICA DEL PERU, INSTITUTO RIVA-AGUERO, ARCHIVO DE MUSICA TRADICIONAL ANDINA
CATHOLIC UNIVERSITY OF PERU, RIVA-AGUERO INSTITUTE, ARCHIVE OF TRADITIONAL ANDEAN MUSIC
Apartado postal 1761
LIMA 100
PERU
Tel.: 51-14-622540 ext. 273
Fax.: 51-14-611785

Collections

Collections of Video, Sound, photographic (color slides).

Sound materials : more than 8000 individual items of field recordings of Andean music of Peru. Cassettes and reel-to-reel tapes. Video : over 200 video recording hours (field recordings of fiestas, rituals and music of the Peruvian Andes) VHS-NTSC.
Video over 200 hours video
Sound over 8000 individual items in nearly 600 tapes (cassette and reel-to-reel)

Access

Catalogue on database.

Access to catalogue.

Access to materials: limited to investigators and advanced students (graduates).
Access on archives premises.

Fees – Copyright

Fees for record and video productions.
Copyright holder is the institution.

PHILIPPINES

QUEZON CITY

_____ 390
UNIVERSITY OF THE PHILIPPINES FILM CENTER ARCHIVES
Magsaysay avenue
P.O. Box 214
QUEZON CITY 1101
PHILIPPINES

Tel.: 63-2-962722
Fax.: 63-2-992863, 63-2-986780
Telex: 63199 ETPIMO PN

Collections
Collections of Film, Video, Sound, stills, music sheet, posters, books and other publications.

Filipino feature-length films ; U.P. Film Center productions of professional and student films ; U.P. Film Center video productions ; Philippine government documentaries, newsfilms and recorded speeches ; audio recordings of lectures on Filipino film history & appreciation, current issues, film-making techniques.
Films 1908 titles
Video 16 titles
Sound 2575 titles

Access
Catalogue on database.

Acces to catalogue: limited access by staff only, but is programmed for publication for use of researchers.

Access to materials: limited. Purchase is for recent U.P. Film Center video productions ; loan of collection limited to Manila ; special screenings on archives premises or within university campus. Access on archives premises, by loan, by purchase.

Fees – Copyright
Fees for research for reuse and production purposes, research by archive staff, facilities and handling, technical evaluation with reports for films not deposited with the archives but requested by film producers.
Pricelist and conditions for use available.
Institution holds no copyright.
Outside of archives premises, screenings are limited to schools or as cultural programs of museums or city governments. Screenings arranged for individual research. For its own productions, U.P. Film Center reserves the rights for television broadcast.

POLAND

WARSAW

_____ 391
ARCHIWUM DOKUMENTACJI MECHANICZNEJ
ARCHIVES OF MECHANICS DOCUMENTATION
Swietojerska street 24
PL – 00-202 WARSAW
POLAND

Tel.: 48-22-311736
Member of ICA.

Collections
Collections of Film, Sound, historical and documentary materials (1919-1990) recorded on gramophone.

Historical and documentary materials (1919-1990) recorded on gramophone records and magnetic tapes. Collection contains problems connected with politics, economics, social relations and culture in Poland. Including : politicians, speeches, interviews with politicians, scientists, economists, artists, eg. poets, writers, composers, painters, etc.
Films 300 titles
Sound about 10000 items of records, 3000 – gr.rec., 7000 – magnetic tapes, 4164 hours of sound

Access
Catalogue indexed on cards.

Access to catalogue.

Access to materials.
Access on archives premises.

Fees – Copyright
Materials available, free of charge.
Copyright holder is the institution.

_____ 392
BIBLIOTEKA NARODOWA W WARSZAWIE, PRACOWNIA DOKUMENTÓW DZWIEKOWYCH
WARSAW NATIONAL LIBRARY, SOUND DEPARTMENT
Al. Niepodleglosci 213
PL – 00-973 WARSZAWA
POLAND

Tel.: 48-22-257241 ext. 398, 399
Member of IFLA.

Collections
Collections of Video, Sound, newspapers, books.

Classical music, pop music, rock music, jazz, folk music and other (eg. sound effects, education records, speeches on records, poetry), discs, CD, cassette-tapes, cylinders, piano-rolls, video CD.
Video 4 titles
Sound 33500 items

Access

Catalogue indexed on cards.

Access to catalogue.

Access to materials: limited for preservation and limited facilities.
Access on archives premises.

Fees – Copyright

Institution holds no copyright.

393

FILMOTEKA NARODOWA W WARSZAWIE

NATIONAL FILMARCHIVE IN WARSAW
ul. Pulawska 61
P.O. Box 65
PL – 00-975 WARSZAWA
POLAND

Tel.: 48-22-455074
Fax.: 48-22-455074
Telex: 813640 Film PL

Member of FIAF.

Collections

Collections of Film, books, posters, magazines, scripts, photos, dialogue lists, production papers.

National and foreign cinema : feature films mostly. Small collection of Polish documentaries and animation films.
Films about 19000 titles

Access

Catalogue on cards.

Acces to catalogue: limited. Reserved to staff and recommended persons.

Access to materials: limited. Reserved to staff and recommended persons.
Access on archives premises, by loan.

Fees – Copyright

Fees for research for reuse and production purposes, research by archive staff, library.
Institution holds no copyright.

394

ODDZIAL ZBIOROW MUZYCZNYCH BIBLIOTEKI UNIWERSYTETU WARSZAWSKIEGO

MUSIC DEPARTMENT OF WARSAW UNIVERSITY LIBRARY
ul. Krakowskie Przedmiescie 32
PL – 00-927 WARSZAWA
POLAND

Tel.: 48-22-223051
Telex: 81 7016 buwar pl

Member of IFLA, IAML.

Collections

Collections of Sound.
Records of polish music.
Sound 450 records

Access

Catalogue indexed on cards.

Access to catalogue: no.

Access to materials: no.

Fees – Copyright

Institution holds no copyright.

PORTUGAL

LISBON

395

BIBLIOTECA NACIONAL, AREA DE MÚSICA

NATIONAL LIBRARY, MUSIC SERVICE
Campo Grande
P.O. Box 83
P – 1751 LISBOA CODEX
PORTUGAL

Tel.: 351-1-7950130, 351-1-7950131, 351-1-7950132, 351-1-7950133, 351-1-7950134
Fax.: 351-1-7933607

Member of IFLA.

Collections

Collections of Sound, scores, books and magazines.

Classical, folk and popular Portuguese music on 33, 45 and 78 rmp discs, CD's and cassette.
Sound about 1000 titles

Access

Catalogue on database.

Acces to catalogue: limited. Catalogue still in progress.

Access to materials: limited. Handling by staff only.
Access on archives premises.

Fees – Copyright
Copyright holder is the institution.

396
CINEMATECA PORTUGUESA
rua Barata Salgueiro 39
P – 1200 LISBOA
PORTUGAL

Tel.: 351-1-546279

Member of FIAF.

Collections
Collections of Film, photos, books, magazines.
Portugese cinema, classical foreign films.
Films 6000 titles

Access
Catalogue on database.
Acces to catalogue: limited for staff only.
Access to materials: limited for legal problems and reasons of preservation.
Access on archives premises, by loan.

Fees – Copyright
Fees for use in TV, new productions, video productions.
Pricelist and conditions for use available.
Institution holds no copyright.
Agreement of right holder is necessary for all external use. Agreement of the depositor may also be necessary for use on the premises.

397
INSTITUTO PORTUGUES DO PATRIMO-NIO CULTURAL
PORTUGUESE INSTITUTE OF CULTURAL PATRIMONY
R. Ocidental do Campo Grande 83-1°
P – 1799 LISBOA Codex
PORTUGAL

Tel.: 351-1-762230

Member of IASA.

Collections
Collections of Sound, scores (20000), books.
The collection of the Musicology Department of the IPPC comprises a few wax cylinders, about 400 piano rolls, about 3000 records (Edison, 78 rpm, 33 1/3 rpm, 45 rpm, CD), magnetic tapes and cassettes. Portuguese music and performers and others (classical and folk music).
Sound about 3400 items

Access
Catalogue on cards.
Access to catalogue.
Access to materials.
Access on archives premises.

Fees – Copyright
No fees are asked, people come only to hear and not to duplicate.

398
RADIOTELEVISÃO PORTUGUESA, E.P. – RTP, ARQUIVOS E DOCUMENTACÃO
av. 5 de Outubro, 197 – 13°
P – 1000 LISBOA
PORTUGAL

Tel.: 351-1-7979633, 351-1-7585501
Fax.: 351-1-7937763, 351-1-7584063
Telex: 42462 RTP AAV P

Member of IFTA.

Collections
Collections of Film, Video, Sound, stills (180000).
National and international news and national TV programmes.
Films 370000 films 35mm and 16mm
Video 200000 videos 1"B, 1"C, Betacam, Betacam SP, VHS, BVU, Beta formats

Access
Catalogue on database.
Acces to catalogue: limited.
Access to materials.
Access by purchase.

Fees – Copyright
Fees for research for reuse and production purposes, research by archive staff, facilities and handling.
Pricelist and conditions for use available.
Copyright holder is the institution.

ROMANIA

BUCAREST

399
ARHIVA NATIONALA DE FILME
ARCHIVE NATIONALE DE FILMS
Iulius Fucik, N° 25, CNC pour ANF, sect.2
C.P. 1-126
7000 BUCAREST
RUMANIA

Tel.: 40-0-107930 int.22
Fax.: 40-0-120417

Member of FIAF.

Collections

Collections of Film, Video, production papers, scores, scripts, censorship documents, photos, posters, books, magazines.

Collection of feature and documentary films.
Films 30000
Video 300

Access

Catalogue on database.

Access to catalogue.

Access to materials.
Access on archives premises, by loan, by hire, by purchase.

Fees - Copyright

Fees for research for reuse and production purposes, research by archive staff, facilities and handling, rent and loan.
Pricelist and conditions for use available.
Copyright holder is the institution.
Various specialized agreements include copyright for the archive.

___

400
BIBLIOTECA CENTRALA UNIVERSITARA
BIBLIOTHEQUE CENTRALE UNIVERSITAIRE
6 rue de la Transilvanie
70778 BUCAREST
RUMANIA

Tel.: 40-0-154240
Fax.: 40-0-132842

Collections

Collections of Film, Video, Sound.

Films 1393
Video 6
Sound 250

RUSSIA

BELYE STOLBY

___

401
GOSFILMOFOND
142050 BELYE STOLBY, Moskovskaia Oblast
RUSSIA

Tel.: 7-095-546.05.16, 7-095-546.05.13

Member of FIAF.

Collections

Collections of Film, books, scripts, dialogue lists, posters, photo stills, magazines, film files.

Russian films (till 1917), Soviet films : feature, animated, popular science. Foreign films : feature, animated, documentaries, popular science.
Films about 50000 titles, 791483 cans

Access

Catalogue indexed on cards.

Acces to catalogue: limited for archive, education and research purposes.

Access to materials: limited.
Access on archives premises.

Fees - Copyright

Fees for research for reuse and production purposes, facilities and handling.
Pricelist and conditions for use available.
The problem is under consideration of legislative bodies, but now free access to films and other material of Russian (till 1917) and Soviet origin.

MOSCOW

___

402
ALL-UNION FUND OF TV AND RADIO PROGRAMMES (TELERADIOFOND)
Shabolovka Str., 37
113162 MOSCOW
RUSSIA

Tel.: 7-095-2340386
Fax.: 7-095-2323339
Telex: 111285 Moscow, "KURK"

Member of IFTA.

Collections

Collections of Film, Video, Sound, programme's scripts, stills.

Philosophy, history, sociology, demography, economic science, State and Law, international relations, culture, morals, traditions and customs, people's education, pedagogics, psychology, linguistics, art, literature, mass communication, religion, church and atheism, natural and exact sciences, industry, agriculture, building industry, communication, water transport, fish industry, municipal economy and services, public health, sport and physical culture, tourism, ecology, cosmos, etc.
Films 195000 entries, 370000 storage units
Video 5100 entries, 11000 videotape recordings

Access

Catalogue indexed on cards.

Access to catalogue.

Access to materials.
Access by purchase.

403
ZENTRALNIJ GOSUDARSTWENNIJ ARCHIV KINOFOTOFONODOKUMENTOW G. MOSKWA
CENTRAL STATE FILM- PHOTO- AND SOUND ARCHIVES OF MOSCOW
ul. Profsoiusnaia, 80
117393 MOSCOW
RUSSIA

Tel.: 7-095-12878-98

Collections
Collections of Film, Sound, photos.

Film- and sounddocuments about the important events in the industrial, scientific and cultural life of Moscow 1939-1982.
Films 1047 doc. units
Sound 1192 doc. units

Access
Catalogue indexed on cards.

Access to catalogue.

Access to materials.
Access on archives premises, by loan.

Fees – Copyright
Fees for research for reuse and production purposes, facilities and handling.
Pricelist and conditions for use available.
Copyright holder is the institution.

VLADIMIR

404
ZENTRALNIJ GOSUDARSTWENNIJ ARCHIV KINOFOTOFONODOKUMENTOW ROSSIA
CENTRAL STATE FILM-, PHOTO- AND SOUND ARCHIVES OF RUSSIA
ul. Stoliarova, 9
600000 VLADIMIR
RUSSIA

Tel.: 7-9222-25538

Collections
Collections of Film, Sound, photos.

Film- and sounddocuments about the industrial, scientific, cultural development of the Russian federation in the years 1971-1979.
Films 892 documents
Sound 1192 sounddocuments

Access
Catalogue indexed on cards.

Access to catalogue.

Access to materials.
Access on archives premises, by loan.

Fees – Copyright
Fees for research for reuse and production purposes, facilities and handling.
Pricelist and conditions for use available.
Copyright holder is the institution.

SAUDI ARABIA

MAKKAH

405
UMM AL-QURA UNIVERSITY, CENTRAL LIBRARY
Aziziyah
P.O. Box 1629
MAKKAH
SAUDI ARABIA

Tel.: 966-2-5574644 (Central)
Fax.: 966-2-55656
Telex: 540026 JAMMKA SJ
Member of IFLA.

Collections
Collections of Film, Video, Sound.

Teaching of various subjects such as sciences and technology; learning English language ; history and geography of Saudi Arabia with special reference to the Holy cities of Makkah and Madina ; Muslim pilgrims and pilgrimages – Saudi Arabia.
Films 22
Video 35
Sound 318

Access
Acces to catalogue: limited. Information is kept on Accession registers.
Access to materials: limited.

RIYADH

406
KING ABDULAZIZ PUBLIC LIBRARY
P.O. Box 86486
RIYADH – 11622
SAUDI ARABIA

Tel.: 966-1-4911280, 966-1-4911304
Fax.: 966-1-4911949

Member of IFLA, FID.

Collections

Collections of Video, Sound.

Collection based on social, educational, science and technology, history, culture, children stories, comics, plays, etc.
Video 350
Sound 300

Access

Catalogue published.

Access to catalogue: Catalogues for video, sound and computer games have already been published and work on transfering into database is in progress.

Access to materials: no. Materials can be searched into the catalogues, and requested to the incharge for availability.
Access on archives premises.

Fees – Copyright

Fees for research by archive staff, facilities and handling. Library has a separate, fully organised audio-visual section, where these materials are kept and relevent services are rendered from this section.
Institution holds no copyright.
We do not imply any copyright condition also we do not copy any material.

407
KING SAUD UNIVERSITY LIBRARIES
Dhiriyya
P.O. Box 22480
RIYADH 11495
SAUDI ARABIA

Tel.: 966-1-4676152
Fax.: 966-1-4676162
Telex: 401019 KSU SJ

Member of IFLA, FID.

Collections

Collections of Film, Video, Sound, slides.

Films 241
Video 5037
Sound 2321

Access

Catalogue on database.

Access to catalogue.

Access to materials: limited.
Access on archives premises.

Fees – Copyright

No fees.
Institution holds no copyright.

SEYCHELLES

MAHÉ

408
NATIONAL ARCHIVES AND MUSEUMS
Victoria
P.O. Box 720
MAHÉ
REPUBLIC OF SEYCHELLES

Member of ICA.

Collections

Collections of Film, Video, Sound.

Films (documentaries) on Seychelles. Videos of major events in Seychelles for the past decade or so. Tapes and cassettes on oral tradition. Political addresses. Records of traditional music.
Films 7 titles
Video 14 titles
Sound 347 reels, 93 cassettes and 5 records

Access

Access to materials.
Access on archives premises.

SINGAPORE

SINGAPORE

409
NATIONAL ARCHIVES
140 Hill Street, Hill Street Building
SINGAPORE 0617
SINGAPORE

Tel.: 65-3300974, 65-3300911
Fax.: 65-3393583

Member of ICA.

Collections

Collections of Film, Video.

Singapore history, english news on Singapore Broadcasting Corporation, curriculum development Institute of Singapore.
Films 1873 reels, 4822 feet
Video 2144 items

Access

Acces to catalogue: limited. In register book and on lists.

Access to materials: limited.
Access on archives premises, by loan.

Fees – Copyright

No fee is imposed.
Archive has rights for academic, non-profit, non-commercial use.

410
NATIONAL UNIVERSITY OF SINGAPORE LIBRARY
10 Kent Ridge Crescent
SINGAPORE 0511
SINGAPORE

Tel.: 65-7722026, 65-7722069
Fax.: 65-7773571
Telex: RS 33943 UNISPO % VMID SCL

Member of IFLA, FID.

Collections
Collections of Film, Video, Sound.

Humanities, social sciences, architecture, building, engineering, medicine, business administration, human resources, management, science and law.
Films 130 titles (16mm)
Video 6031 titles
Sound 564 titles

Access
Catalogue on database.

Acces to catalogue: limited to Members of the University Library and participating libraries of the Singapore Integrated Library Automation Service (SILAS), the national database.

Access to materials: limited to Members of the University Library.
Access on archives premises, by loan.

Fees – Copyright
Pricelist and conditions for use available.
Copyright holder is the institution.
Use is limited to members of the University Library and dependent on the sales conditions of the items.

411
ORAL HISTORY DEPARTMENT
Hill Street Building, 140 Hill Street
SINGAPORE 0617
SINGAPORE

Tel.: 65-3300912
Fax.: 65-3395697

Member of IASA.

Collections
Collections of Sound, pictures.

The social, cultural, economical and political aspects of Singapore's history.
Sound 11590 reels of tapes

Access
Catalogue on database.
Access to catalogue.

Access to materials except those restricted by legal agreements.
Access on archives premises.

Fees – Copyright
Pricelist and conditions for use available.
Copyright holder is the institution.
For purchase, the copyright holder's permission is needed.

SLOVAK REPUBLIC

BRATISLAVA

412
SLOVENSKA TELEVIZIA
SLOVAK TELEVISION
PROGRAM FONDS, SLOVAK TELEVISION
Asmolovova 28
845 45 BRATISLAVA
SLOVAK REPUBLIC

Tel.: 42-7-723 086
Fax.: 42-7-726 341
Telex: 922 77 TVS MD

Collections
Collections of Film, Video, Sound, photographs, music, scenarios, papers.

Collection of materials from all spheres of TV creation.
Films 90000 titles
Video 17000 titles
Sound 15000 titles

Access
Catalogue on database.
Access to catalogue.

Access to materials: limited only for order.
Access on archives premises, by loan, by hire.

Fees – Copyright
Fees for research for reuse and production purposes, research by archive staff, facilities and handling.
Pricelist and conditions for use available.
Copyright holder is the institution.

413
SLOVENSKY ROZHLAS
SLOVAK RADIO
ARCHIVE OF SLOVAK RADIO
rue Mytna 1
812 90 BRATISLAVA
SLOVAK REPUBLIC

Tel.: 42-7-491 611
Fax.: 42-7-498 923
Telex: 933 52

Collections

Collections of Sound.

Radio broadcast from Slovak Radio – politics, culture, literature, sports, speeches, theatre plays, music, features. Interviews with important personalities from politics, economy, culture, literature, etc.
Sound 11500 tapes

Access

Catalogue indexed on cards.

Access to catalogue.

Access to materials.
Access by loan, by purchase.

Fees – Copyright

No fee to pay for radio boradcasters, students and researchers. Other users have to pay.
Pricelist and conditions for use available.
Copyright holder is the institution.
Fees for access, lending and sales.

SLOVENIA

LJUBLJANA

NARODNA IN UNIVERZITETNA KNJIZNICA, GLASBENA ZBIRKA
NATIONAL AND UNIVERSITY LIBRARY, MUSIC DEPARTMENT
Turjaska 1
P.P.259
61001 LJUBLJANA
SLOVENIJA

Tel.: 38-61-213052
Fax.: 38-61-150134 3 AM
Telex: 32285 NUKLJB YU

Member of IFLA.

Collections

Collections of Video, Sound, scores, books, magazines.

Classical music, popular music, folk music, acquired by legal deposit : sound recordings on cassettes (language courses, literary texts, children's literature), video recordings on VHS videocassettes (motion pictures, cartoons, documentary recordings, courses...).
Video 214 items
Sound 13804 items

Access

Catalogue on database.

Access to catalogue: For use inside the library only.

Access to materials: limited.
Access on archives premises.

Fees – Copyright

Fees for facilities and handling.
Pricelist and conditions for use available.

SOLOMON ISLANDS

HONIARA

NATIONAL ARCHIVES OF SOLOMON ISLANDS
Hibiscus Avenue
P.O. Box 780
HONIARA
SOLOMON ISLANDS

Tel.: 677-21426
Fax.: 677-21397
Telex: HQ 66311

Member of ICA.

Collections

Collections of Film, Video, Sound.

The collection is more or less on Solomon Island Affairs. That is to say it consists of the above with regard to social, cultural, political & religious practices of the Solomon Islands.
Films 12
Video 7
Sound 300-400

Access

Catalogue indexed on cards.

Acces to catalogue: limited due to legal problems.

Access to materials: limited due to legal problems.
Access on archives premises.

Fees – Copyright

Institution holds no copyright.
Unless stated in the original documents or items, copyright regulations still apply to whatever we preserve at the National Archives of Solomon Islands. Such a regulation can only be altered by the chief justice of this Nation.

SOUTH AFRICA

GRAHAMSTOON

_____ 416
SOUTH AFRICAN LIBRARY FOR THE BLIND
High Street
P.O. Box 115
GRAHAMSTOON 6140
SOUTH AFRICA

Tel.: 27-461-27226
Fax.: 27-461-27650

Collections
Collections of Sound.

Audio book library.
Sound 7000 titles

Access
Catalogue on database.

Access to catalogue on request.

Access to materials.
Access on archives premises, by loan, by purchase.

Fees – Copyright
Fees for purchase.
Pricelist and conditions for use available.
If you purchase the book you have to apply for copyright.

JOHANNESBURG

_____ 417
JOHANNESBURG PUBLIC LIBRARY
Market Square
2001 JOHANNESBURG
SOUTH AFRICA

Tel.: 27-11-8363787
Fax.: 27-11-8366607

Member of IFLA.

Collections
Collections of Sound.

Sound 968 (gramophone records, compact discs, cassettes)

Access
Catalogue on cards.

Access to catalogue.

Access to materials.
Access by loan.

NOORDBRUG

_____ 418
POTCHEFSTROOM UNIVERSITY FOR CHE, FERDINAND POSTMA LIBRARY
Private Bag X05
2522 NOORDBRUG
SOUTH AFRICA

Tel.: 27-148-992000
Fax.: 27-148-992999
Telex: 3-46019
Electronic mail: fpbcjhl.puknet@smtpqw.puk.ac.za
Member of IFLA.

Collections
Collections of Film, Video, Sound.
General.
Films 13 titles
Video 177 titles
Sound 7390 titles

Access
Catalogue on database.

Access to catalogue.

Access to materials.
Access by loan.

Fees – Copyright
No fees.

PRETORIA

_____ 419
SOUTH AFRICAN NATIONAL FILM, VIDEO AND SOUND ARCHIVES
698 Churchstreet East, Arcadia Pretoria 0002
Private Bag X236
0001 PRETORIA
SOUTH AFRICA

Tel.: 27-12-3439767
Fax.: 27-12-3445143

Member of IASA.

Collections
Collections of Film, Video, Sound, books, scenarios, photos, dias, posters, microfilms, clippings, documents, objects.

Audio visual material made in or about South Africa.
Films 68173 reels
Video 8485 units
Sound 35346 records and tapes

Access
Catalogue on database.

Access to materials.
Access on archives premises.

Fees – Copyright

Fees for facilities and handling.
Pricelist and conditions for use available.
Copyright is respected even if material is in public domain. Material is only released for duplication with copyright holders written permission.

SPAIN

BARCELONA

_____ 420
ARXIU D'AUDIOVISUALS DE LA GENE-RALITAT DE CATALUNYA (FILMOTECA)
AUDIOVISUAL ARCHIVE OF GENERALITAT DE CATALUNYA (FILMOTECA)
Gran Via 184 "La campana" building
E – 08004 BARCELONA
SPAIN

Tel.: 34-3-3313550
Fax.: 34-3-4322322

Member of FIAF.

Collections

Collections of Film, Video, photo, posters, books, magazines, news papers.

Films in general, Catalan films.
Films 7500 titles
Video 4000 titles

Access

Catalogue on cards.

Acces to catalogue: limited. Aimed at image professionals.

Access to materials: limited. Aimed at image professionals.

Fees – Copyright

Fees: Possible with preview consulting in each case.

_____ 421
TELEVISIO DE CATALUNYA S.A.
Motor way A-2 (exit Sant Just) – Sant Joan Despi
P.O. Box 30300
E – 08080 BARCELONA
SPAIN

Tel.: 34-3-4730333
Fax.: 34-3-4731438
Telex: 53280 TVDC E

Member of IFTA.

Collections

Collections of Video.

All TV programmes produced by Televisió de Catalunya and broadcasted through its two channels (TV3 since 1984, CANAL 33 since 1989), including news, sports, documentary, entertainment and fiction. It includes also a selection of rough material from news, sports or documentary programmes.
Video about 80000 holdings (video-tapes and video-reels)

Access

Catalogue on database.

Acces to catalogue: limited for staff only. Listing on request.

Access to materials.
Access on archives premises, by purchase.

Fees – Copyright

Fees for research for reuse and production purposes, research by archive staff, facilities and handling, copyright.
Pricelist and conditions for use available.
Copyright holder is the institution.

BELLATERRA

_____ 422
UNIVERSITAT AUTONOMA DE BARCELONA : BIBLIOTECA DE FOR-MACIÓ DEL PROFESSORAT
Campus Universitario de Bellaterra. Edificio G
E – 08193 BELLATERRA
SPAIN

Tel.: 34-93-5811932
Fax.: 34-93-5812007

Collections

Collections of Film, Video, Sound.

Themes : education, pedagogics, psychology, geography, history, physics, biology. Classical music. Teaching language, reading and music. Folk music.
Films 4 titles
Video 954 titles
Sound 310 cassettes + 150 compact-discs

Access

Catalogue indexed on cards.

Access to catalogue.

Access to materials: limited. Only to professors as teaching material.

MADRID

_____ 423
BIBLIOTECA NACIONAL, SERVICIO DE PARTITURAS, REGISTROS SONOROS Y AUDIOVISUALES
Paseo de Recoletos 20
E – MADRID
SPAIN

Tel.: 34-1-5807859
Fax.: 34-1-5775634

Member of IASA.

Collections
Collections of Video, Sound, reference materials, books, scores, posters, programs.

Entries from a legal deposit of Spanish production. Includes also collections prior to legal deposit law. Donations of private collections and acquisition of foreign publications.
Video 16000
Sound 200000

Access
Catalogue on database.

Access to catalogue.

Access to materials: limited. Some collections only accessible through copies made in the service.
Access on archives premises.

Fees – Copyright
Pricelist and conditions for use available.

_____ 424
FILMOTECA ESPAÑOLA
Ctra. Dehesa de la Villa s/n
E – 28040 MADRID
SPAIN

Tel.: 34-1-5490011
Fax.: 34-1-5497348

Member of FIAF.

Collections
Collections of Film, Video, books, magazines, stills, posters, records, scripts, museum pieces, production and distribution records.

Spanish cinema, Spanish newsreels, Spanish civil war.
Films 18000 titles
Video 4500 titles
Sound 5000 music sound track (records) and magnetic sound tracks

Access
Catalogue on cards.

Access to catalogue: no. Reserved to staff.

Access to materials: limited due to preservation, legal and staff limitations.
Access on archives premises, by loan, by purchase.

Fees – Copyright
Fees for research for reuse and production purposes, royalties.
Pricelist and conditions for use available.
Copyright holder is the institution.
Purchase is accessible only for materials owned by the archive (Spanish newsreels) and under contract for one production use.

OVIEDO

_____ 425
BIBLIOTECA DE ASTURIAS "RAMÓN PÉREZ DE AYALA", SECCIÓN DE FONOTECA, FILMOTECA Y VIDEOTECA REGIONAL
Plaza Daoíz y Velarde, 11
E – 33009 OVIEDO
SPAIN

Tel.: 34-85-218095, 34-85-211397
Fax.: 34-85-228576

Member of IFLA.

Collections
Collections of Film, Video, Sound.

Videos : education, natural science, humanities, towns of the world, Spanish towns, tourist guides, languages, research, human body, animals, biology, ecology, physics, opera, classical music, biographies, religion, children films, sports, paintings, industrial development. Sound recordings : classical music, pop, jazz, traditional music, religious, opera, Zarzuela.
Films 11
Video 1675
Sound 4450

Access
Catalogue on database.

Access to catalogue.

Access to materials.
Access on archives premises, by loan.

Fees – Copyright
Institution holds no copyright.

PAMPLONA

_____ 426
UNIVERSIDAD DE NAVARRA, SERVICIO DE BIBLIOTECAS
Campus Universitario, Edificio de Bibliotecas

P.O. Box 177
E – 31080 PAMPLONA
SPAIN

Tel.: 34-948-252700
Fax.: 34-948-178269
Telex: 37917-UNAV E
Electronic mail: ZARATIEGUI bibl UNAV ES

Member of IFLA.

Collections

Collections of Sound.

Classic and Spanish folkloric music.
Sound 349 records

Access

Catalogue on cards.

Access to catalogue.

Access to materials.
Access by loan, by hire.

RENTERIA

_____ 427

ERESBIL – ARCHIVO DE COMPOSITORES VASCOS
BASQUE COMPOSERS ARCHIVES
Martin Echeverria, 15
P.O. Box 203
E – 20100 RENTERIA
SPAIN

Tel.: 34-43-521466
Fax.: 34-43-529706

Member of IASA, IAML.

Collections

Collections of Sound, scores.

Music of Basque composers, and music recorded or related to Basque Country (classical, ethnical, folk, pop-rock, children's, oral poetry, "bertsolaritza").
Sound 2500 LP's, 975 s., 500 78 rpm, 1300 cas., 400 CD's, 30 open reels

Access

Catalogue on cards.

Acces to catalogue: limited.

Access to materials: limited.
Access by purchase.

Fees – Copyright

Fees for facilities and handling.
Institution holds no copyright.

SAN SEBASTIAN

_____ 428

FILMOTECA VASCA-EUSKADIKO FILMATEGIA
Plaza Oquendo, s/n°
Apartado Correos 1017
E – 20004 SAN SEBASTIAN
SPAIN

Tel.: 34-43-421356
Fax.: 34-43-421976

Collections

Collections of Film, Video, Sound, photos, posters.

Films about 350 titles
Video about 1300 titles
Sound 250 tapes

Access

Catalogue on database.

Acces to catalogue: limited.

Access to materials: limited.
Access on archives premises, by purchase.

Fees – Copyright

Fees for facilities and handling.
Pricelist and conditions for use available.
Copyright holder is the institution.
Only historical and documentary material is the property of the filmoteca.

SANTANDER

_____ 429

UNIVERSIDAD DE CANTABRIA, BIBLIOTECA UNIVERSITARIA
Avda Los Castros
E – 39005 SANTANDER
SPAIN

Tel.: 34-42-201180
Fax.: 34-42-201183
Telex: 35861

Member of IFLA.

Collections

Collections of Video, Sound, microforms, filmstrips.

Videocassettes, filmstrips, sound recordings for teaching purposes, organised as a small collection of non-book materials inside the library.
Video 150
Sound 200

Access

Catalogue on database.

Access to catalogue: Access via online public access catalogs or printed lists.

Access to materials.
Access on archives premises, by loan.

Fees – Copyright

No fees.
Institution holds no copyright.

VALENCIA

_____ 430
FILMOTECA DE LA GENERALITAT VALENCIANA
Plaza Ayuntamiento, 17
E – 46002 VALENCIA
SPAIN

Tel.: 34-6-3512336
Fax.: 34-6-3525079

Member of FIAF.

Collections

Collections of Film, Video, scripts, photos, posters.

Documentaries (history, arts, industry, travel, ...) and feature films.
Films 823 titles
Video 1785 titles

Access

Catalogue on database.

Access to catalogue.

Access to materials: limited to researchers, historians, public or cultural entities, students.
Access on archives premises, by loan.

Fees – Copyright

No tarifs. There are agreements between the archive and channels of public TV.
Institution holds no copyright.
Photographic, videographic and cinematographic reproduction requires agreement of copyright holder.

_____ 431
RADIOTELEVISIÓ VALENCIANA, UNITAT DE DOCUMENTACIÓ
RADIOTELEVISION VALENCIANA
Polígon Acces Ademuz s/n
E – 46100 BURJASSOT VALENCIA
SPAIN

Tel.: 34-6-3641100
Fax.: 34-6-3631350
Telex: 61023

Collections

Collections of Video, Sound.

Television broadcasts, music records and radio broadcasts. Main topics covered are : current affairs, sports, drama and comedy soaps and TV contests.
Video 20000 tapes
Sound 3500 tapes

Access

Catalogue on database.

Access to catalogue: no.

Access to materials.
Access by purchase.

Fees – Copyright

Fees for facilities and handling.
Pricelist and conditions for use available.
Copyright holder is the institution.
Copyright conditions for access not yet settled.

ZARAGOZA

_____ 432
PATRONATO MUNICIPAL FILMOTECA DE ZARAGOZA
C/Domingo Miral s/n Cuartel de Palafox
E – 80009 ZARAGOZA
SPAIN

Tel.: 34-976-551184

Collections

Collections of Film, Video, Sound, bibliographics, books, magazines, scripts, catalogues, pamphlets, posters, photographs, slides.

Documentary and filmic material on Aragon themes and from Aragon authors. Spanish cinema. All kinds of documentaries and features.
Films about 2000 titles
Video about 400 titles
Sound about 1500 titles

Access

Catalogue on cards.

Acces to catalogue: limited. Catalogue under way. Work started two years ago.

Access to materials: limited due to problems of space and staff.
Access on archives premises.

Fees – Copyright

Consultation of catalogue, study and research on the premises.

SRI LANKA

COLOMBO

433
DEPARTMENT OF NATIONAL ARCHIVES
Reid Avenue
P.O. Box 1414
07 COLOMBO
SRI LANKA

Tel.: 94-1-694523, 94-1-696917
Telex: ARCHIVES
Member of ICA.

Collections
Collections of Film, Video, Sound.

Speeches of former Presidents of Sri Lanka, appearances at public and official functions of former President of Sri Lanka, folk songs of Sri Lanka.
Films 43
Video 40
Sound magnetic tapes : 550, discs : 17, audio-cassettes : 300 (NOS:)

Access
Catalogue indexed on cards.

Access to catalogue.

Access to materials: limited. Only for bona fide research with the approval from the depositing agency or institution.
Access on archives premises.

Fees – Copyright
No fees are charged for using the collection. Copyright or right to access is given only with the approval of the institution or the individual depositing the material in the National Archives.

434
NATIONAL FILM CORPORATION OF SRI LANKA
FILMARCHIVES OF THE NATIONAL FILM CORPORATION
Govt. film unit premises, Polhengoda, Narahenpita
COLOMBO 5
SRI LANKA

Fax.: 94-1-580721
Telex: 21537 METALIX CE, 22933 METALIX CE

Collections
Collections of Film.

Picture and sound negatives of 180 locally produced full length feature films, dupe negatives of 71 full length films, positive prints of one feature film and negatives of 60 shorts & trailers.
Films 5377 cans

Access
Catalogue published.

Access to catalogue but only as a list of title of films.

Access to materials: limited only when required by producer/owner of each film for the purpose of making new prints.
Access on archives premises.

Fees – Copyright
No such fee is charged at the initial stage of the Archive as the films stored at the moment are only for permanent storage.
Institution holds no copyright.
Since the films belong to private individuals they are to be contacted for purpose of copyright.

435
SRI LANKA NATIONAL LIBRARY SERVICES BOARD
NATIONAL LIBRARY OF SRI LANKA
Independence Avenue
P.O. Box 1764
COLOMBO
SRI LANKA

Tel.: 94-1-698847, 94-1-685199, 94-1-685201
Fax.: 94-1-685201

Member of IFLA.

Collections
Collections of Video, Sound, slides, micro films and micro fiches.

Sri Lankan collection : records, audio and video cassettes. Folk culture collection : records, slides, audio and video cassettes.
Video 37
Sound 755

Access
Catalogue on cards.

Access to catalogue.

Access to materials.
Access on archives premises, by loan.

Fees – Copyright
Fees for research for reuse and production purposes, research by archive staff, Inter Library Lending : charges for photocopying the microfiches and microfilms.
Institution holds no copyright.
Library holds rights for research and private studies.

SUDAN

KHARTOUM

436

DAR AL-WATHAIQ OL-QUMIYYIA
THE NATIONAL RECORDS OFFICE
Al-Jumhuryyia Street
P.O. Box 1914 Khartoum
KHARTOUM
SUDAN

Tel.: 249-11-81995, 249-11-84255
Telex: Watjaiq – Khartoum

Member of ICA.

Collections
Collections of Film, Sound, photographs and slides.
Video 200
Sound 100

Access
Access to catalogue.

Access to materials: limited. There may be some restrictions according to the type of documents.
Access on archives premises.

Fees – Copyright
Fees for research for reuse and production purposes, facilities and handling.
Most of the moving images held in the NRO are accessible. Those documents which belong to International bodies such as the African Branch of the International Council of Archives (Ecarbica) and other Institutions could not be published by the NRO without having a written permission from the branch concerned.

SWEDEN

GOETEBORG

437

GÖTEBORGS UNIVERSITETSBIBLIOTEK, LJUD- OCH VIDEOARKIVET
GÖTEBORG UNIVERSITY LIBRARY, SOUND AND VIDEO ARCHIVES
Renströmsgatan 4
Box 5096
S – 402 22 GÖTEBORG
SWEDEN

Tel.: 46-31-631715
Fax.: 46-31-163797
Telex: 20896 UBGBG S

Member of IASA, IFLA.

Collections
Collections of Video, Sound, playmanuscripts.

Theatre performances from Göteborg and Stockholm. Poetry. Folk music and classical music.
Video 200 videocassettes
Sound 23000 phonogram (78 rpm, LP, CD), 2000 magnetic tapes and cassette tapes

Access
Catalogue indexed on cards.

Access to catalogue.

Access to materials: limited for students and researchers only.
Access on archives premises.

Fees – Copyright
Institution holds no copyright.

STOCKHOLM

438

ARKIVET FÖR LJUD OCH BILD (ALB)
THE SWEDISH NATIONAL ARCHIVE OF RECORDED SOUND AND MOVING IMAGES
Regeringsgatan 65
Box 7371
S – 103 91 STOCKHOLM
SWEDEN

Tel.: 46-8-143960
Fax.: 46-8-206968

Member of IFTA, IASA.

Collections
Collections of Video, Sound.

Recordings of radio- and TV-broadcasts ; Swedish and foreign feature films, shortfilms and commercials shown to the public in Sweden (the films are transferred to videotape before storing) ; the national production of phonograms and videograms and the foreign production imported to Sweden and with special Swedish interest – all of the above from 1979 onwards. Collections of older recordings, donated to or purchased by ALB.
Video 25000 titles (film and video), 60000 tapes (tv)
Sound 202000 items (phonograms), 66000 tapes (radio)

Access
Catalogue on database.

Access to catalogue.

Access to materials: limited for serious research purpose only ; copyright limitations.
Access on archives premises.

Fees – Copyright

Researchers pay a small fee for their study copies. Pricelist and conditions for use available.
Institution holds no copyright.
Researchers fill out an application which has to be approved by the archive. Copies of the collection may be studied on the archive premises or in certain other institutions. Deliverers under the Legal Deposit Act may order copies of their own material. For older material, where the copyright have expired, copies may be ordered by the public, but for personal use only.

439

ARMÉ- MARIN- OCH FLYGFILM (AMF)
ASSOCIATION ARMY- NAVY- AND AIR FORCE FILMS
Skeppargatan 61
S – 114 59 STOCKHOLM
SWEDEN

Tel.: 46-8-6670940
Fax.: 46-8-6636741

Collections

Collections of Film, Video.
Films 6000 titles

Access

Catalogue on database.
Access to catalogue.
Access to materials.
Access by loan, by hire, by purchase.

Fees – Copyright

Fees for research for reuse and production purposes, research by archive staff, facilities and handling.
Some titles require right holders permission.

440

RIKSARKIVET
NATIONAL ARCHIVES
Fyrverkarbacken 13-17
P.O. Box 12541
S – 102 29 STOCKHOLM
SWEDEN

Tel.: 46-8-7376350
Fax.: 46-8-7376474

Member of ICA.

Collections

Collections of Film, Video, Sound, documentation.
Various units from official state authorities (agencies) and private persons, institutions (agencies).
Films about 200 units
Video about 30 units
Sound about 2000 units

Access

A computerized register is on work based on different kinds of specifications, inventories, etc. (there has never been established a card-register system).

Limited access to certain items according to secrecy regulations (state agencies) or private secrecy (private archives).

Fees – Copyright

No fees for the time being.
There is no copyright except for recordings by the National Archives themselves. Generally there is no copyright by itself connected to the possession of certain archival units of collections.

441

STIFTERLSEN SVENSKA FILMINSTITUTET, CINEMATEKET
SWEDISH FILM INSTITUTE
Borgvägen 5
Box 27 126
S – 102 52 STOCKHOLM
SWEDEN

Tel.: 46-8-6651100
Fax.: 46-8-6611820
Telex: 133 26 FILMINS S

Member of FIAF.

Collections

Collections of Film, 35000 books, 1200 mags (260 subscriptions), clipping files on 15000 persons, 50000 films, posters about 35000, stills over 1000000 to about 40000 films.

Only feature films : 13000 titles, about 8000 titles are features from the last 30 years.
Films 13000 titles (8000 long, 5000 shorts), about 17000 prints

Access

Catalogue on database.
Acces to catalogue: limited.
Access to materials: limited.
Access on archives premises.

Fees – Copyright

Fees for research for reuse and production purposes, research by archive staff, facilities and handling, Nothing is free of charge.
Pricelist and conditions for use available.
Institution holds no copyright.
Most of the material is deposit by copyright owner. Use of material outside archive premises need written permisssion from copyright owner.

442
SVERIGES RIKSRADIO, GRAMMO-FONARKIVET
SWEDISH NATIONAL RADIO CO, RECORD LIBRARY
Oxenstiernsgatan 20
S - 10510 STOCKHOLM
SWEDEN

Tel.: 46-8-7841764
Fax.: 46-8-7843471
Telex: 10000 SRCENT S

Member of IASA.

Collections
Collections of Sound.

Commercially recorded sound on cylinders, piano rolls, 78s, LPs, 45s, cassettes and CDs. For public broadcasting purposes since 1925. Music of all kinds and spoken word.
Sound about 750000 items

Access
Catalogue on database.

Acces to catalogue: limited only for the National Archive of Sound and Moving Images and the Swedish rights society (STIM) today.

Access to materials: limited.
Access on archives premises.

Fees – Copyright
Fees only for limited public access : i.e. research (minimum graduate students) and copying (commercial/institutional/private) within copyright limitations.
Pricelist and conditions for use available.
Institution holds no copyright.

443
SVERIGES RIKSRADIO : PROGRAM-ARKIVET
SWEDISH RADIO PROGRAMME ARCHIVES
Oxenstiernsgatan 20
S - 105 10 STOCKHOLM
SWEDEN

Tel.: 46-8-7841535
Fax.: 46-8-7842285

Member of IASA.

Collections
Collections of Sound.

Selection of radio programmes on magnetic tapes from 1931.
Sound about 180000 tapes

Access
Catalogue on database.
Access to materials: no.
Access by purchase.

Fees – Copyright
Pricelist and conditions for use available.

444
SVERIGES TELEVISION AB
SWEDISH TELEVISION, PROGRAMSERVICE
Oxenstiernsgatan 20
S - 105 10 STOCKHOLM
SWEDEN

Tel.: 46-8-7840000
Fax.: 46-8-6604000
Telex: 10000 SR CENT

Member of IFTA.

Collections
Collections of Film, Video, stills (5 million historic international press photos).

Own TV productions since 1955. Swedish filmindustries news reels and short films 1898-1955. Several other cultural and industrial collections.
Films about 30000 hours
Video about 40000 videotapes and about 2000 hours news items

Access
Catalogue on database.

Acces to catalogue: limited on commercial conditions through our Film and Video Sales 46-8-7844000.

Access to materials: limited on commercial conditions through our Film and Video Sales 46-8-7844000.
Access on archives premises, by purchase.

Fees – Copyright
Fees for research for reuse and production purposes, research by archive staff, facilities and handling.
Pricelist and conditions for use available.
Copyright holder is the institution.
Certain parts of our material may have other copyright holders as well.

UPPSALA

445
DIALEKT- OCH FOLKMINNESARKIVET
INSTITUTE OF DIALECT AND FOLKLORE RESEARCH
Östra Ågatan 27
Box 1743

S - 751 47 UPPSALA
SWEDEN
Tel.: 46-18-156360
Fax.: 46-18-151342
Member of IASA.

Collections

Collections of Sound.

Access

Catalogue on database.

Access to catalogue.

Fees – Copyright

Fees for research by archive staff.
Copyright holder is the institution.

SWITZERLAND

BERN

_____ 446
SCHWEIZERISCHE NATIONALBIBLIOTHEK
SWISS NATIONAL LIBRARY
Hallwylstrasse 15
CH – 3003 BERNE
SWITZERLAND
Tel.: 41-31-61.89.11
Fax.: 41-31-61.84.63
Telex: 912 691 SLB ch
Member of IFLA.

Collections

Collections of Sound.

Part of the collection is deposited in the National Phonothek in Lugano, mostly documents with spoken word.
Sound 7754 titles

Access

Catalogue on cards.

Acces to catalogue: limited due to security and preservation.

Access to materials: limited on premises only.

Fees – Copyright

Fees for research by archive staff.

_____ 447
SCHWEIZERISCHES BUNDESARCHIV
ARCHIVES FEDERALES SUISSES
Archivstrasse 24
CH – 3003 BERN
SWITZERLAND
Tel.: 41-31-61.89.89
Fax.: 41-31-61.78.23
Member of ICA.

Collections

Collections of Film, Video, Sound.

Film and video : Swiss newsreels, foreign newsreels (censured), documentaries. Sound : parliamentary sessions from 1982 onwards.
Films 5000 m
Video 70 cassettes
Sound 28 tapes, 45 discs

Access

Catalogue on database.

Acces to catalogue: limited.

Access to materials.
Access on archives premises.

Fees – Copyright

Fees for copies.
Pricelist and conditions for use available.
Copyright holder is the institution.

GENEVA

_____ 448
DISCOTHEQUE MUNICIPALE – BIBLIOTHEQUES MUNICIPALES DE LA VILLE DE GENEVE
2, Cité-Vieusseux
CH – 1203 GENEVE
SWITZERLAND
Tel.: 41-22-344.31.25
Member of IFLA.

Collections

Collections of Video, Sound, documentation.

Classical music, jazz, filmmusic, pop, rock, songs, folklore, childrens music.
Video 100
Sound 15000 LP, 15000 CD, 900 cassettes

Access

Catalogue on cards.

Access to catalogue.

Access to materials.
Access on archives premises, by hire.

Fees – Copyright

The Swiss copyright law is under revision.

449
DISCOTHEQUE MUNICIPALE – BIBLIOTHEQUES MUNICIPALES DE LA VILLE DE GENEVE
rue des Minoteries, 5-7
CH – 1205 GENEVE
SWITZERLAND

Tel.: 41-22-20.58.38

Member of IFLA.

Collections
Collections of Sound.

Classical music, ethnomusic, folklore, pop, rock, jazz, songs, childrens music.
Sound 16000 LP, 3500 cassettes, 20000 CD

Access
Catalogue on cards.

Access to catalogue.

Access to materials.
Access by loan.

Fees – Copyright
The Swiss copyright law is under revision.

450
INTERNATIONAL LABOUR OFFICE
4, route des Morillons
CH – 1211 GENEVA 22
SWITZERLAND

Tel.: 41-22-799.61.11
Fax.: 41-22-798.85.85
Telex: 41.56.47 ILO CH

Member of IFLA.

Collections
Collections of Video.

Collection comprises videocassettes produced by the International Labour Organization for public information or training purposes. Subjects covered include : management development, employment policy, occupational safety and health, women workers, apartheid, rural employment.
Video 38 videocassettes

Access
Catalogue on database.

Access to catalogue.

Access to materials.
Access on archives premises.

Fees – Copyright
Copyright holder is the institution.

451
MEDIATHEQUE DE LA CITE – BIBLIOTHEQUES MUNICIPALES DE LA VILLE DE GENEVE
10, rue de la Tour-de-Boël
CH – 1204 GENEVE
SWITZERLAND

Tel.: 41-22-312.00.73

Member of IFLA.

Collections
Collections of Video, Sound, slides, multimedia kits.

This collection is aimed at children (5-17 years), created in 1991. Only documentary material.
Video 700 video VHS – videodisques
Sound 100 CD – 100 cassettes – 500 slides/sound cassettes

Access
Catalogue on database.

Access to catalogue.

Access to materials: no.
Access by loan.

Fees – Copyright
The Swiss copyright law is under revision.

452
MUSEE D'ART ET D'HISTOIRE
BIBLIOTHEQUE D'ART ET D'ARCHEOLOGIE
5, promenade du Pin
CH – 1204 GENEVE
SWITZERLAND

Tel.: 41-22-29.60.33 (changing in 1992)
Fax.: 41-22-21.17.06

Member of IFLA.

Collections
Collections of Video, Sound, slides, images on paper, microforms.

Painting, sculpture, archeology, applied arts, architecture, prehistory, museology, conservation, restoration.
Video 137 titles
Sound 12 titles

Access
Catalogue on database.

Access to catalogue.

Access to materials: limited. Free access to slides one by one. Video consultation on the premises.
Access on archives premises, by loan.

Fees – Copyright
Museum holds copyright on own productions only.

SWITZERLAND – GENEVA

453
TELEVISION SUISSE ROMANDE (TSR), SERVICE DOCUMENTATION ET ARCHIVES
20, quai Ernest-Ansermet
Case 234
CH – 1211 GENEVA 8
SWITZERLAND

Tel.: 41-22-29.33.33
Fax.: 41-22-28.37.87
Telex: 427 701

Member of IFTA.

Collections

Collections of Film, Video.

Local and national actualities. Magazines : politics, economy and social (1959-). Agriculture (1960-77). Arts (1960-). Mountain district (1973-80). Sciences (1965-). Medicine (1960-). Sports. Literature (1960-). Archeology, ethnology (1960-80). Cinema : interviews, portraits (1960-). Consumers (1976-). Education (1964-).
Films 90000 documents (film and video)

Access

Catalogue on database.

Acces to catalogue: limited.

Access to materials: limited.
Access by purchase.

Fees – Copyright

Fees for research for reuse and production purposes, research by archive staff.
Copyright holder is the institution.

LA CHAUX-DE-FONDS

454
BIBLIOTHEQUE DE LA VILLE, DEPARTEMENT AUDIO-VISUEL (DAV)
33, rue du Progrès
CH – 2300 LA CHAUX-DE-FONDS (NE)
SWITZERLAND

Tel.: 41-39-28.46.12

Collections

Collections of Film, Video, Sound, press clippings, photos, posters.

Cantonal archives concerning the canton of Neuchâtel. Works made by persons from Neuchâtel.
Films 100
Video 1000
Sound 1750

Access

Catalogue indexed on cards.

Access to catalogue: Catalogue in preparation.

Access to materials: limited. Under control of staff for reasons of preservation and legal problems.
Access on archives premises.

Fees – Copyright

Fees for copyright.
Authorization of copyright holder is necessary for use of documents (TV, cinema, radio, historical research). Copyright holder may ask for payment of fees. The institution does not charge for material which it owns, except for commercial use.

LAUSANNE

455
CINEMATHEQUE SUISSE LAUSANNE
ARCHIVES DU CINE-JOURNAL SUISSE
3, allée E. Ansermet
2512
CH – 1002 LAUSANNE
SWITZERLAND

Tel.: 41-21-23.74.40
Fax.: 41-21-20.48.88
Telex: 454 430 sfalch

Member of FIAF.

Collections

Collections of Film.
Swiss Newsreel 1940-1975.

Access

Catalogue on cards.

Acces to catalogue: limited.

Access to materials: limited.
Access by purchase.

Fees – Copyright

Fees for research for reuse and production purposes.
Pricelist and conditions for use available.
Copyright holder is the institution.

456
RADIO-TELEVISION SUISSE ROMANDE, SERVICE DOCUMENTATION ET ARCHIVES DE LA RADIO
40, av. du Temple
Case postale 78
CH – 1010 LAUSANNE
SWITZERLAND

Tel.: 41-21-318.11.11
Fax.: 41-21-652.37.19
Telex: 454 130

Member of IASA.

Collections

Collections of Sound.

Radio production from 1930 on records, tapes. Commercial records used for radio production.
Sound discs : 170000 (Lausanne), 120000 (Genève) – tapes : 80000

Access

Catalogue on database.

Acces to catalogue: limited.

Access to materials: limited. Sound archives are reserved for radio productions. Request for consultation and external copies are accepted occasionally.
Access on archives premises.

Fees – Copyright

Fees for research by archive staff, facilities and handling, possibly for copies.
Copyright holder is the institution.
The institution holds the rights for radiodiffusion.
For another usage agreement of copyright holder is requested.

LUGANO

_____ 457

FONOTECA NAZIONALE SVIZZERA/ PHONOTHEQUE NATIONALE SUISSE/ SCHWEIZERISCHE LANDESPHONOTHEK
SWISS NATIONAL SOUND ARCHIVE
Via Foce 1
Casella postale
CH – 6906 LUGANO 6
SWITZERLAND

Tel.: 41-91-52.65.96
Fax.: 41-91-52.61.69

Member of IASA.

Collections

Collections of Video, Sound.

Into the Swiss National Sound Archives all those recordings of commercial and non-commercial origin will be brought together, which can contribute to the documentation of the history and culture of the country.
Video 100
Sound 60000

Access

Catalogue on database.

Acces to catalogue: limited only with the help of a staff member.

Access to materials: limited due to preservation, legal problems.
Access on archives premises.

Fees – Copyright

No fees.
Institution holds no copyright.
For unpublished materials the agreement of the producer(s) is needed.

ZURICH

_____ 458

SCHWEIZER FERNSEHEN DRS
TELEVISION DE LA SUISSE ALEMANIQUE
Fernsehstr. 1-4
Postfach
CH – 8052 ZÜRICH
SWITZERLAND

Tel.: 41-1-305.61.11 (Film- und Videodok : 41-1-305.58.96)
Fax.: 41-1-305.56.60, 41-1-305.58.87
Telex: 823 823

Member of IFTA.

Collections

Collections of Film, Video, Sound, photos, stills (dias).

DRS collects since 1958 all its own productions (only very few earlier films), news, documentaries, all subjects. Cataloguing since 1987 with TEC VAX 11/75Q.
Films 52000 reels = 8200000 meter
Video about 22000 items, Beta SP : 12000

Access

Catalogue on database.

Acces to catalogue: limited to be used only for sales department and program makers. Exceptions can be granted by the Sales Department.

Access to materials: limited.
Access on archives premises, by purchase.

Fees – Copyright

Fees for research for reuse and production purposes, research by archive staff, facilities and handling.
Pricelist and conditions for use available.
Copyright holder is the institution.

_____ 459

ZENTRALBIBLIOTHEK ZÜRICH
ZURICH CENTRAL LIBRARY
Zähringerplatz 6
Postfach
CH – 8025 ZÜRICH
SWITZERLAND

Tel.: 41-1-261.72.72
Fax.: 41-1-262.03.73

Member of IFLA.

Collections

Collections of Sound.

Sound recordings, principally of classical music.
Sound 28000 sound recordings (records, CDs, cassette tapes)

Access

Catalogue on cards.

Access to catalogue.

Access to materials.
Access on archives premises.

Fees – Copyright

Institution holds no copyright.
Sound recordings may be listened to during library opening hours ; copies may not be made, and therefore there are no copyright conditions for access.

SYRIA

DAMASCUS

_____ 460

MAKTABET AL-ASSAD
ASSAD NATIONAL LIBRARY
Malki Street
P.O. Box 3639
DAMASCUS
SYRIA

Tel.: 963-11-338255
Telex: 419134

Member of IFLA.

Collections

Collections of Video, Sound.

All sorts of information.
Video 260
Sound 131

Access

Catalogue on database.

Acces to catalogue: limited inside the library up till now.

Access to materials.

Fees – Copyright

No fees.
Copyright holder is the institution.

TANZANIA

DARESSALAM

_____ 461

AUDIO VISUAL INSTITUTE, FILM ARCHIVES
New Bagamoyo Road
P.O. Box 9310
DAR ES SALAAM
TANZANIA

Tel.: 255-51-72601, 255-51-72602, 255-51-72603, 255-51-72604

Collections

Collections of Film, Video.

We preserve 16mm & 35mm films and video tapes on agriculture, health, news reels and documentaries on social and political activities.
Films 800
Video 50

Access

Catalogue on cards.

Access to materials: limited due to preservation and use within the premises.

Fees – Copyright

The Institute holds copyright for its own productions. Producers who deposit films to the archives hold the copyright.

THAILAND

BANGKOK

_____ 462

NATIONAL ARCHIVES OF THAILAND
Samsen Road
BANGKOK 10300
THAILAND

Tel.: 66-2-2823829
Fax.: 66-2-2816947

Member of ICA.

Collections

Collections of Film, Video, sound, books, magazines, scripts, stills, lobby cards, censorship documents, posters, production papers.

Concerning arts and culture of the nation. TV news from Thai TV Channel 9 and Channel 3, information films from government organizations, Usis Bangkok films collection, King Prajadhipok's film collection, animated films collection, family films, Thai feature films.

Films 50000 items of TV news, 1800 titles of documentaries, 500 titles of features
Video 699 hrs
Sound 2120 hrs

Access

Catalogue indexed on cards.

Access to catalogue.

Access to materials.
Access on archives premises, by purchase.

Fees – Copyright

Fees for research for reuse and production purposes.
Pricelist and conditions for use available.
Institution holds no copyright.
Only for research purpose. Films copying service could be obtained if the user gets a permission paper from the copyright owner.

THE NATIONAL FILM ARCHIVE
4 Chao Fa Road
BANGKOK 10200
THAILAND

Tel.: 66-2-2821847, 66-2-2820170
Fax.: 66-2-2821846

Member of FIAF.

Collections

Collections of Film, Video, Sound, related materials are mostly those of Thai films. Books and periodical collection has no specialization.

Specialized in Thai films, films about Thailand or about Thai people only.
Films 62000 titles (60000 newsreels, 1550 documentaries, 450 feature films)
Video 250
Sound 398

Access

Catalogue indexed on cards.

Access on archives premises.

Fees – Copyright

Fees for making copy.
Institution holds no copyright.
Those who wish to have a copy of any archive film and video materials are required written permission from copyright owner of each material except for education use which is required an official request from head of educational insitution.

TUNISIA

TUNIS

CENTRE DE DOCUMENTATION NATIONALE
4, rue Ibn Nadim – Cité Montplaisir
1002 – TUNIS
TUNESIA

Tel.: 216-1-894.266
Fax.: 216-1-792.241

Member of ICA, IFLA.

Collections

Collections of Sound.

Records and cassettes of speeches of president Bourguiba. Film : newsreels from Tunesia and foreign.
Sound 291 discs + 177 cassettes

Access

Catalogue on cards.
Access to catalogue.

Access to materials: limited.
Access on archives premises.

Fees – Copyright

Fees for research for reuse and production purposes, research by archive staff, facilities and handling, Free consultation on the premises.
Copyright holder is the institution.
No duplication. User must take notes when viewing or hearing.

TURKEY

ANKARA

BILKENT UNIVERSITESI KÜTÜPHANESI
BILKENT UNIVERSITY LIBRARY
06533 BILKENT ANKARA
TURKEY

Tel.: 90-4-266 44 72
Fax.: 90-4-266 43 91
Telex: 42 999 tcsm tr
Electronic mail: (interbit) Phyllis@trbilun

Member of IFLA.

Collections

Collections of Video, Sound, books accompanied by sound recordings or "talking books".

Fine arts, English learning, music.
Video 32 titles
Sound 193 cassettes + 2120 phonograph records

TURKEY – ANKARA

Access
Catalogue on database.

Access to catalogue.

Access to materials: limited.
Access on archives premises.

Fees – Copyright
Institution holds no copyright.

466

MILLÎ KÜTÜPHANE BASKANLIGI
PRESIDENCY OF NATIONAL LIBRARY
Bahçelievler son durak
06490 ANKARA
TURKEY

Tel.: 90-4-222 38 12
Fax.: 90-4-223 04 51

Member of IFLA.

Collections
Collections of Video, Sound.

The collection contains video cassettes including art films on Turks and tapes including the Turkish music, the folk music and the other specific countries' musics.
Video 61
Sound 7482

Access
Catalogue on cards.

Access to catalogue.

Access to materials.
Access on archives premises.

Fees – Copyright
Free of charge.
Copyright holder is the institution.

ISTANBUL

467

SINEMA TV ENSTITÜSÜ
TURKISH FILM AND TV INSTITUTE
80700 Kislaönü-Besiktas
ISTANBUL
TURKEY

Tel.: 90-1-166 10 96
Fax.: 91-1-167 65 99

Member of FIAF.

Collections
Collections of Film, Video, Sound, photographs (neg-pos), scripts, posters, books, magazines, cuttings from newspapers, censorship documents, all kinds of documents concerning cinema and TV.

Archive of the Institute keeps original negatives and positives of Turkish documentaries and fiction films ; and also copies of classical films belonging to World Cinema.
Films 4250 films (negative, positive)
Video 1085 video cassettes (1 inch, U-Matic, VHS, Beta)
Sound 100 bands, 85 sound films (magnetic, optic)

Access
Catalogue indexed on cards.

Acces to catalogue: limited. Only the staff of the Archive is permitted tu use the catalogues.

Access to materials: limited.
Access on archives premises, by loan.

Fees – Copyright
Fees for research by archive staff. Culture societies, universities, researchers, scientists and cinematographers can use the materials of the Archive without payment. However, they are not allowed to take them out of the Institute. In some special cases, a copy can be taken by paying the cost price of material and also its copyright fee. In our Archive, there are materials which their cultural and commercial usage rights belonging to the Institute as well as there are some with only the cultural usage rights belong to the Institute. If the material will be used for commercial purpose a permission document which mentions the person has the right to use the material in this purpose must be brought. All copies given from the Archive have got the symbol of the Institute, and it is obliged to be shown with this symbol.

UNITED KINGDOM

ABERYSTWYTH

468

LLYFRGELL GENEDLAETHOL CYMRU
NATIONAL LIBRARY OF WALES
UK – ABERYSTWYTH, DYFED
U.K.

Tel.: 44-970-623816
Fax.: 44-970-615709

Member of IASA, ICA, IFLA.

Collections
Collections of Film, Video, Sound, large collection of photographs.

Mainly material relating to Wales or in the Welsh language. Sound recordings include published audio records, broadcast radio programmes and original recordings. Video recordings comprise largely broadcast television programmes including the entire output of S4C (The Welsh Fourth Channel).

Films over 100 titles
Video over 20000 hours
Sound over 5000 hours

Access

Catalogue on database.

Access to catalogue.

Access to materials: Minimum 24 hrs notice required.
Access on archives premises.

Fees – Copyright

Fees for research for reuse and production purposes.
Institution holds no copyright.
Material freely available for viewing on premises only. All other usage requires copyright clearance.

_____ 469

UNIVERSITY COLLEGE OF WALES ABERYSTWYTH
INFORMATION AND LIBRARY STUDIES LIBRARY
Llanbadarn Fawr
UK – ABERYSTWYTH, DYFED SY23 3AS
U.K.

Tel.: 44-970-622417
Fax.: 44-970-622190
Electronic mail: BTGOLD 79:ZOZ9

Member of ICA, IFLA.

Collections

Collections of Film, Video, Sound, scripts of series of recorded interviews with eminent librarians & authors.

Collection concentrates on librarianship and information science with small number of titles on computing, management & childrens literature.
Films 250
Video 400
Sound 2000

Access

Catalogue on database.

Access to catalogue.

Access to materials: limited. Most materials are for reference use only.
Access on archives premises, by loan.

Fees – Copyright

Fees for research for reuse and production purposes.
Institution holds no copyright.

BEAULIEU

_____ 470

NATIONAL MOTOR MUSEUM, FILM AND VIDEO LIBRARY
UK – BEAULIEU, BROCKENHURST HAMPSHIRE SO42 7ZN
U.K.

Tel.: 44-590-612345 ext. 239
Fax.: 44-590-612655

Collections

Collections of Film, Video, Sound, photographs.

Collection covers all areas of motoring from 1890s to present day. Also includes Ford and Vauxhall film collection, plus motorsport, etc.
Films about 20000 (film + video)
Sound relatively small at present

Access

Catalogue indexed on cards.

Acces to catalogue: limited. Available by appointment during normal working hours.

Access to materials: limited.
Access on archives premises.

Fees – Copyright

Fees for research for reuse and production purposes, facilities and handling, footage fees.
Copyright holder is the institution.
Written details of programme/project to be submitted prior to viewing material.

BIRMINGHAM

_____ 471

BIRMINGHAM CENTRAL LIBRARY, ARCHIVES DIVISION
CHARLES PARKER ARCHIVE
Chamberlain square
UK – BIRMINGHAM B3 3HQ
U.K.

Tel.: 44-21-2354217
Fax.: 44-21-2334458

Member of IASA.

Collections

Collections of Film, Sound, transcripts and recording documentation, background material (pamphlets, books, etc.) to subject coverage.

Charles Parker (d.1980) was a B.B.C. radio producer in Birmingham. The archive contains tapes made for the B.B.C. and also in his own time. Subjects covered are very wide, but especially folk music revival, radical theatre & politics, revolutionary China, adolescence, ethnic minority experience, songs and life experiences of working people.

Films 20 cans
Sound about 5000 hours of recordings

Access

No catalogue yet produced. Catalogue will become available in sections as produced.

Access to materials: limited. Only catalogued material generally available.
Access on archives premises.

Fees – Copyright

If agreement of copyright owners can be obtained for copying, reproduction fees may be charged. Institution holds no copyright.
Some material is B.B.C. copyright and available for consultation only without written permission of B.B.C. Much other material is subject to copyright interests of trustees of the archive and individual performers and also available for consultation only.

BRENTFORD

472

BBC TELEVISION LIBRARY SERVICES
Reynard Mills Industrial Estate, Windmill Road
UK – BRENTFORD, MIDDLESEX, TW8 9NF
U.K.

Tel.: 44-81-7588406
Fax.: 44-81-5699374
Telex: 265781

Member of IFTA.

Collections

Collections of Film, Video, stills, music, gramophone records.

Film & VT Library holds selected BBC Television output since 1948 with a very limited amount of pre-war originated material. The BBC Photograph Library and Archive is the BBC's unique collection of 2 million BBC copyright images dating back to the earliest days of radio and television broadcasting, including programmes, personalities, equipment and premises. Supporting collection of music and gramophone records.
Films 500000 reels
Video 350000 spools/cassettes

Access

Catalogue on database.

Acces to catalogue: limited. Direct access available only to BBC users.

Access to materials: limited.
Access on archives premises.

Fees – Copyright

Fees for research for reuse and production purposes, research by archive staff, facilities and handling.
Pricelist and conditions for use available.
Copyright holder is the institution.
Material is available from the Archive for BBC users only. BBC Enterprises provide a service for commercial users. Selected material is available for bona fide researchers at the National Film Archive.

CAERNARTON

473

GWASANAETH ARCHIFAU AC AMGUEDDFGYDD GWYNEDD
GWYNEDD ARCHIVES AND MUSEUMS SERVICE
County Offices
UK – CAERNARTON LL55 ISH
U.K.

Tel.: 44-286-679095
Fax.: 44-286-679637

Member of IASA.

Collections

Collections of Sound.

Oral history tapes, mainly collected from informants in period 1980-1987.
Sound 750 cassettes

Access

Catalogue indexed on cards.

Acces to catalogue: limited.

Access to materials.
Access on archives premises.

Fees – Copyright

Fees for research by archive staff.
Copyright holder is the institution.

CARDIFF

474

AMGUEDDFA WERIN CYMRU
WELSH FOLK MUSEUM
St. Fagans
UK – CARDIFF CF5 6XB
U.K.

Tel.: 44-222-569441
Fax.: 44-222-578413

Member of IASA.

Collections

Collections of Film, Video, Sound, some tape transcripts, plus books, articles and cassettes based on sound archive material. Also the Museum's collections of artefacts, documents, and photographs.

Fieldwork recordings from all parts of Wales, illustrating various aspects of Welsh oral tradition and dialect. Mainly Welch-language material, although there are many English recordings. Also a substantial number of off-air recordings of radio and TV broadcasts on maters relevant to the name of the Museum ; as well as a limited collection of commercial discs and 16mm film.
Films about 100 hrs
Video about 80 hrs
Sound about 4500 hrs of audio tape + 830 discs

Access

Catalogue indexed on cards.

Acces to catalogue: limited. Supervised access for bona fide researchers.

Access to materials: limited by prior arrangement only.
Access on archives premises.

Fees – Copyright

Fees for research for reuse and production purposes, facilities and handling, No charge for on-site listening facilities.
With most of the sound recordings, the interviewee retains copyright in his/her contribution, and permission must be sought for copying or public performance of the material. The Museum does not hold the copyright in all of its film/video collection, only those made by its own fieldworkers.

CLITHEROE

_____ 475
NORTH WEST SOUND ARCHIVE (UK)
Clitheroe Castle
UK – CLITHEROE, LANCASHIRE
U.K.

Tel.: 44-200-27897
Fax.: 44-200-26339

Member of IASA.

Collections

Collections of Sound, photos & documents which complement the sound collections. Two computer databases : a) children's playsongs ; b) a 10000 word regional dictionary, incl. dialect.

Folk music, canals, railways, coalmining, dialect, textiles, local radio progs, radio astronomy, jewish history, homelife, World War I, World War II, oral history, birdsong, regional & historic sounds, musichall, hat-making, engineering, aeronautics, fishing, Salford docks, Liverpool docks, Solidarity (Poland) interviews.
Sound about 85000 items

Access

Catalogue on database.

Access to catalogue.

Access to materials: Staff access at HQ, copies used by public, loan service & out-stations also supply.
Access on archives premises, by loan, by hire, by purchase.

Fees – Copyright

Fees for research for reuse and production purposes, facilities and handling.
Institution holds no copyright.

DENHAM

_____ 476
BRITISH MOVIETONEWS LIMITED
North Orbital Road
UK – DENHAM UB9 5HQ
U.K.

Tel.: 44-895-833071
Fax.: 44-895-834893

Collections

Collections of Film.

Newsreels covering the period 1929-1979.
Films over 5000 newsreels on 35mm film

Access

Catalogue on cards.

Access to catalogue.

Access to materials.
Access on archives premises.

Fees – Copyright

Fees for research for reuse and production purposes, research by archive staff, facilities and handling.
Pricelist and conditions for use available.
Copyright holder is the institution.

EDINBURGH

477
EDINBURGH UNIVERSITY LIBRARY, THE UNIVERSITY OF EDINBURGH
George Square
UK – EDINBURGH EH8 9LJ
U.K.

Tel.: 44-31-6501000
Fax.: 44-31-6679780
Telex: 727442 (UNIVED G)

Member of IFLA.

Collections
Collections of Video, Sound.

Sound and video collection supporting music teaching in the University.
Video 100 cassettes
Sound 7000 vinyl discs, 500 CD's

Access
Catalogue on cards.

Access to catalogue.

Access to materials.
Access on archives premises.

Fees – Copyright
Institution holds no copyright.

478
SCHOOL OF SCOTTISH STUDIES, UNIVERSITY OF EDINBURGH
27 George Square
UK – EDINBURGH EH8 9LD
U.K.

Tel.: 44-31-6504160
Fax.: 44-31-6620772
Telex: 727442 (UNIVED C)

Member of IASA.

Collections
Collections of Film, Video, Sound, transcripts, summaries and catalogues of sound recordings (which are the vast majority of the collection).

Ethnological, ethnomusicological, linguistic, onomastic and folklore recordings, especially folksongs, dialect, traditional tales and oral history, in Gaelic and Lowland Scots, from fieldwork in Scotland, with some videotapes and a few films and ancillary and comparative written (MS, typescript and printed) material. Also John Levy ethnomusicology coll. (mostly Asian), Will Forret (popular music) and deposited Scottish oral history tapes.
Films 3 hours
Video 250 hours
Sound 8250 hours (estimated, not including back-up copies and duplicates)

Access
Catalogue on database.

Acces to catalogue: limited for approved researchers and enquirers.

Access to materials: limited. On application to Archivist and Director : a few copies may be made with informant's/performer's permission.
Access on archives premises, by purchase.

Fees – Copyright
Fees for research for reuse and production purposes, research by archive staff, facilities and handling, copies (sound or video tape, transcripts). Pricelist and conditions for use available.
Permission required from : Archivist to consult catalogue and transcript ; Archivist, Director and usually fieldworker or depositor to hear or see recordings ; all these plus informant/performer (unless copyright assigned to Archive) to study in depth, obtain copies, publish or broadcast. Some recordings under complete embargo.

GATESHEAD, TYNE AND WEAR

479
THE NORTHERN FILM & TELEVISION ARCHIVE
36 Bottle Bank
UK – GATESHEAD, TYNE & WEAR NE8 2AR
U.K.

Tel.: 44-91-4773601, 44-91-4775532
Fax.: 44-91-4783681

Collections
Collections of Film, Video.

Mainly post-1945, of film and video relevant to the region (North East England), especially its industries. Large collection, for instance, on coal mining.
Films some 1500 catalogued items in all, mainly video, with some film

Access
Catalogue on database.

Access to catalogue by prior arrangement.

Access to materials also by prior arrangement.
Access on archives premises.

Fees – Copyright
Fees for research for reuse and production purposes, research by archive staff, facilities and handling.
Institution holds no copyright.
Copyright holders permission required for purchase especially for use in productions.

GLASGOW

_____ **480**
BBC SCOTLAND, LIBRARY SERVICES
Queen Margaret Drive
UK – G12 8DG, GLASGOW
U.K.

Tel.: 44-41-3302880
Fax.: 44-41-3340614
Telex: 779221

Member of IASA.

Collections
Collections of Film, Video, Sound, programme documentation.

Work-in-progress, transmission library and archive for output of BBC Scotland (regional division of British Broadcasting Corporation).
Films 12000 reels
Video 20000 tapes
Sound 20000 tapes, 50000 vinyl + CD recordings

Access
Catalogue on database.

Acces to catalogue: limited, fee-based service only.

Access to materials: limited, fee-based service.
Access on archives premises, by purchase.

Fees – Copyright
Fees for research for reuse and production purposes, facilities and handling, external use.
Copyright holder is the institution.
BBC broadcast material usually bound by mixed rights of BBC and performers, scriptwriters, etc.

_____ **481**
THE SCOTTISH FILM ARCHIVE
74 Victoria Crescent Road
UK – GLASGOW G12 9JN
U.K.

Tel.: 44-41-3344445
Fax.: 44-41-3348132

Member of FIAF, IAMHIST.

Collections
Collections of Film, printed and manuscript records of film production and cinema exhibition industries. Small collection of stills, posters, books and periodicals.

Principally non-fiction, related to Scottish cultural, industrial and political history. Contains professional and amateur productions, educational, sponsored and news footage, and broadcast materials.
Films 16000 titles

Access
Catalogue on database.

Acces to catalogue: limited. Only card catalogue can be accessed, and this exists for a proportion of the collection only.

Access to materials: limited to viewing copies, and by copyright considerations.
Access on archives premises, by loan, by hire, by purchase.

Fees – Copyright
Fees for research for reuse and production purposes, facilities and handling.
Pricelist and conditions for use available.
Copyright holder is the institution.
The institution holds rights for a proportion of the titles in the Archive. Access by loan, hire and purchase is only allowed subject to the permission of the rights owner. Viewings on Archive's premises can be allowed by prior appointment and without prior copyright consent.

HADLEIGH

_____ **482**
BOULTON-HAWKER FILMS LTD
28 George Street
UK – HADLEIGH, IPSWICH IP7 5BG
U.K.

Tel.: 44-473-822235
Fax.: 44-473-824519

Collections
Collections of Film.

Films on geography of Europe, Africa, Middle East, India.
Films 51

Access
Catalogue published.

Access to catalogue: Catalogue on request.

Access to materials: limited.
Access on archives premises, by hire.

Fees – Copyright
Fees for facilities and handling.
Pricelist and conditions for use available.
Copyright holder is the institution.
Access on premises by arrangement or by hire of prints.

HOLYWOOD

_____ 483
ULSTER FOLK AND TRANSPORT MUSEUM
Cultra
UK – HOLYWOOD, BT18 OEU
U.K.

Tel.: 44-232-428428
Fax.: 44-2317-4786

Member of IASA.

Collections
Collections of Film, Video, Sound, documentation archive and library.

Collections of cultural and historical significance including archival holdings of broadcasters, recording studios, local collectors, etc.
Films 1000 items
Video 600 items
Sound 12000 items

Access
Catalogue on database.

Access to catalogue.

Access to materials: limited, subject to limitation imposed by copyright and performing rights legislation.
Access on archives premises, by purchase.

Fees – Copyright
Some fees are imposed for the use of visual images. Fees also apply to audio copies of archival material – provided on a non profit making basis. Pricelist and conditions for use available.
The Museum holds a wide variety of archival material which equally varies in terms of the copyright conditions which apply.

IVER

_____ 484
BRITISH PATHÉ NEWS
Pinewood Studios
UK – IVER, BUCKS, SLO ONH
U.K.

Tel.: 44-753-630361
Fax.: 44-753-655365

Collections
Collections of Film, Video, much production data.

News archive covering 1896-1970.
Films 50 million feet or 3000 hours

Access
Catalogue on database.

Access to catalogue: Indexes may also be searched at Central London Office (telephone 44-71-3230407).

Access to materials: limited. Materials are all original and are sent to laboratory for copies to be made for licensees.
Access on archives premises.

Fees – Copyright
Fees for research for reuse and production purposes, research by archive staff, facilities and handling, licensing for TV, video and other media. Pricelist and conditions for use available.
Copyright holder is the institution.
British Pathé News owns all copyright of the material in the Archive and can therefore grant all forms of licenses wordwide. Potential licensees in North America should apply through WPA Film Library (101-708-385-8535).

LEEDS

_____ 485
ARCHIVE FILM AGENCY
21 Lidgett Park Avenue
UK – LS8 1EU LEEDS
U.K.

Tel.: 44-532-662454

Collections
Collections of Film, production notes, reviews, etc. 50000 stills from British Feature Films.

Fiction, non fiction and newsreel from 1900 to mid 30's. Fiction subjects : British music hall, comedy, drama, westerns and animation. Non fiction and newsreel subjects : transport, sport, fishing, sailing, music hall (British), travelogue, dancing and stunts, automobile and aircraft.
Films about 6000 cans

Access
Catalogue indexed on cards.

Access to catalogue: no.

Access to materials.
Access on archives premises, by loan.

Fees – Copyright
Fees for research for reuse and production purposes, facilities and handling, Fees for viewing off the premises, on VHS format.
Pricelist and conditions for use available.
Institution holds no copyright.
Where copyright exists the researcher/user is required to seek permission from the rights holder when loaning, hiring or purchasing their material.

486
CHAMELEON FILM & STOCK SHOT LIBRARY
The Magistretti Building
UK – LEEDS LS1 4RB
U.K.

Tel.: 44-532-434017
Fax.: 44-532-431267

Collections
Collections of Film.

The collection includes over one million feet of stock shots on 16mm film from contemporary documentary programmes. There is also a small collection of one hour long adventure documentaries (also on film).
Films over one million feet

Access
Catalogue indexed on cards.

Access to catalogue.

Access to materials.
Access on archives premises, by purchase.

Fees – Copyright
Fees for research for reuse and production purposes.
Pricelist and conditions for use available.
Copyright holder is the institution.
Permissions can be granted for the use of any material in the collection for use in any medium.

LONDON

487
BRITISH BROADCASTING CORPORATION
BBC SOUND LIBRARY
Broadcasting House
UK – LONDON W1A 1AA
U.K.

Tel.: 44-71-9274850
Fax.: 44-71-4362770

Member of IASA.

Collections
Collections of Sound.

Archive comprises recordings from BBC radio programme output although there are some recordings from pre-broadcasting period, all types.
Sound 500000 recordings

Access
Catalogue on database.

Acces to catalogue: limited. Some information held at NSA research facilities available at cost.

Access to materials: limited. Licensing service available.
Access on archives premises, by purchase.

Fees – Copyright
Fees for research for reuse and production purposes, research by archive staff, facilities and handling.
Pricelist and conditions for use available.
Copyright holder is the institution.
BBC has institutional rights. Artists/performers also have rights to be cleared before reuse.

488
BRITISH LIBRARY, NATIONAL SOUND ARCHIVE
29 Exhibition Road
UK – LONDON SW7 2AS
U.K.

Tel.: 44-71-5896603
Fax.: 44-71-8238970

Member of IASA, IFLA.

Collections
Collections of Video, Sound, A secondary printed reference collection is maintained to support the use of the primary collection of sound. Notable strengths are commercial record catalogues and relevant periodical literature. A collection of 240 examples of early playback equipment is also held.

Commercially issued and non-commercial sound recordings dating back to the 1890s, including a wide range of formats from wax cylinder through magnetic tape to compact disc. Subject areas include western art music, jazz, popular music, international music, poetry & drama, oral history, languages dialect, wildlife sounds, and industro-mechanical sound. Related broadcast material, both radio & television, is recorded off-air. A comprehensive collection of popular music videos is maintained.
Video 6100 video cassettes, small number of laser discs and CD-Vs
Sound 800000 discs, 52000 hours of tape recording

Access
Catalogue on database.

Acces to catalogue: limited.

Access to materials.
Access on archives premises.

Fees – Copyright
Fees for research for reuse and production purposes, research by archive staff, transcription service available (subject to copyright clearances).
Pricelist and conditions for use available.

Permission of copyright holder(s) is not required for the free listening service offered on the premises. It is required for playing off the premises, or for making copies for customers of the Archive.

489
BRITISH LIBRARY, ORIENTAL AND INDIA OFFICE COLLECTIONS
INDIA OFFICE RECORDS
197 Blackfriars Road
UK – LONDON SE1 8NG
U.K.

Tel.: 44-71-4127000
Fax.: 44-71-4127858
Telex: 21462
Member of ICA.

Collections

Collections of Sound, typescript transcripts of many of the interviews.

Tape recorded interviews with persons (mainly British but some Indian) who worked or lived in India or Burma under British rule chiefly between 1920 and 1947. Subjects include : social life and leisure pursuits of British in India, relations between British and Indians, second World War in Burma, events leading up to independence in India and Burma ; lives of civil servants, police, army officers, businessmen, forest officers, medical service, planters, missionaries, and their wives.
Sound 203 interviews

Access

Catalogue indexed on cards.

Access to catalogue: Part published, part typescript, with unified access via card index.

Access to materials: limited. Generally available to most of the tape recordings, but some are closed because of special copyright problems.
Access on archives premises.

Fees – Copyright

Fees for research for reuse and production purposes. Fees would normally be charged only for use for a commercial purpose. If a transcript exists a copy can be purchased subject to copyright restrictions.
Copyright is variously owned, sometimes by Institution, sometimes by interviewee, and sometimes by both jointly. Apart from those interviews subject to special copyright problems, access on the archive premises is generally open to all members of the public for the purpose of research or private study, and if a transcript exists a copy can be provided for the same purpose. Users wishing to publish excerpts from the interviews must obtain permission of the copyright owners.

490
BRITISH MEDICAL ASSOCIATION FILM LIBRARY
BMA House, Tavistock Square
UK – LONDON W5 4BH
U.K.

Tel.: 44-71-3836690
Fax.: 44-71-3882544
Telex: 9312131899 NL G
Electronic mail: 14:BMX030

Collections

Collections of Film, Video.

Health and medical subjects. Includes archive of teaching films dating back to 1923.
Films 900 16mm prints
Video 500 VHS and U-Matic

Access

Catalogue on database.

Acces to catalogue: limited. Membership available for relevant institutions/commercial organisations. Non members at the film librarians discretion.

Access to materials: limited. Membership available for relevant institutions/commercial organisations. Non members at the film librarians discretion.
Access on archives premises.

Fees – Copyright

Fees for research for reuse and production purposes, research by archive staff.
Pricelist and conditions for use available.
Archive films are copyright films. Current films are a variety of copyright films. Details of copyright holders on file.

491
HUNTLEY FILM ARCHIVES LTD
22 Islington Green
UK – LONDON N1 8DU
U.K.

Tel.: 44-71-2269260
Fax.: 44-71-7040847

Collections

Collections of Film, Sound, some British production stills, pre-cinematic equipment and toys, early projectors, magic lanterns, early posters and cinematic magazines.

1894 to 1960 documentary, black and white film library specialising in TRANSPORT (trains, aviation, trams, cars), DANCE (classical, popular, ethic), TRAVEL AND FOREIGN LOCATIONS, SILENT FEATURES and COMEDIES, FARMING, INDUSTRY, SOCIAL HISTORY (fashion, schools, housing, etc.).
Films about 10000 reels
Sound about 4000 78 rpm discs

Access

Catalogue indexed on cards.

Access to catalogue: no.

Access to materials: Phone or fax inquiries, then viewing on the premises or VHS, brochure available on request.
Access on archives premises.

Fees – Copyright

Fees for research for reuse and production purposes, research by archive staff, facilities and handling.
Pricelist and conditions for use available.
Copyright holder is the institution.
Copyright arrangements are dealt with in-house.

492

IMPERIAL WAR MUSEUM, DEPARTMENT OF FILM

Lambeth Road
UK – LONDON SE1 6HZ
U.K.

Tel.: 44-71-4165000
Fax.: 44-71-4165379

Member of FIAF, IFTA, IAMHIST.

Collections

Collections of Film, Video, cameraman's "dopesheets" for record film ; production files, scripts etc. for some film and television material. Large still photograph collection held in separate Department of Photographs.

All the collections of the Imperial War Museum relate in some way to the causes, the course and the consequences of conflict since August 1914. The majority of films are official British record, information, documentary and newsreelmaterial ; significant minority collections of non-British film and of television material are also held.
Films 100000 cans
Video 3750 tapes

Access

Catalogue on database.

Acces to catalogue: limited. Generally, some degree of supervision of researchers by staff is recommended, because of the specialist nature of much of the collections.

Access to materials: limited. Access is limited only by archival considerations (eg no viewing of unique material) or in accordance with the donor's wishes or instructions.
Access on archives premises, by loan, by hire, by purchase.

Fees – Copyright

Fees for research for reuse and production purposes, research by archive staff, facilities and handling.
Pricelist and conditions for use available.
Material held may be IWM copyright, British Crown copyright (which the IWM is licensed to administer) or have copyright vested in outside owners. IWM will release non-copyright material for reuse or production only on clearance of rights, which is user's responsibility.

493

IMPERIAL WAR MUSEUM, DEPARTMENT OF SOUND RECORDS

Lambeth Road
UK – LONDON SE1 6HZ
U.K.

Tel.: 44-71-4165363
Fax.: 44-71-4165379

Member of IASA.

Collections

Collections of Sound.

Spoken word collection : oral history (eyewitness accounts of civilian and military experience of 20th Century conflicts), speeches/broadcasts, also some sound effects.
Sound about 16000 hours

Access

Catalogue published.

Access to catalogue: Computers not available for public use but we can print out relevant sections ; printed catalogues are sold ; CD-ROM in progress.

Access to materials by appointment.
Access on archives premises, by purchase.

Fees – Copyright

No charge for access and research ; copyright fees payable for publication.
Pricelist and conditions for use available.
Copyright holder is the institution.
Most of collection is fully accessible for research/ education – also available for sale.

494

INDEPENDENT TELEVISION NEWS LTD (ITN)

ITN LIBRARY SALES
200 Gray's Inn Road
UK – LONDON WC1X 8XZ
U.K.

Tel.: 44-71-4304480
Fax.: 44-71-4304453

Member of IFTA.

Collections

Collections of Film, Video, Sound.

News footage from 1955 to present day on film and videotape computerised access from 1980 to date. Fast and efficient research and supply of material.

Access

Catalogue on database.

Access to catalogue.

Access to materials.
Access on archives premises.

Fees – Copyright

Fees for research for reuse and production purposes, research by archive staff, facilities and handling.
Pricelist and conditions for use available.
Copyright holder is the institution.
ITN Library Sales can supply non-ITN material but client must obtain permission of the copyright holder.

495

INDEX STOCK SHOTS
12 Charlotte Mews
UK – LONDON W1P 1LN
U.K.

Tel.: 44-71-6310134
Fax.: 44-71-4368737

Collections

Collections of Film, Video.

Stock footage of international locations, aircraft, wildlife, industry, time-lapse photography. Majority of footage shot on 35mm film and mastered on digital videotape.
Films impossible to quantify

Access

Catalogue on cards.

Access to catalogue: no.

Access to materials.
Access on archives premises, by loan.

Fees – Copyright

Fees for research for reuse and production purposes, research by archive staff, facilities and handling. Royalties payable on footage used.
Pricelist and conditions for use available.
Copyright holder is the institution.

496

KING'S COLLEGE LONDON
LIDDELL HART CENTRE FOR MILITARY ARCHIVES
King's College London, Strand
UK – LONDON WC2R 2LS
U.K.

Tel.: 44-71-8732187, 44-71-8732015
Fax.: 44-71-8720207

Collections

Collections of Sound.

Radio interviews of Air Vice Marshal Menaul on South Africa, Falkland conflict, Nato. BBC coverage of the Gulf War 1991.
Films 3
Video 24
Sound 277 audio cassette tapes

Access

Access to catalogue: No catalogue.

Access to materials.
Access on archives premises.

Fees – Copyright

Pricelist and conditions for use available.
Institution holds no copyright.

497

NATIONAL FILM ARCHIVE
21 Stephen Street
UK – LONDON W1P 1PL
U.K.

Tel.: 44-71-2551444
Fax.: 44-71-4367950
Telex: 27624 BFILDNG

Member of FIAF, IFTA, IAMHIST.

Collections

Collections of Film, Video, Sound, mainly stills, transparencies, posters, designs, and various documentation (eg letters, memorabilia).

National heritage collection comprising broad range of films, videos and TV programmes from 1895 to present day which exemplify art and history of the cinema and TV and record life, history, science, sociology and portraiture in the 20th century. Features, shorts, documentaries, newsreels, animation, amateur films, home movies and videos on all gauges and formats. Special responsibility assumed for British cinema and TV production.
Films 140000 titles
Video 35000 titles
Sound small number of related sound tapes

Access

Catalogue on database.

Access to catalogue: On-site catalogue accessible to public usually by appointment. Some published catalogues. All telephone enquirires and letters answered.

Access to materials: limited. Research viewings on premises ; loans to BFI cinemas and FIAF archives; copies made for copyright owners ; Production Library.

Access on archives premises, by loan, by hire, by purchase.

Fees – Copyright

Fees for research for reuse and production purposes, facilities and handling, loans to festivals, etc.
Pricelist and conditions for use available.
Institution holds no copyright.
All use of Archive's films and videos off the premises subject to prior written consent of copyright owner if any. If non, letter of indemnity must be supplied by user if so requested.

_____ 498

NATIONAL MARITIME MUSEUM
Romney Road, Greenwich
UK – LONDON SE10 9NF
U.K.

Tel.: 44-81-8584422
Fax.: 44-81-3126632

Collections

Collections of Film, Video, Sound.

This museum collects film material on all maritime topics and is predominantly documentary in character although a few feature films are held. Subjects covered include : fishing, the last days of sail, trade and commerce by sea, naval power, yachting, ocean liners.
Films about 600 films
Video about 200 videos
Sound about 500 tapes

Access

Catalogue on cards.

Acces to catalogue: limited. Typescript catalogue and index is available for use on premises, but has not been published.

Access to materials by appointment.
Access on archives premises.

Fees – Copyright

Fees for research for reuse and production purposes, facilities and handling.
Copyright on a good proportion of the collection is not held by this Museum, and copyright must be cleared with holder before material can be released. Where copyright is held by this Museum, reproduction fees are payable. Charges are by negotiation and depend on intended use, medium and frequency.

_____ 499

THE NATURAL HISTORY MUSEUM
Cromwell Road
UK – LONDON SW7 5BD
U.K.

Tel.: 44-71-9389238
Fax.: 44-71-9389290

Collections

Collections of Video, Sound.

All items relate to the Museum – its staff, research work, collections or exhibitions.
Video 20
Sound 50

Access

Catalogue on cards.

Access to catalogue.

Access on archives premises.

Fees – Copyright

Fees for research for reuse and production purposes, research by archive staff.

_____ 500

THAMES TELEVISION PLC
FILM AND VIDEOTAPE LIBRARY
306 Euston Road
UK – LONDON NW1 3BB
U.K.

Tel.: 44-71-3879494
Fax.: 44-71-3833982
Telex: 22816 LONDTV G

Member of IFTA.

Collections

Collections of Film, Video.

Programmes transmitted by Thames Television from 1968 onwards. Stock shot library of worldwide locations, current affairs and documentary material (eg English rural life and social history). Drama, light entertainment, children, school, the arts, documentaries, current affairs, news (especially London and S.E. England).
Films 50000 cans
Video 97000 tapes

Access

Catalogue on database.

Access to catalogue: by staff only.

Access to materials via library sales for sequence licenses.
Access by loan, by purchase.

Fees – Copyright

Fees for research for reuse and production purposes, research by archive staff, facilities and handling. Footage available for use by programme and commercial producers and researchers. Pricelist and conditions for use available. Copyright holder is the institution.

501

VISNEWS LIMITED
VISNEWS LIBRARY
Cumberland Avenue
UK – LONDON NW10 7EH
U.K.

Tel.: 44-81-4534338
Fax.: 44-81-9650620
Telex: 22678

Member of IFTA.

Collections

Collections of Film, Video.

News reels + television news items.
Films 60 million feet (film + video)

Access

Catalogue indexed on cards.

Access to catalogue.

Access to materials.
Access on archives premises, by purchase.

Fees – Copyright

Fees for research for reuse and production purposes, research by archive staff, facilities and handling, royalties.
Pricelist and conditions for use available.
Copyright holder is the institution.
Where we have accessed other broadcaster material agreement is sought from copyright holder before material is supplied. Most sports material requires clearance from sponsors.

MANCHESTER

502

NORTH WEST FILM ARCHIVE AT MANCHESTER POLYTECHNIC
Minshull House, 47-49 Chorlton Street
UK – MANCHESTER, M1 3EU
U.K.

Tel.: 44-61-2473097, 44-61-2473098
Fax.: 44-61-2365319

Collections

Collections of Film, Video, Sound, complementary collections of photographs, ephemera, documentation and taped interviews relating to the region's film and cinema industries.

From the 1890s to the present day, all films relate to life in the North West of England. Home movies, cinema newsreels, advertising and promotional material, educational and travel films are all represented, illustrating themes such as street life, work, the textile industry, leisure, entertainment, celebrations, healthcare, housing and wartime experiences in the region. Material on video is now also collected to reflect contemporary life.
Films about 17000 cans
Video about 400 cassettes, mainly for access
Sound 50 x 5" reels of interview

Access

Catalogue on database.

Access to catalogue.

Access to materials: limited due to preservation.
Access on archives premises, by loan, by hire, by purchase.

Fees – Copyright

Fees for research for reuse and production purposes, research by archive staff, facilities and handling. Sliding scale of charges for certain kinds of public services but no charge in many cases. Pricelist and conditions for use available.
Institution holds no copyright.
Viewing is unconditional – supply requires copyright permission in advance.

MILTON KEYNES

503

OPEN UNIVERSITY LIBRARY
Walton Hall
UK – MILTON KEYNES, MK7 6AA
U.K.

Member of IASA.

Collections

Collections of Video, Sound, related materials.

Open University teaching materials, distance learning. Faculties : arts, social sciences, mathematics, education science, technology, business.
Video 5500
Sound 4000

Access

Catalogue on database.

Acces to catalogue: limited, on-site access only.

Access to materials: limited. Viewing facility on site.

Access on archives premises, by purchase.

Fees – Copyright

Fees for research for reuse and production purposes, facilities and handling.
Pricelist and conditions for use available.
For copyright contact Rights Manager Open University.

SANOY

_____ 504
ROYAL SOCIETY FOR THE PROTECTION OF BIRDS
The Looge
UK – SANOY, BEDFORDSHIRE SG19 1EY
U.K.
Tel.: 44-767-680551
Fax.: 44-767-692365

Collections

Collections of Film.

UK and European birds and habitats plus various other wildlife.
Films 1000000 ft

Access

Catalogue indexed on cards.
Acces to catalogue: limited.
Access to materials.
Access on archives premises, by loan.

Fees – Copyright

Fees for research for reuse and production purposes, research by archive staff, facilities and handling.
Pricelist and conditions for use available.
Copyright holder is the institution.

SHEFFIELD

_____ 505
SHEFFIELD UNIVERSITY LIBRARY
UK – SHEFFIELD S10 2TN
U.K.
Tel.: 44-742-768555 ext. 4803
Fax.: 44-742-739826
Telex: 547216 UGSHEF G
Electronic mail: LB1MSH@UK.AC.SHEFFIELD.PRIMEA
Member of IFLA.

Collections

Collections of Video, Sound, slides, kits.

General support material.
Video 530 video cassettes
Sound 502 sound cassettes

Access

Catalogue on database.
Access to catalogue.
Access to materials.
Access on archives premises.

Fees – Copyright

Pricelist and conditions for use available.
Institution holds no copyright.
Access as specified by copyright holder.

SOLIHULL

_____ 506
SOLIHULL LIBRARIES & ARTS DEPT, MUSIC LIBRARY
Homer Rd
UK – SOLIHULL, WEST MIDLANDS B91 3RG
U.K.
Tel.: 44-21-7046983
Fax.: 44-21-7046991

Collections

Collections of Sound, books & scores.

CDs, cassettes, LPs, language courses, talking books, scores & books for loan to the public.
Sound about 15000

Access

Catalogue on database.
Access to catalogue.
Access to materials.
Access by loan, by hire.

Fees – Copyright

Fees for facilities and handling.
Pricelist and conditions for use available.

WALSALL

_____ 507
WALSALL LOCAL HISTORY CENTRE
Leisure Services
UK – ESSEX ST. WALSALL WS2
U.K.
Member of IASA.

Collections

Collections of Film, Video, Sound.

All collections unless otherwise stated relate to Walsall MBC. Oral history recordings : World War I, World War II, social conditions, transport. Video film b&w sound : civil & national events, local history. Gramophone : Frank Mullings, local tenor + misc. local artists.
Films 20 (dating 1936-1970's) (film + video)
Sound 500 oral history recordings dating 1970-1991, 40+ song

Access

Catalogue indexed on cards.

Access to catalogue: Only part of the oral history collection has been catalogued.

Access to materials: Listening copies available for catalogued recordings.
Access on archives premises, by purchase.

Fees – Copyright

A copyright fee will be levied at the discretion of the Local History Centre for use by profit making bodies.
Copyright holder is the institution.

WINCHESTER

_____ 508

WESSEX FILM AND SOUND ARCHIVE
20 Southgate Street
UK – WINCHESTER, HAMPSHIRE, SO23 9EF
U.K.

Tel.: 44-962-847742

Collections

Collections of Film, Video, Sound, photographs and written/printed documentation, ephemera, equipment of historical interest.

Cinefilms, sound and video recordings of local interest, to Hampshire and surrounding counties of England.
Films 1400 reels
Video 130 tapes
Sound 2000 tapes and discs

Access

Catalogue on database.

Access to catalogue.

Access to materials: limited copies only, presentations made off the premises also.
Access on archives premises, by loan, by purchase.

Fees – Copyright

Fees for research for reuse and production purposes, facilities and handling.
Pricelist and conditions for use available.
All copied items may be researched on archive premises, but only some items may be hired or purchased, due to copyright restrictions. Copyright holders and the owners of deposits in the archive must give permission before their material can be used commercially or non-commercially.

U.S.A

ALBUQUERQUE

_____ 509

UNIVERSITY OF NEW MEXICO GENERAL LIBRARY : FINE ARTS LIBRARY
JOHN DONALD ROBB ARCHIVE OF SOUTHWESTERN MUSIC
Fine Arts Center
ALBUQUERQUE, NM 87131-1501
USA

Tel.: 1-505-277-2357
Fax.: 1-505-277-6019
Electronic mail: BITNET: JWRIGHT@UNMB

Collections

Collections of Sound.

Audio tapes of indigenous music of the Southwest United States. Hispanic, Native American, cowboy, railroad songs and music. Collection consists of field recordings deposited by collectors.
Sound 1200 hours, 25000 titles

Access

Catalogue on database.

Access to catalogue on location and OCLC database.

Access to materials: Some restrictions on individual collections.
Access on archives premises.

Fees – Copyright

Fees for research by archive staff, facilities and handling.
Pricelist and conditions for use available.
Institution holds no copyright.
Conditions for access vary with collector.

ANN ARBOR

_____ 510

UNIVERSITY OF MICHIGAN
BENTLEY HISTORICAL LIBRARY
1150 Beal Ave
ANN ARBOR, MICHIGAN 48109-2113
USA

Tel.: 1-313-764-3482
Fax.: 1-313-936-1333

Collections

Collections of Sound, various manuscript records : transcripts, correspondence, sheet music, etc.

Predominantly spoken materials. Topics include : University of Michigan history, special seminars and conferences, etc. Various aspects of Michigan history : politics, social movements, social activism, civil rights, Sixties' radicalism, oral history.
Sound about 11000 items in various formats

Access
Catalogue on cards.

Acces to catalogue: limited. Approximately 25% of sound collection is indexed in card catalog which is open to the public. Reference staff available for further assistance.

Access to materials.
Access on archives premises.

Fees – Copyright
Fees to be determined.
Copyright holder is the institution.
In most cases the institution holds copyright and access is determined by regular copyright law. When donor retains copyright, researchers must request and receive written permission from the donor.

BERKELEY

_____ 511
PACIFIC FILM ARCHIVE
University Art Museum, 2625 Durant Ave
BERKELEY, CA 94720
USA

Tel.: 1-415-642-1412
Fax.: 1-415-642-4889
Telex: 9103667114 UC BERK BERK
Member of FIAF.

Collections
Collections of Film, Video, books, periodicals, clippings, press kits, still photographs, posters.

Areas of concentration in Japanese and Soviet cinema, international animation, and the American avant garde. The collection also includes an international selection of feature films and documentaries, and some historical footage of the San Francisco Bay Area.
Films 6000 titles
Video 100 titles

Access
Catalogue on database.

Acces to catalogue: limited on-site access to inventory cards, and to published volume cataloging 150 Japanese titles. Full on-line cataloging for the collection is not yet completed.

Access to materials: limited, all materials available for on-site study use only. Materials are not available for licensing or re-use.
Access on archives premises.

Fees – Copyright
Fees for research by archive staff, facilities and handling, University Art Museum membership includes discounts on research screenings. Institution holds no copyright.

_____ 512
UNIVERSITY OF CALIFORNIA, BERKELEY
MEDIA RESOURCES CENTER, MOFFITT LIBRARY
BERKELEY, California 94720
USA

Tel.: 1-415-643-8566, 1-415-642-8197
Fax.: 1-415-643-7891
Electronic mail: ghandman@library.berkeley.edu
Member of IFLA.

Collections
Collections of Video, Sound, laser disk ; computer-interactive laser disks.

A broad, interdisciplinary collection of materials supporting research and study on the UC Berkeley campus. Collection includes commercial and locally-produced documentary materials ; dramatic works ; literary adaptations ; interviews and speeches ; training films and related instructional material.
Video 4000 titles
Sound 2500 (audiocassette – largely spoken word)

Access
Catalogue on database.

Access to catalogue: Dial-up access available to the online catalog (via internet and other networks).

Access to materials: limited. Materials are intended largely for on-site use and for use in UCB classrooms. Interlibrary loan within UC system only.
Access on archives premises.

BETHESDA

_____ 513
NATIONAL LIBRARY OF MEDICINE, HISTORICAL AUDIOVISUALS COLLECTION
8600 Rockville Pike
BETHESDA, MARYLAND 20894
USA

Tel.: 1-301-496-8949
Fax.: 1-301-402-0872

Collections

Collections of Film, Video, scripts, reviews, stills, correspondence and production files, etc.

This repository of historical medical footage, ranging in date from 1910 to 1970, includes medical teaching films, documentation of experiments, health promotional films, and films depicting significant persons, events, facilities, equipment, and the evolution of film for medical purposes. Total collection includes approximately 4000 titles.
Films 1800000 feet
Video 520 hours

Access

Catalogue on database.

Access to catalogue: Online catalog contains full collection. Online access is available in many countries. Printed catalogue is a yearly cumulation of newly accepted items.

Access to materials: Materials are accessible through onsite viewing, loan, and sale (barring any copyright or other restrictions). However, materials are only available for loan in the United States. Access on archives premises, by loan, by purchase.

Fees – Copyright

No fees are levied ; however, we ask for credit at the end of the film, if a producer uses our footage in his production.
Pricelist and conditions for use available.
Institution holds no copyright.
In order to make a copy of our footage, we require that copyright permission be received or that the footage be in the public domain.

BEVERLY HILLS

_____ 514

ACADEMY OF MOTION PICTURE ARTS AND SCIENCES, ACADEMY FILM ARCHIVE
Center for Motion Picture Study, 333 SO. La Cienega Blvd.
Beverly Hills 90211
USA

Tel.: 1-213-247-3027
Fax.: 1-213-657-5193

Member of FIAF.

Collections

Collections of Film, Video, Sound, early cinema apparati ; also Academy Library (Margaret Herrick Library) contains vast holdings of original material on cinema.

US silent film, Academy Awards broadcasts, Méliès films, Blackhawk film collection, Academy war film collection.
Films 10000
Video 2000
Sound 200

Access

Catalogue on cards.

Access to catalogue: no.

Access to materials: limited by appointment.
Access on archives premises.

Fees – Copyright

Institution holds no copyright.

BLUE HILL FALLS

_____ 515

NORTHEAST HISTORIC FILM
Route 175
BLUE HILL FALLS, MAINE
USA

Tel.: 1-207-374-2736
Fax.: 1-207-374-2082

Collections

Collections of Film, Video.

Regional moving image collections for the northeastern United States : the states of Maine, New Hampshire and Vermont. Collections include two television stations' news, features, sports and commercials from 1953-1977, also home movies, industrial films and dramatic works. Rural life, domestic life, cold war US, forestry, agriculture.
Films 2 million feet
Video 1000 hours

Access

Catalogue on database.

Access to catalogue: 4000 records on line. Call or write for information.

Access to materials: Reference videotapes available for much of the collection where rights permit.
Access on archives premises, by loan, by purchase.

Fees – Copyright

Fees for research by archive staff, facilities and handling.
Pricelist and conditions for use available.
Copyright of some materials held by institution ; some collections reference rights only. Inquire for information.

BOSTON

516

NEW ENGLAND CONSERVATORY OF MUSIC
FIRESTONE AUDIO LIBRARY
290 Huntington Ave
BOSTON, MA 02115
USA

Tel.: 1-617-262-1120

Member of IASA.

Collections

Collections of Video, Sound.

Archives comprise Conservatory concerts and recitals since 1969.
Video 250 videocassettes
Sound 15500 LPs, 600 CDs, 4000 cassette tapes

Access

Access to catalogue: Older materials on cards, newer in database.

Access to materials: limited closed stacks – staff retrieval.

Access on archives premises.

517

SIMMONS COLLEGE, COLLEGE ARCHIVES
300 The Fenway
BOSTON, MASSACHUSETTS 02115
USA

Tel.: 1-617-738-3141
Fax.: 1-617-738-2099

Member of ICA, IFLA.

Collections

Collections of Film, Video, Sound.

Relating to special events at Simmons College.
Films 10 items
Video 100 items
Sound 60 items

Access

Catalogue on cards.

Acces to catalogue: limited.

Access to materials: limited.
Access on archives premises.

Fees – Copyright

Fees for research for reuse and production purposes.
Copyright holder is the institution.

BOWLING GREEN

518

BOWLING GREEN STATE UNIVERSITY, MUSIC LIBRARY AND SOUND RECORDINGS ARCHIVES
BOWLING GREEN, OHIO 43403-0179
USA

Tel.: 1-419-372-2307
Fax.: 1-419-372-7996

Member of IASA.

Collections

Collections of Sound, books, periodicals, sheet music, catalogues, pictures, posters, promotional material.

Popular music, jazz, country music, blues, comedy, poetry, prose, drama, speeches, sermons, radio shows, juvenile, folk, disco, rap, musicals, sound + rock music, cajun, zydeco, calypso, reggae, polkas, documentaries.
Sound over 550000 recordings

Access

Catalogue on database.

Access to catalogue.

Access to materials.
Access on archives premises.

Fees – Copyright

Fees for research for reuse and production purposes, research by archive staff.
Pricelist and conditions for use available.
Institution holds no copyright.

BROOKLYN

519

THE BROOKLYN MUSEUM
200 Eastern Parkway
BROOKLYN, NY 11238
USA

Tel.: 1-718-638-5000
Fax.: 1-718-638-3731
Electronic mail: bm.bml

Member of IFLA.

Collections

Collections of Film, Video.

Ethnographic films, documentaries on art, documentaries on Brooklyn Museum exhibitions/collections, interviews with artists, documentation of installation of shows, educational films, some "art" films and tapes, films and videos produced by The Brooklyn Museum.
Films about 200
Video about 450

Fees – Copyright

Copyright holder is the institution.

BUFFALO

_____ 520

STATE UNIVERSITY OF NEW YORK AT BUFFALO, MUSIC LIBRARY
Baird Hall
BUFFALO, NY
USA

Tel.: 1-716-636-2924
Fax.: 1-716-636-3824
Electronic mail: BM.SML@RLG.BITNET

Collections

Collections of Video, Sound.

Commercially-issued classical, jazz, popular, and world music recordings. The collection supports programs and courses offered by the University's Music Department. Also about 150 cassettes of faculty recitals and concerts in the archive of the CCPA. Videos : operas, jazz, world music.
Video 75 titles
Sound 26000 discs, cassettes and CDs ; unprocessed backlog of about 12000 items

Access

Catalogue on database.

Access to catalogue: There is a published catalog for "Evenings for New Music" concerts sponsored by the Center of the Creative and Performing Arts, 1964-1977.

Access to materials: limited. All must be used in the Library ; application for use of archival tapes must be made in writing one week in advance. Access on archives premises.

Fees – Copyright

Pricelist and conditions for use available.

BURBANK

_____ 521

THE WALT DISNEY COMPANY
WALT DISNEY ARCHIVES
500 S. Buena Vista St.
BURBANK, CALIFORNIA 91521
USA

Tel.: 1-818-560-5424

Member of ASIFA.

Collections

Collections of Video, Sound, related materials.

Everything Disney : production files, business records, products, etc.

Video 1750
Sound 2000 phonograph records, 800 audio tapes

Access

Access to catalogue: Many different catalogs and methods of access.

Access to materials: limited by appointment only. Access on archives premises.

Fees – Copyright

Copyright holder is the institution.

CAMBRIDGE

_____ 522

HARVARD UNIVERSITY, MUSIC LIBRARY
CAMBRIDGE, MA 02138
USA

Tel.: 1-617-495-2794

Member of IASA.

Collections

Collections of Video, Sound.

Research collection of Academic Music Library, with strengths in opera, jazz, ethnic folk music, historical performances.
Video 237
Sound 37835

Access

Catalogue on database.

Access to materials.
Access on archives premises.

CHICAGO

_____ 523

CHICAGO PUBLIC LIBRARY, SPECIAL COLLECTIONS – THE CHICAGO THEATER ARCHIVES
400 S, State Street
CHICAGO, IL. 60604
USA

Member of IFLA.

Collections

Collections of Video.

The Chicago Theater Archive includes videotapes of select Chicago productions and interviews with local playwrights. The tapes are a small part of an extensive theater archive which includes photos, scripts, programs, posters, audio tapes, and set drawings from a variety of Chicago theaters.
Video 63 videotapes

Access

Access to catalogue.

Access to materials: Some of the tapes have limited access because they are Equity (union) productions, but waivers are available.
Access on archives premises.

Fees – Copyright

Institution holds no copyright.

524

SCHOOL OF THE ART INSTITUTE OF CHICAGO
JOHN M. FLAXMAN LIBRARY
37 South Wabash
CHICAGO, ILLINOIS 60603
USA

Tel.: 1-312-899-5097

Member of IFLA.

Collections

Collections of Film, Video, Sound.

Films for the study of filmmaking. Videos for instructional and informational use. Audio cassettes, disks and CDs to support curriculum. Classical, jazz, ethnic, spoken word, sound, sound art, experimental.
Films 452 titles
Video 182 titles
Sound 2500 items

Access

Catalogue on cards.

Access to catalogue: Card catalogue in library.

Access to materials: Films for classroom use only. Video for in-house use. Audio materials circulate mostly not at all.
Access on archives premises, by loan.

Fees – Copyright

No fees.
Institution holds no copyright.
None of the materials can be legally copied.

DENTON

525

UNIVERSITY OF NORTH TEXAS MEDIA LIBRARY
111 Chilton Hall, Chestnut at Ave. C
P.O. Box 12898
DENTON, TEXAS 76203-2898
USA

Tel.: 1-817-565-2480
Fax.: 1-817-565-2599

Collections

Collections of Film, Video, Sound, laser discs (12"), filmstrips, slides.

From all disciplines, a large collection of films, videos, and slides comprise the Gerontological Film & Video Collection. Own many opera videorecordings. Cataloging done on OCLC, in-house PC-based booking system in use.
Films 1451 titles, 2004 film prints
Video 1493 titles, 2331 video copies (this includes VHS and U-Matic), 55 laser videodiscs
Sound 1150 phonodiscs (vinyl LPs), 1101 phonotapes (audiocassettes & a few reel-to-reel)

Access

Catalogue on database.

Acces to catalogue: Card catalogue available in the Media Library ; media holdings in VTLS database for the entire libraries. Records tagged onto in the OCLC database.

Access to materials: Closed stack library. Items are available for viewing/consultation in the Media Library. Rental requests processed on a case-by-case basis.
Access on archives premises, by loan.

Fees – Copyright

Fees for rental.
Pricelist and conditions for use available.
Institution holds no copyright.

EVANSTON

526

NORTHWESTERN UNIVERSITY LIBRARY
MITCHELL MEDIA CENTER
1935 Sheridan Road
EVANSTON, IL 60208
USA

Tel.: 1-708-491-7678
Fax.: 1-708-491-8306

Member of IFLA.

Collections

Collections of Video.

Collection devoted to documentary films in the social sciences and humanities ; performing arts (drama, dance, opera) ; and feature films (silent films to current releases).
Video 4000 NTSC format 1/2" VHS videotapes ; 200 laser discs

Access

Catalogue on database.

Access to catalogue: All holdings are represented in LUIS, the Library's on-line card catalog.

Access to materials: limited to this non-circulating collection limited to Northwestern University Faculty, staff and students.
Access on archives premises.

Fees – Copyright

Institution holds no copyright.
Northwestern University Library follows all current United States copyright laws regarding the duplication of videotapes.

IOWA

___ 527
UNIVERSITY OF IOWA LIBRARIES, SPECIAL COLLECTIONS DEPARTMENT
ARTISTS' TELEVISION PROJECT
IOWA CITY, IA 52242
USA

Tel.: 1-319-335-5921
Fax.: 1-319-335-5830

Collections

Collections of Video.

Collection consists of original video works produced by individual artists in conjunction with the Artists' Television Network (ATN) of New York during the mid-1970s through the mid-1980s.
Video about 420 titles in 3/4" U-Matic videotape cassettes ; some also on VHS

Access

Access to catalogue: Only inventory list.
Access to materials: limited.
Access on archives premises.

Fees – Copyright

Institution holds no copyright.
Interested persons would need to contact the original artist.

JAMAICA

___ 528
QUEENS BOROUGH PUBLIC LIBRARY
89-11 Merrick Blvd.
JAMAICA, N.Y. 11432
USA

Tel.: 1-718-990-0830
Fax.: 1-718-291-8936

Collections

Collections of Film, Video.

16mm films on a variety of subjects available to organized non-profit groups. Videocassettes available for borrowing.
Films 3200 titles
Video 8000 titles

Access

Catalogue on database.
Access to catalogue.
Access to materials: limited.
Access by loan.

Fees – Copyright

Fees for overdue loans.
Institution holds no copyright.

LEWISTON

___ 529
BATES COLLEGE, THE EDMUND S. MUSKIE ARCHIVES
LEWISTON, MAINE 04240
USA

Tel.: 1-207-786-6354
Fax.: 1-207-786-6123

Collections

Collections of Film, Video, Sound.

Collection documenting Muskie's political career and the political history of Maine and the United States from 1954 to 1980. Recordings contain interviews, campaign spots, speeches and other public appearances.
Films 185 reels, ranging from 1 to 30 minutes
Video 69 tapes
Sound 600 cassettes, 400 reel to reel recordings

Access

Catalogue on database.
Access to catalogue: Finding aid for sound has not been completed.
Access to materials: Film and videotape have been duplicated on videotape for reference use.
Access on archives premises.

Fees – Copyright

Access is open and free. Small fee for reproduction.
Copyright holder is the institution.
Material is available for research and copying, provided that Archives is cited as source.

LONG BEACH

___ 530
CALIFORNIA STATE UNIVERSITY, LONG BEACH
1250 Bellflower Blvd
LONG BEACH, CA 90840-1901
USA

Tel.: 1-301-985-4047
Fax.: 1-301-985-1703

Member of IFLA.

Collections

Collections of Film, Video, Sound.

Phonodiscs, audiocassettes, video cassettes, video discs, 16mm films, and compact audio discs containing music, spoken, and instructional material suitable for support of university-level curricular programs.
Films 1053
Video 6586
Sound 17144

Access

Catalogue on database.

Access to catalogue: Dial-up access : 1-301-985-1691. Internet access : COAST.lib.csulb.edu (VT100 emulation).

Access to materials only to library card holders in-house ; items loaned to other libraries through inter-library loan.

Fees – Copyright

Institution holds no copyright.

LOS ANGELES

___ 531

NATIONAL CENTER FOR FILM AND VIDEO PRESERVATION AT THE AMERICAN FILM INSTITUTE
2021 North Western Avenue
P.O. Box 27999
LOS ANGELES, CALIFORNIA 90027
USA

Tel.: 1-213-856-7637
Fax.: 1-213-467-4578

Member of FIAF, IFTA, IAMHIST.

Collections

Collections of Film, Video, books, photographs, scripts (both film and television), posters, special collections, periodicals.

The American Film Institute (AFI) Collection includes over 21000 titles and consists primarily of theatrical features and shorts (1894-present), as well as a substantial number of newsreels, documentaries, and television programs. The AFI Collection is housed by the Library of Congress and a number of other archives in the U.S. All types of film and videotape elements are included in the AFI Collection. Most films originally received on nitrate stock. In many cases, viewing copies are not yet available.

Access

Catalogue on database.

Acces to catalogue: The NCFVP at AFI is not a custodial archive. While information on the AFI Collection may be obtained directly from the Center, information regarding access should be obtained from the Library of Congress and other appropriate archives.

Access to materials: limited.

Fees – Copyright

Institution holds no copyright.
Some material in the public domain. Rights generally retained by original source or producer. Users must assume full responsibility for copyright search and/or securing any necessary clearances or authorizations required for reuse of the material. Contact the appropriate archive holding materials in the AFI Collection for information about licensing, research, handling and duplication fees and services.

___ 532

UNIVERSITY OF CALIFORNIA LOS ANGELES GRADUATE SCHOOL OF LIBRARY, INFORMATION SCIENCE
GSLIS Lab
300 Circle Dr. North, 405 Hilgard Ave
LOS ANGELES 90024
USA

Tel.: 1-213-206-9263

Member of IFLA.

Collections

Collections of Film, Video, Sound.

Audiovisual material collected to support instruction in library and information science.
Films 79 various formats
Video 11 VHS
Sound 99 cassettes

Access

Catalogue on cards.

Acces to catalogue: limited to students, faculty and staff of UCLA/GSLIS only.

Access to materials: limited to students, faculty and staff of UCLA/GSLIS only.
Access on archives premises.

MADISON

___ 533

WISCONSIN CENTER FOR FILM AND THEATER RESEARCH
WCFTR FILM & PHOTO ARCHIVE
816 State Street
MADISON, WISCONSIN 53706
USA

Tel.: 1-608-264-6466
Fax.: 1-608-264-6404
Electronic mail: mefducey@vms.macc.wisc.edu

Member of FIAF.

Collections

Collections of Film, Video, 2 million film, tv & theatre still photographs ; over 300 manuscripts collections with scripts, production, distribution and financial files & personal correspondence.

A collection documenting 20th century performing arts in America, in particular the history of cinema and television in the USA. Hollywood films of 1930's and 40's, Broadway theatre of the 40's and 50's and American television from the 1950's to the early 1980's are well represented.

Access

Catalogue on database.

Acces to catalogue: On-site access to card catalogue and to feature films database (limited database). No off-site catalogue available at this time.

Access to materials: Catalogued materials available for on-site research by qualified scholars with appointments.
Access on archives premises.

Fees – Copyright

Fees for research by archive staff.
Institution holds no copyright.
WCFTR does not hold rights to any films in its collections. Copyright clearance must be secured from appropriate source before anything other than on-site scholarly research is permitted.

MURFREESBORO

_____ 534

CENTER FOR POPULAR MUSIC
Middle Tennessee State University
P.O. Box 41
MURFREESBORO, TN 37132
USA

Tel.: 1-615-898-2449
Fax.: 1-615-898-2530

Collections

Collections of Video, Sound, monographs, serials, sheet music, vertical files, manuscript collections, photographs, posters, ephemera.

Collection represents diversity of American popular music synchronically & diachronically ; focuses on rock & roll and vernacular religious music in depth; recognizes the importance of regional, ethnic & other vernacular traditions in shaping American popular music ; and pays special attention to the contributions of the Southeast in general & Tennessee in particular, to the history of American popular music.
Video 598
Sound 55569

Access

Catalogue on database.

Access to catalogue.

Access to materials: Sound recording and video tapes are available only for those engaged in research leading to a public product.
Access on archives premises.

Fees – Copyright

Fees for research by archive staff, facilities and handling.
Pricelist and conditions for use available.
Institution holds no copyright.
Subject to standard U.S. copyright restrictions.

NASHVILLE

_____ 535

VANDERBILT TELEVISION NEWS ARCHIVE
110 21st Avenue South, Suite 704
NASHVILLE, TN 37203
USA

Tel.: 1-615-322-2927
Fax.: 1-615-343-8250

Member of ICA.

Collections

Collections of Video.

Collection includes ABC, CBS and NBC evening news broadcasts, special reports and selected news programs from August 5, 1968 to present ; PBS special reports and selected news programs from August 5, 1968 to present ; and CNN PrimeNews, special reports and selected news programs from January 1989 to present.
Video over 21000 evening news programs and over 7000 hours of special broadcasts

Access

Catalogue published.

Access to catalogue: Our publication, Television News Index & Abstracts, is published monthly. We also have in-house lists of pre-1989 special broadcasts and of programs too recent for latest publication.

Access to materials: We loan duplications of programs and make custom compilations of individual news items from many evening news broadcasts.
Access on archives premises, by loan.

Fees – Copyright

Fees for loan services to help defray operating expenses. Subsidized discount given to academic clients and to US government and US state/city government agencies.
Pricelist and conditions for use available.
Institution holds no copyright.
The Vanderbilt Television News Archive operates under the fair use clause of Public Law 94-553. Borrowers are responsible for abiding by that law and when necessary for obtaining permission from the copyright holder(s).

536

VANDERBILT UNIVERSITY LIBRARY, SPECIAL COLLECTIONS

419 21st Avenue South
NASHVILLE, TN 37240-0007
USA

Tel.: 1-615-322-2807

Collections

Collections of Film, Video, Sound.

Film and video : Vanderbilt University Football and Basketball Games. Film and video : Vanderbilt University Special Events and Promotional Programs. Sound – Radio Transcripts, Francis Robinson Collection (Metropolitan Opera, New York), Cole Lecture Series (Divinity School).
Films 1200 reels
Video 200 reels
Sound 500 phonograph records, 150 cassette tapes

Access

Catalogue on database.

Acces to catalogue: Francis Robinson Collection has catalog ; Football and Basketball films are on database ; Cole Lecture Series is on database ; other collections are not indexed.

Access to materials: Vanderbilt University Special Events and Promotional Programs and Radio Transcripts have limited access.
Access on archives premises.

Fees – Copyright

Fees for research by archive staff, Reproduction.
Pricelist and conditions for use available.
Copyright holder is the institution.

NEW HAVEN

537

YALE UNIVERSITY – THE FORTUNOFF VIDEO ARCHIVE OF HOLOCAUST TESTIMONIES

Sterling Memorial Library, Room 331 C
NEW HAVEN, CONNECTICUT
USA

Tel.: 1-203-432-1879

Collections

Collections of Video.

Testimonies of jewish survivers of concentration camps and ghettos during the Nazi period.
Video 2300

Access

Catalogue on database.

Access to catalogue.

Access to materials: limited for research only.
Access on archives premises.

Fees – Copyright

Copyright partly with the institution, the interviewe and the interviewer.

NEW YORK

538

ANTHOLOGY FILM ARCHIVES

32-34 Second Avenue
10003 NEW YORK, NY
USA

Tel.: 1-212-505-5181
Fax.: 1-212-477-2714

Member of FIAF.

Collections

Collections of Film, Video, Sound, reference library with 5000 books, 20000 periodicals, 3000 stills, clippings and manuscripts.

Anthology's film collection concentrates on the personal/avant-garde film and video production. US avant-garde collection, with choice international films. Our "Essential Cinema" collection covers samples of film art, from Lumiere to Kubelka.
Films 7000 cans (prints and printing material) for over 4000 titles, mostly 16mm
Video 2000 videotapes, in diverse formats : one-inch, 3/4-inch, half-inch, etc.
Sound 250 audio tapes, preserving lectures and interviews with filmmakers

Access

Catalogue on cards.

Acces to catalogue: At the moment, the catalogue records are being upgraded into a computer database. Until we reach our goal of a printed catalogue, access is restricted to staff.

Access to materials: Due to lack of proper 35mm viewing equipment, our 35mm collection is limited to projection.
Access on archives premises, by purchase.

Fees – Copyright

Fees for research for reuse and production purposes, research by archive staff, facilities and handling.
While we hold rights to most of the collection, some items are restricted by their depositor/owners. We refer people to the rights owners in those cases.

539

THE METROPOLITAN MUSEUM OF ART, FILM AND VIDEO ARCHIVE : EDUCATION DEPARTMENT
1000 Fifth Avenue
NEW YORK, NY
USA

Tel.: 1-212-879-5500 x2090
Fax.: 1-212-879-3879

Collections

Collections of Film, Video.

The Metropolitan Museum of Art's film and video archive numbers over 1300 titles which date back to 1898. The Archive reflects the encyclopedic nature of the Metropolitan's collections and documents the visual arts historically, culturally and aesthetically.
Films 875
Video 500

Access

Catalogue on database.

Access to catalogue by request. Also available through the Program for Art on Film, a joint venture of the Metropolitan Museum of Art and The Getty Museum.

Access to materials: Materials may be viewed by individual scholars, educators and film and video professionals by appointment only.
Access on archives premises.

Fees – Copyright

Institution holds no copyright.

540

MUSEUM OF JEWISH HERITAGE
342 Madison Ave, Suite 706
NEW YORK, NY 10173
USA

Tel.: 1-212-687-9141
Fax.: 1-212-573-9847
Member of IFTA.

Collections

Collections of Film, Video, Sound.

A small but growing collection of films relating to Jewish life in Europe & North Africa before World War II, the Holocaust and its aftermath, and Jewish life in the USA from colonial times to the present. Also oral and video testimonies of survivors, rescuers & liberators.
Films 37 reels of film. 17 are unique material
Video 230 testimonies
Sound 3030 testimonies from the Center for Holocaust Studies Collection

Access

Catalogue on database.

Acces to catalogue: All material is in the process of being catalogued on computer.

Access to materials: Call for information.
Access on archives premises.

Fees – Copyright

Fees: Call for information.
Copyright holder is the institution.
Access taken on a case by case basis. Call for information.

541

THE MUSEUM OF MODERN ART, DEPARTMENT OF FILM
11 West 53rd Street
NEW YORK, NY 10019
USA

Tel.: 1-212-708-9613 (viewing), 1-212-708-9605 (loans, other access)
Fax.: 1-212-708-9531
Telex: 62370 Modart NYK

Member of FIAF.

Collections

Collections of Film, Video, still photographs, set designs, posters, periodicals, books, scripts, press cuttings, music, slides, production and corporate records, etc.

The collection is international, from beginnings of cinema and video to present, film and video are collected as an art form and as important to history of the media, but in general excluding newsreels and television. It is not a stock shot library.

Films 11000 titles
Video 1000 titles

Access

Catalogue on database.

Acces to catalogue: A limited catalog published in 1986 and a limited card catalog are available for consultation and staff will research requests for information within its time limits ; there are no subject listings.

Access to materials: Prints that are protected by preservation materials are accessible for viewing for advanced research purposes and, with owner's permission, for loan to nonprofit institutions.
Access on archives premises, by loan.

Fees – Copyright

Fees for research for reuse and production purposes, research by archive staff, facilities and handling, viewing, loan fees.
Pricelist and conditions for use available.
Institution holds no copyright.
No copyright permission needed to view prints on premises. Copyright owner and sometimes also the donor must give permission in writing for loans, or any copying. Archive will give guidance as to necessary permissions. The archive's preservation work has priority over outside lab orders.

_____ 542

NBC NEWS
NBC NEWS ARCHIVES
30 Rockefeller Plaza, Room 902
NEW YORK, NY 10112
USA

Tel.: 1-212-664-3797
Fax.: 1-212-957-8917

Member of IFTA.

Collections

Collections of Film, Video, transcripts of news broadcasts.

Film and video holdings of generic stock shots, worldwide news events and documentaries from the mid-1940's to present. Limited footage of events prior to that time.
Films 100000000 feet
Video 500000 cassettes (including 1" and 2")

Access

Catalogue on database.

Acces to catalogue: limited.

Access to materials: limited.
Access on archives premises, by hire, by purchase.

Fees – Copyright

Fees for research by archive staff, facilities and handling.
Pricelist and conditions for use available.
Copyright holder is the institution.

_____ 543

THE NEW YORK PUBLIC LIBRARY
THE THEATRE ON FILM AND TAPE ARCHIVE (TOFT)
40 Lincoln Center Plaza
NEW YORK, NY 10023-7498
USA

Tel.: 1-212-870-1641
Fax.: 1-212-787-3852

Collections

Collections of Film, Video.

Collection of films and videotapes of : live performances of Broadway, off-Broadway and regional theatre productions ; dialogues with distinguished theatre personalities ; and theatre-related films and television programs.
Films 1821 titles (film + video)

Access

Catalogue on cards.

Access to catalogue for viewing on premises. List of holdings available for a fee.

Access to materials: For viewing on premises by qualified students, theatre professionals and researchers. No loan, no copies can be made.
Access on archives premises.

Fees – Copyright

Fees for purchase of list of holdings.
Copyright holder is the institution.

_____ 544

NEW YORK PUBLIC LIBRARY
RODGERS & HAMMERSTEIN ARCHIVES OF RECORDED SOUND
40 Lincoln Center Plaza
NEW YORK, NY 10023-7498
USA

Tel.: 1-212-870-1663
Fax.: 1-212-787-3852

Member of IASA.

Collections

Collections of Video, Sound.

General recording collection in all known formats from cylinder to compact disc. Subject matter includes all types of music, spoken word, broadcast, etc. Many special collections of unpublished, non-commercial recordings.
Video 1500 items
Sound 480000 items

Access

Catalogue on database.

Access to catalogue: For listening on premises : open to public. No loan. Tape copies can be made of out-of-print, published recordings.

Access to materials.
Access on archives premises.

Fees – Copyright

Fees for tape copies of out-of-print recordings. Institution holds no copyright.

_____ 545

THE NEW YORK PUBLIC LIBRARY, DANCE COLLECTION
40 Lincoln Center Plaza
NEW YORK, NY 10023
USA

Tel.: 1-212-870-1657
Fax.: 1-212-799-7975

Collections

Collections of Film, Video, Sound, bibliographies, reviews, press kits.

The Dance Collection includes all types of material relating to dance : books, periodicals, programs, photographs, prints, original designs, scrapbooks, notation scores, clippings files, as well as film/video and oral history.
Films 2454 titles
Video 6053 titles
Sound 4650 hours

Access

Catalogue on database.

Access to catalogue.

Access to materials: A few audio and visual materials have restrictions of prior permission by the author or producing organization.
Access on archives premises.

_____ 546

NEW YORK UNIVERSITY AVERY FISHER CENTER FOR MUSIC AND MEDIA
70 Washington Square South
NEW YORK, NY 10012
USA

Tel.: 1-212-998-2580
Fax.: 1-212-995-4070

Collections

Collections of Video, Sound.

Video collection emphases : performing arts, film and TV, video art, journalism and mass media.
Music emphases : Verdi archive, collection of musical theatre.

Video 3000
Sound 30000

Access

Catalogue on database.

Access to catalogue.

Access to materials: limited. Special permission required. Collections are for the most part restricted to use by NYU.
Access on archives premises.

Fees – Copyright

Institution holds no copyright.

_____ 547

SHERMAN GRINBERG FILM LIBRARIES, INC.
630 Ninth Avenue
NEW YORK CITY, NY. 10036
USA

Tel.: 1-212-765-5170
Fax.: 1-212-262-1532

Collections

Collections of Film, Video.

Stock footage library specializing in news. Spans years 1900 to present. Stock footage from Hollywood Studios, MGM and 20th Century Fox. Many small collections.
Films 100 million feet
Video 1 million video cassettes

Access

Catalogue on database.

Access to catalogue: no.

Access to materials.
Access on archives premises.

Fees – Copyright

Fees for research for reuse and production purposes, research by archive staff, facilities and handling.
Pricelist and conditions for use available.
Copyright holder is the institution.
Access by license contract for one specific purpose (title) in perpetuity. Cannot be reused with payment to Grinberg. License fees predicated by use i.e. markets as TV, theatrical, educational, etc.

_____ 548

UNITED NATIONS HQ
UN VISUAL MATERIALS LIBRARY
UN Plaza Room S-805/N
NEW YORK, NY 10017
USA

Tel.: 1-212-963-7318, 1-212-963-7319
Fax.: 1-212-963-0765

Collections

Collections of Film, Video, Sound.

Archives of the UN Activities since 1945. Production out-takes since 1945.
Films about 50000 cans
Video about 25000 hours

Access

Catalogue indexed on cards.

Access to catalogue.

Access to materials.
Access on archives premises.

Fees – Copyright

Fees for facilities and handling, royalties.
Pricelist and conditions for use available.
Copyright holder is the institution.
Any footage incorporated into a production is subject to Library Royalties.

549

UPITN
1915 Broadway
NEW YORK, NY
USA

Tel.: 1-212-362-4440
Fax.: 1-212-496-1269

Collections

Collections of Film, Video.

Collection is composed of news footage shot by WTN (formerly UPITN) cameramen. It is primarily international after 1977 in content. Before 1963-77 we also shot news widely in the USA.
Films 100000 items
Video 30000

Access

Catalogue on database.

Access to catalogue.

Access to materials.
Access on archives premises.

Fees – Copyright

Fees for research for reuse and production purposes, research by archive staff, facilities and handling.
Pricelist and conditions for use available.
Copyright holder is the institution.

PITTSBURGH

550

UNIVERSITY OF PITTSBURGH, SCHOOL OF LIBRARY AND INFORMATION SCIENCE LIBRARY
MISTER ROGERS NEIGHBORHOOD ARCHIVES
135 North Bellefield Ave, Room 312, University of Pittsburgh, SLIS Library
ENR PENNSYLVANIA
USA

Tel.: 1-412-624-4710
Fax.: 1-412-624-4062
Electronic mail: ETM@V

Member of IFLA.

Collections

Collections of Video, scripts, production notes, clippings + puppets.

800 programs produced for a children's television (public) program. Production tapes for 30 years of a show called "Mister Rogers Neighborhood" shown on National Public Television.
Video 420 tapes

Access

Catalogue on database.

Access to catalogue: Available through the University OPAC "PITTCAT" through 1985. 1985to date available via manual search on cards.

Access to materials: limited in room use of materials.
Access on archives premises.

Fees – Copyright

Institution holds no copyright.
For educational purposes only Family Communications, Inc. grants final priviledge for "Mister Rogers Neighborhood" show.

PULLMAN

551

WASHINGTON STATE UNIVERSITY
WSU INSTRUCTIONAL MEDIA SERVICES
HISTORICAL MEDIA COLLECTIONS
Holland Library
PULLMAN, WASH. 99164-5602
USA

Tel.: 1-509-335-7587
Fax.: 1-509-335-4392
Electronic mail: Bitnet + Internet SEMINGSOaW-SUVM1@.WSU.EDU

Member of IFLA.

Collections

Collections of Film, Video, Sound.

Historical collections of media materials used for educational purposes and general interest.
Films 3500
Video 300
Sound 4500

Access

Catalogue on database.

Access to catalogue: Film/Video catalogs and special lists available (some for fee, inquire).

Access to materials: Some materials may carry access restrictions, inquire.
Access on archives premises, by loan, by hire.

Fees – Copyright

Fees for research for reuse and production purposes, facilities and handling.
Pricelist and conditions for use available.
Institution holds no copyright.
User must guarantee that item will not be copied without permission from copyright holder.

ROCHESTER

_____ 552
EASTMAN SCHOOL OF MUSIC
EASTMAN AUDIO ARCHIVE (DEPARTMENT OF RECORDING ARTS & SERVICES)
24 Gibbs Street
ROCHESTER, NY 14604
USA

Tel.: 1-716-274-1130
Fax.: 1-716-263-2807

Collections

Collections of Sound.

Live recordings made at the Eastman School of Music 1933-present. Features recordings of the works and performances of Howard Hanson and other major American composers.
Sound 21000 tapes, 6700 instantaneous disks

Access

Catalogue on database.

Access to catalogue.

Listening sessions scheduled by appointments only.
Access on archives premises.

Fees – Copyright

Copyright holder is the institution.

_____ 553
INTERNATIONAL MUSEUM OF PHOTOGRAPHY AT GEORGE EASTMAN HOUSE
900 East Ave
ROCHESTER, NY 14607
USA

Tel.: 1-716-271-3361
Fax.: 1-716-271-3970

Member of FIAF, IAMHIST.

Collections

Collections of Film, Video, film stills (3 million), posters (10000), star portraits, industry documents.

Film collections are rich in American, French and German silents, as well as American studio films from 1930s to 1950s : MGM, DeMille. Focus on American independent documentary from 1960s.
Films 14000 titles
Video 500 titles

Access

Catalogue on database.

Acces to catalogue: limited.

Access to materials: limited, depending on preservation status.
Access on archives premises, by loan, by purchase.

Fees – Copyright

Fees for research for reuse and production purposes, facilities and handling.
Pricelist and conditions for use available.
Institution holds no copyright.

SANTA BARBARA

_____ 554
UNIVERSITY OF CALIFORNIA, SANTA BARBARA, ARTS LIBRARY
ARCHIVE OF RECORDED VOCAL MUSIC
SANTA BARBARA, CALIFORNIA 93106
USA

Tel.: 1-805-893-2641
Fax.: 1-805-893-4676
Electronic mail: LB10SILV@UCSBUXA.bitnet

Member of IASA, IFLA, IAML.

Collections

Collections of Sound.

Collection devoted to Lieder and Opera. Representative collection of major singers. Includes the Anthony Boucher Collection.
Sound 29405

Access

Acces to catalogue: limited, about 5000 items cataloged on in house catalog.

Access to materials: limited by appointment – subject to tape copying.
Access on archives premises.

Fees – Copyright

Fees for research for reuse and production purposes, facilities and handling.
Copyright holder is the institution.

ST. LOUIS

_____ 555
WASHINGTON UNIVERSITY, LIBRARIES, UNIVERSITY ARCHIVES
One Brookings Drive
Campus Box 1061
ST. LOUIS, MISSOURI
USA

Tel.: 1-314-935-5444
Fax.: 1-314-935-4719

Collections

Collections of Sound.

Official records of Washington University ; manuscript collections related to 20th century St. Louis history, primarily political, social welfare, business, and transportation history. Record Group UA 4 : Series 1. Washington University Public Affairs Office, Recordings of Assembly Series Lectures and University Events, 1949- (ongoing).
Sound about 800 items (audiotape)

Access

Catalogue on database.
Staff will search the database for patrons.
Access to materials.
Access on archives premises.

Fees – Copyright

Institution holds no copyright.
Recordings may not be quoted in a publication or re-broadcast without permission of the speaker and of the University Archivist.

STANFORD

_____ 556
STANFORD UNIVERSITY, MEDIA CENTER
MEYER LIBRARY
STANFORD, CA 94305-3093
USA

Member of IFLA.

Collections

Collections of Film, Video.

Materials representing Latino culture, history and politics. Dance performances and interviews with Hanya Holmes and her contemporaries.
Films 20
Video 300

Access

Catalogue on database.
Access to catalogue.
Access to materials: limited.
Access on archives premises.

Fees – Copyright

No fees.
Institution holds no copyright.

STORRS

_____ 557
UNIVERSITY OF CONNECTICUT, HOMER BABBIDGE LIBRARY
CHARLES E. CULPEPER LIBRARY
369 Fairfield Road
P.O. Box U-5AV
STORRS, CONNECTICUT 06268
USA

Tel.: 1-203-486-2375
Fax.: 1-203-486-3593

Member of IFLA.

Collections

Collections of Video, Sound, related print documentation.

Video : PBS and BBC programming, Shakespeare's plays, locally (university) produced programs ; broad range of other topics. Audio : writers reading their own and others' works ; poetry, plays, short stories, criticism, lectures ; National Women's Studies Association lectures.
Video 2500 video cassette titles
Sound 2000 audio cassette titles

Access

Catalogue on database.
Acces to catalogue: limited within Babbidge Library.
Access to materials: limited, available to University students and staff, and to community borrowers on fee basis. Video only on archive premises accessible.
Access on archives premises, by loan.

Fees – Copyright

Fees for community (non-University) borrowers.
Institution holds no copyright.

SYRACUSE

558
SYRACUSE UNIVERSITY, BELFER AUDIO LABORATORY AND ARCHIVE
222 Waverly Avenue
SYRACUSE, NEW YORK 13244-2010
USA

Tel.: 1-315-443-3477
Fax.: 1-315-443-9510

Member of IASA.

Collections

Collections of Sound, record catalogs, record discographies, historical and technological materials.

Sound recordings in all formats, both commercial and one-of-a-kind – Discs, cylinders, tape, wire. Classical and popular music, broadcasts and sound tracks, test pressings, spoken word.
Sound about 300000 total items

Access

Catalogue on database.

Acces to catalogue: limited. Cylinders, acetate discs and 78 rpm discs are accessible through microfilm and computer listings.

Access to materials: limited. Cassette copies are provided for researchers who have copyright permissions.
Access on archives premises, by hire.

Fees – Copyright

Fees for research for reuse and production purposes.
Pricelist and conditions for use available.
Institution holds no copyright.
Tapes which are made for use outside the institution must have copyright clearance in advance in writing, this is the responsibility of the researcher.

WALTHAM

559
NATIONAL CENTER FOR JEWISH FILM
Lown 102 Brandeis University
WALTHAM, MA 02254-9110
USA

Tel.: 1-617-8997044
Fax.: 1-617-7362070

Collections

Collections of Film, stills, scripts, posters, etc.

Jewish content film materials, collection of Yiddish language features, documentary footage of Jews around the world.

Films about 1000 cans
Video about 300 for research – about 100 for sale to home

Access

Catalogue on cards.

Access to catalogue by appointment.

Access to materials: 16mm & 35mm screening by appointment.
Access on archives premises, by hire.

Fees – Copyright

Fees for research for reuse and production purposes, research by archive staff, facilities and handling.
Pricelist and conditions for use available.
Copyright holder is the institution.

WASHINGTON

560
GALLAUDET UNIVERSITY ARCHIVES
800 Florida Ave, N.E.
WASHINGTON, DC 20002
USA

Tel.: 1-202-651-5209
Fax.: 1-202-651-5213

Member of IFLA.

Collections

Collections of Film, Video.

George W. Veditz Film Collection is dedicated to the preservation of visual materials which relate to the history of Deaf people in America and Deaf culture with a primary emphasis on native language of the deaf-American Sign Language. Collection includes film excerpts from reunions, addresses, sports events, dramas, and commencement exercis.

Access

Catalogue on cards.

Access to catalogue.

Access to materials: limited.
Access on archives premises.

Fees – Copyright

Fees for research for reuse and production purposes, facilities and handling.

561
HUMAN STUDIES FILM ARCHIVES
NHB E307 Smithsonian Institution
WASHINGTON, DC 20560
USA

Tel.: 1-202-357-3349
Fax.: 1-202-357-2208

Member of FIAF.

Collections

Collections of Film, Video, Sound, manuscripts, dissertations, field notes, field diaries, shooting logs, etc.

Anthropological film and video documenting traditional peoples and cultures worldwide. Holdings range from 1908 through 1991 and include edited and unedited, black and white and color, silent and sound, historic and contemporary materials.
Films about 5 million feet of original 16mm film
Video about 150 hours of original video
Sound all sound materials associated with moving image collections

Access

Catalogue on database.

Access to catalogue.

Access to materials: As long as there are reference copies.
Access on archives premises.

Fees – Copyright

Fees for duplication of materials in the collections.
Pricelist and conditions for use available.
Copyright on case by base basis. HSFA holds copy right for some materials. Filmmaker, company, or family holds rights for other materials.

562

LIBRARY OF CONGRESS – MOTION PICTURE, BROADCASTING & RECORDED SOUND DIVISION
10 First Street, S.E.
WASHINGTON, DC
USA

Tel.: 1-202-707-5840
Fax.: 1-202-707-2371

Member of FIAF, IFTA, IASA, IAMHIST.

Collections

Collections of Film, Video, Sound, books, posters, scripts, lobby cards, and other materials related to the field. Also stills.

Collections are general and cover all subjects. Particular strengths include : American feature films, early cinema, entertainment television and television news and documentaries, radio and classical music.
Films 410283 items
Video 533723 items
Sound 2105515 items

Access

Catalogue on database.

Access to catalogue.

Access to materials: Viewing of moving image materials is limited to individuals performing scholarly research ; loan generally limited to other archives. Copying for purchase only permitted with written permission from copyright claimant.
Access on archives premises, by loan, by purchase.

Fees – Copyright

Fees for copying only.
Pricelist and conditions for use available.
Institution holds no copyright.
Viewing and auditing permitted ; copying permitted only with written permission from copyright claimant. For sound recording sales only.

563

NATIONAL ARCHIVES AND RECORDS ADMINISTRATION – MOTION PICTURE, SOUND AND VIDEO BRANCH
WASHINGTON, DC 20408
USA

Tel.: 1-202-501-5446
Fax.: 1-202-501-5778

Member of FIAF, ICA.

Collections

Collections of Film, Video, Sound, card catalogs and selected production files.

The permanently valuable audiovisual records of the U.S. Government dating from the 1890s to the present era together with donated newsfilm, newsreels, documentaries and broadcast materials relating to news and public affairs. These are unique copies. There are also 2 or 3 copies of each item for preservation and access needs.
Films 150000 reels
Video 40000 reels + cassettes
Sound 160000 sound recordings

Access

Catalogue on database.

Access to catalogue: Selected portions are published. Access provided to all requestors.

Access to materials: Access provided to all requestors and copies of unrestricted items may be purchased.
Access on archives premises, by purchase.

Fees – Copyright

Fees for photocopies of catalog cards and for the sale of audiovisual copies.
Pricelist and conditions for use available.
There are no restrictions governing access on premises. Materials of U.S. Government origin may be copied and sold without restriction ; the US Government does not copyright its materials. Donated materials from the private sector may require written permission for reproduction and sale.

URUGUAY

MONTEVIDEO

_____ 564
ARCHIVO NACIONAL DE LA IMAGEN – SODRE
Sarandi 430 1° piso
Casilla de Correo 1412
MONTEVIDEO 11000
URUGUAY

Tel.: 598-2-955493
Fax.: 598-2-963240
Telex: Telex UY 6553

Member of FIAF.

Collections
Collections of Film, Video, photo, documentation.

International and national collection of film and videos in different formats.
Films 1200
Video 800

Access
Catalogue published, on cards.

Access to catalogue.

Access to materials.
Access on archives premises, by loan.

Fees – Copyright
No fees.
Pricelist and conditions for use available.
Copyrightholder is partially the institution.

_____ 565
CINEMATECA URUGUAYA
Lorenzo Carnelli 1311
P.O. Box 1170, MONTEVIDEO
11200 MONTEVIDEO
URUGUAY

Tel.: 598-2-482460, 598-2-495795
Fax.: 598-2-494572
Telex: 22043 CIMTECA UY

Member of FIAF.

Collections
Collections of Film, Video.

Historical events, national and foreign ; sports, culture, politics, music.
Films about 1100 titles
Video about 50 titles

Access
Catalogue on cards.

Acces to catalogue: limited to archive staff. Upon individual request. Decided on case by case.

Access to materials: limited due to legal and technical reasons.
Access on archives premises, by purchase.

Fees – Copyright
Fees for facilities and handling.
In some cases rights are with the archive. In other cases archive can obtain rights from rightholder. In other cases the user has to obtain authorization from copyrightholder.

VATICAN CITY

VATICAN CITY

_____ 566
CENTRO TELEVISIVO VATICANO
VATICAN TELEVISION CENTER
Palazzo Belvedere
00120 VATICAN CITY
VATICAN CITY STATE

Tel.: 39-6-6985233, 39-6-6985467, 39-6-6985300
Fax.: 39-6-6985192

Collections
Collections of Video.

Activity of Pope John Paul II.
Video 6000 videocassettes

Access
Catalogue on database.

Acces to catalogue: limited by staff only.

Access to materials: limited due to limited facilities.
Access by purchase.

Fees – Copyright
Copyright holder is the institution.

_____ 567
FILMOTECA VATICANA
VATICAN FILM LIBRARY
Palazzo San Carlo
00120 VATICAN CITY
VATICAN CITY STATE

Tel.: 39-6-6983197
Fax.: 39-6-6985373
Telex: 2019 PCCS VA

Member of FIAF.

Collections
Collections of Film, Video, Sound, books, magazines.

Materials on religions, Pope's travels, life and history of the Church, life of the saints, anthropology, actualities, commercial films of moral and artistic interest.
Films 700 titles
Video 1800 titles
Sound 1000 titles

Access

Catalogue on cards.

Acces to catalogue: limited on the premises for students and recommended researchers.

Access to materials: limited for students and recommended researchers.
Access on archives premises.

Fees – Copyright

Fees for reimbursement of handling costs.
Legislation on copyright in preparation.

568

RADIO VATICANA
00120 CITTA' DEL VATICANO
VATICAN CITY STATE

Tel.: 39-6-6983945
Fax.: 39-6-6983237
Telex: 504-2023

Member of IASA.

Collections

Collections of Sound.

Popes' speeches (starting with Pius XI).
Sound 8000 magnetic tapes (chronological)

Access

Acces to catalogue: limited on request.

Access to materials: limited on request.

Fees – Copyright

Copyright holder is the institution.

VENEZUELA

CARACAS

569

BIBLIOTECA NACIONAL DE VENEZUELA
ARCHIVO AUDIOVISUAL DE VENEZUELA
Calle Soledad con Las Piedritas, Edif. Rogi, Zona Industrial, La Trinidad
Apartado Postal 6525
CARACAS 1010
VENEZUELA

Tel.: 58-2-9418011 ext. 200/206
Fax.: 58-2-9415219
Telex: 28120 IASBN

Member of FIAF, IFTA, IFLA.

Collections

Collections of Film, Video, Sound, files, slides, scores, musical manuscripts, photos, posters, designs, postcards.

Social science, history, arts, classical music, folkloric and popular music, politics.
Films 18361 items
Video 15774 items
Sound 35000 items

Access

Catalogue on database.

Access to catalogue.

Access to materials: limited due to conservation.
Access on archives premises, by purchase.

Fees – Copyright

Fees for facilities and handling, by signed agreement for projection and exhibition.
Pricelist and conditions for use available.
Copyright holder is the institution.
User works on the premises. Archive has copyright with some exceptions.

570

UNIVERSIDAD SIMON BOLIVAR
Valle de Sartenejas Los Guayabitos, Edo. Miranda
P.O. Box 89000
1086-A CARACAS
VENEZUELA

Tel.: 58-2-9635062
Fax.: 58-2-939421
Telex: 21910

Member of IFLA.

Collections

Collections of Film, Sound.

Library is specialized in science and technology and has a small collection of AV materials on chemistry, biology, ecology, etc. Also some cassettes and records of classical and folkloric music.
Films 37
Sound 15

Access

Catalogue on cards.

Acces to catalogue: limited.

Access to materials: limited.
Access by loan.

VIETNAM

HANOI

571

VIEN NGHE THUAT VA LUU TRU DIEN ANH VIET NAM
VIETNAM FILM INSTITUTE
VIETNAM FILM ARCHIVES (The former name)
115 – Ngoc Khanh Street
HANOI
VIETNAM
Tel.: 844-2.43451
Member of FIAF.

Collections

Collections of Film, Video, posters, scenarios, books, magazines.
Culture, industry, agriculture, education, sports, music, transport, folklore, history, war,...
Films 62000 reels
Video 600 tapes

Access

Catalogue published.
Access to catalogue.
Access to materials: limited.
Access on archives premises.

Fees – Copyright

Fees for research for reuse and production purposes, research by archive staff.
Pricelist and conditions for use available.
Copyright holder is the institution.
Access an spot for research and sale.

YUGOSLAVIA

BELGRADE

572

JUGOSLOVENSKA KINOTEKA
Knez Mihailova 19
P.O. Box 67
11000 BEOGRAD
YUGOSLAVIA
Tel.: 38-11-622555
Fax.: 38-11-622587
Member of FIAF.

Collections

Collections of Film, stills, posters, books, magazines, screenplays.
Feature and non-feature films, 35mm and 16mm, sound and silent, on acetate and nitrate stock.
Films 80000 prints

Access

Catalogue indexed on cards.
Acces to catalogue: limited by staff only.
Access to materials: limited depending on technical condition of film stock.
Access on archives premises, by loan.

Fees – Copyright

Fees for research for reuse and production purposes, research by archive staff, facilities and handling, copyright (if the archive is the copyright holder).
In case of access by loan the copyright holders permission is needed. (If the archive is not the copyright holder).

NOVI SAD

573

BIBLIOTEKA MATICE SRPSKE
Matice Srpske Br. 1
21000 NOVI SAD
YUGOSLAVIA
Tel.: 38-21-615599
Fax.: 38-21-28574
Telex: 38-21-64367 BMS YU
Electronic mail: JUPAK 512110003022
Member of IFLA.

Collections

Collections of Sound.
The collection contains Yugoslav records and cassettes.
Sound 15000 musical records, 6000 cassettes

Access

Catalogue on database.
Access to materials: limited.
Access on archives premises.

Fees – Copyright

Institution holds no copyright.

SKOPJE

574

KINOTEKA NA MAKEDONIJA
Bul. Goce Delcev bb
P.O. Box 161
91000 SKOPJE
YUGOSLAVIA
Tel.: 38-91-228064, 38-91-211579
Fax.: 38-91-220062
Electronic mail: UBBG::IN%"BAZAFILM% NUBSK@YUBGEF51"
Member of FIAF.

Collections

Collections of Film, Video, Sound, written documentation, books, stills, posters, old aparatus.

The Cinematheque of Macedonia possesses collections of : national Macedonian feature and documentary production, archive film stock, shooted in Macedonia from 1905-1945, significant Yugoslav films, as well as world significant film achievments.
Films 6000 feature and documentary films
Video 300 feature films
Sound 400 recording units of film music and researching (interviews)

Access

Catalogue on database.

Acces to catalogue: limited.

Access to materials: limited.
Access by loan, by hire, by purchase.

Fees – Copyright

Fees for research for reuse and production purposes, research by archive staff.
Pricelist and conditions for use available.
Institution holds no copyright.
For the Macedonian production the copyright holder is the production company "Vardar Film" and "FRZ" – Skopje. For the archive film stock a permission is requested from the Ministry of Culture of the Government of Macedonia, and the copyrights for the Yugoslav films have their producers.

ZAMBIA

LUSAKA

MULTIMEDIA ZAMBIA
MULTIMEDIA ZAMBIA AUDIO VISUALS ARCHIVE
Bishops Road
Kabulonga P.O. Box 320199
101001 LUSAKA
ZAMBIA

Tel.: 260-1-264117
Fax.: 260-1-264117
Telex: ZA 40340

Collections

Collections of Film, Video, Sound.

We have both film 16mm, video Umatic & VHS and audio tapes.
Films 25
Video 125
Sound 2000

Access

Catalogue published.

Access to catalogue: Our catalogue is now outdated and we are revising the re-print since we have acquired new material.

Access to materials.
Access on archives premises.

Fees – Copyright

Fees for research for reuse and production purposes, research by archive staff.
Pricelist and conditions for use available.
Copyright holder is the institution.
Multimedia Zambia has the copyrights for video films it has produced via : 1. The fight against the spread of aids. 2. Musical tape with David Livingstone Teachers' Training College Choir.

UNIVERSITY OF ZAMBIA
Great East Road
P.O. Box 32379
LUSAKA
ZAMBIA

Tel.: 260-1-213221
Fax.: 260-1-253952
Telex: ZA44370

Member of IFLA.

Collections

Collections of Film, Video, Sound, microfiche, microcards.

Economics, language, literature (oral), parliamentary debates, daily newspapers, history, music, poetry, politics.
Films 2800
Sound 200

Access

Catalogue indexed on cards.

Access to catalogue.

Access to materials: limited for preservation, only serious researchers allowed access.
Access on archives premises.

Fees – Copyright

Pricelist and conditions for use available.
Copyright holder is the institution.

ZIMBABWE

HARARE

NATIONAL ARCHIVES OF ZIMBABWE _____ 577
Borrowdale Rd, Gun Hill
P.Bag 7729 CAUSEWAY
HARARE
ZIMBABWE

Tel.: 263-4-792741

Member of FIAF, ICA, IFLA.

Collections

Collections of Film, Video, Sound, posters, photographs, cuttings on film and music in Zimbabwe, production notes for all films made in Zimbabwe 1953-1963 (plus a few others).

Audiovisual materials produced in Zimbabwe or relating to Zimbabwe including some broadcast material.

Films 1000 titles, 20000 reels (estimate)
Video 45 tapes (44 titles)
Sound 320 reel to reel tapes, 500 cassette tapes, 12500 gramophone records, 1 CD

Access

Catalogue on database.

Access to catalogue.

Access to materials: Limited with regard to Zimbabwe Broadcasting Corporation material – access to these collection with their permission. Access on archives premises.

Fees – Copyright

Fees for research for reuse and production purposes, facilities and handling, for commercial use of material, and for copying using telecine equipment.
Pricelist and conditions for use available.
Broadcasting Company's materials : copyright remains with them. Films and videos produced by commercial companies : copyright is with those companies. Government productions made since 1980 : copyright with the Ministry of Information.
Pre-1980 films : copyright with National Archives.

Index

Subjects of Collection

Abbey of la Grainetière 187
Aboriginal music 018
Aboriginals 009, 013, 095
Abu Dhabi 001
Academy Awards broadcasts 514
Academy war film collection 514
Accidents 114
Actors interviewed 179
Adelaide 007
Administration 410
Advertising films 204
Aeronautics 475
Africa 072, 312, 482
African cinema 072
Agriculture 060, 087, 095, 146, 159, 218, 257, 276, 313, 321, 383, 402, 453, 461, 515, 571
Aids 575
Air force films 439
Aircraft 485, 495
Albania 002, 003
Alberta 074
Algeria 004, 166
Alps 453
Alsthom, Belfort 173
Amateur films 026, 188, 192, 194, 281, 497
Amateur video production 167
Amiens 168
Amsterdam 341
Andean fiestas, rituals 389
Andean music 389
Angers 169, 170
Angola 005
Animals 218, 425
Animated images 180
Animation films 048, 067, 068, 080, 091, 131, 178, 193, 221, 228, 247, 294, 310, 393, 462, 485, 497, 511
Anjou 169
Anthropology 321, 561, 567
Apartheid 450
Applied arts 452
Applied science 326
Arab music 206
Aragon 432

Archeology 174, 452, 453
Architecture 171, 174, 179, 203, 410, 452
Archivism 169
Argentina 006
Arhus 136
Army 186
Army films 439
Arnhem 346
Art 048, 089, 126, 217, 246, 338, 462, 500, 519, 539
Art films 006, 202, 466, 539
Art history 054, 174, 184, 358
Artists 048
Artists interviewed 372, 391, 413
Artists Television Network 527
Arts 087, 114, 282, 311, 430, 453, 503, 569
Asia 478
Auschwitz 262
Australia 007–013, 015–018, 020–024, 026–031
Australian music 023
Austria 032, 034, 035, 038–043
Authors 141, 142, 155, 250
Authors interviewed 273
Avant-garde films 538
Avantgarde, American 511
Aviation 207, 321
Baden-Baden 225, 226
Baden-Württemberg 258, 259
Bagneux 171
Bangladesh 044
Barbie, Klaus 199
Basketball 536
Basque composers 427
Basque music 427
Bauer-Müller collection 379
Béarn 210
Beauty 204
Beethoven collection 379
Belfort 173
Belgium 045, 051
Berlin 230, 232, 234
Bermuda 057
Besançon 174
Biology 046, 246, 425

Birds 504
Birmingham 471
Blackhawk film collection 514
Blues 518
Bolivia 058
Bordeaux 179
Botswana 059, 060
Boucher, Anthony 554
Bourguiba 464
Brazil 061, 062, 064, 065
British Columbia 093
British in India 489
Brno 128
Broadway 543
Broken Hill Proprietary Company 027
Brooklyn Museum 519
Brunei 066
Bulgaria 067–071
Burma 489
Business 091, 307, 503
Canada 074–076, 078, 080–083, 088–090, 093, 095
Canals 475
Cars 204
Castres 182
Catalan films 420
Catalunya 421
Catastrophies 197
Censor cuts 277
Ceremonies 060, 092
Chapell of Mont des Alouettes 187
Chemistry 053, 103, 326
Chicago 523
Children 267
Children films 451
Children holiday camps 171
Children programs 203
Children television 550
Childrens literature 254
Childrens music 448, 449
Chile 096, 098, 099
Chilean folklore 096
China 100, 102–106, 267, 317, 471
Chinese music 267
Church 567
Circus artists 142
Civil rights 510
Classical music 002, 011, 016, 023, 038, 071, 077, 078, 112, 116–120, 123, 125, 134, 136, 233, 235, 252, 259, 267, 273, 275, 293, 300, 309, 317, 353, 357, 362, 392, 397, 414, 425, 426, 437, 448, 449, 459, 488, 520, 558, 569
Clémenceau, Georges 187
Coal mining 475, 479
Cold war 515

Collections for the blind 019, 138, 251, 345, 355, 378, 416
Colleu collection 212
Colombia 108
Colonies, Netherlands 354
Comedies 485, 491
Commerce 095, 321
Communication 089, 208, 291
Communist parties history 298
Communist Party 162
Composers, American 552
Computer programming 307
Computing 469
Concentration camps 537
Concerts 516, 520
Congo 109
Conservation 452
Contemporary music 065, 135, 264, 340, 343, 372
Convocation ceremony 370
Corrèze 222
Corse, Haute- 172
Cosmos 402
Costa Rica 110
Côtes-d'Armor 214
Country music 518
Cowboy music 509
Crafts 218
Criminology 056
Croatia 111
Cuba 112, 114, 116–127
Culture 068, 321, 391, 402–404, 415, 462, 481, 497
Czechoslovakia 130–134, 412
Daily life 180, 183
Dance 070, 134, 203, 267, 485, 491, 526, 545, 556
De Gaulle, Charles 187
Deaf people 560
Defence 321
DeMille, Cecil B. 553
Denmark 136–144
Design 203
Dialects 041, 159, 160, 248, 285, 300, 478, 488
Disney, Walt 521
Diving 219
Documentaries 003, 004, 006, 011, 018, 050, 067, 068, 072, 091, 108, 126, 131, 158, 178, 221, 228, 240, 247, 263, 264, 267, 269, 271, 272, 277–279, 281, 290, 294, 310, 324, 328, 335, 353, 376, 390, 399, 421, 430, 434, 438, 444, 447, 458, 461, 463, 467, 485, 497, 500, 511, 512, 526, 531, 541, 553, 563, 574
Domestic life 515
Dordogne 211
Drama 081, 118, 124, 272, 500, 526

Drink 204
Düsseldorf 240
Dutch Radio Union 344
Eastern Churches 289
Eastern Europe 269
Ecole Polytechnique Palaiseau 198
Ecology 103, 402, 425
Economics 179, 291, 307, 325, 576
Economy 004, 114, 146, 148, 240, 251, 278, 453
Ecuador 145
Education 014, 087, 089, 115, 267, 276, 291, 326, 336, 425, 453, 571
Education materials 307
Education science 503
Eichmann, Adolf 290
Election campaigns 332
Emigration, Jewish 286
Employment 450
Engineering 287, 311, 410
Entertainment 089, 324, 336, 421, 500, 502
Environment 013, 015, 031, 089, 192, 208, 276, 306
Estonia 146
Ethnic music 300
Ethnographic films 160
Ethnography 009, 165, 167, 191, 243, 260, 519
Ethnology 145, 180, 184, 222
Ethnomusic 231, 264, 265, 359, 449, 569
Ethnomusicology 201, 242, 252
Europe 482
European fair 217
Expeditions 219
Experimental films 006, 202
Exploration 219
Falkland conflict 496
Farming 491
Farming community 382
Fashion 203, 204, 491
Feature films 310, 315, 316, 353, 357, 376, 413, 434, 438, 441, 462, 463, 467, 526
Fiction films 003, 006, 011, 050, 067, 068, 072, 108, 126, 131, 158, 196, 221, 228, 246, 247, 261, 263, 267, 269, 271, 277–279, 294, 335, 399, 485, 497, 511, 531, 533, 541, 553, 574
Fiction films, silent 491
Field recordings 016, 041, 386
Fiji 147
Filipino film history 390
Filipino films 390
Filmmakers interviewed 273, 277
Filmmusic 448
Films made by artists 202
Fine arts 326
Finland 150–162, 164, 165
Fishing 218, 475, 485, 498

Flanders 045
Flemish 045
Flori, François 172
Folk art 435
Folk dances 327
Folk music 002, 011, 041, 070, 118, 121, 136, 156, 160, 165, 184, 273, 275, 289, 293, 295–297, 300, 312, 313, 321, 324, 327, 359, 362, 392, 397, 408, 414, 437, 448, 466, 471, 475, 478, 518, 522, 534
Folk music, European 235
Folk music, non-european 235
Folk song music 433
Folklore 145, 156, 159, 165, 571
Folkloric music 216, 265
Food 204
Football 536
Ford film collection 470
Forestry 515
Forret, Will collection 478
Fougeres 185
France 186, 199, 201, 205, 215
Frankfurt 242
French Revolution 214
Furniture 204
Gaelic 478
Game shows 267
Garonne, Haute- 220
Geography 087, 103, 193, 338, 482
Germany 225–230, 232–243, 245, 247, 248, 250, 251, 253, 255–259, 261, 262
Gerontology 525
Ghettos 537
Göteborg 437
Gramophone Co, Ltd. 134
Graphic arts 065
Graz 032
Greece 263
Grieg, Edvard 371
Guehenno, Jean 185
Guinea 264
Guinea-Bissau 265
Gulf War 010, 496
Habitats 504
Hampshire 508
Handicapes 174
Hanson, Howard 552
Health 089, 091, 174, 179, 321, 461
Health promotion 513
Healthcare 502
Henie, Sonja 372
Heritage 208
Hessen 262
Hispanic music 509
Historical performances 522

History 306, 311, 313, 317, 324–326, 328, 329, 344, 348, 354, 391, 402–404
Holmes, Hanya 556
Holocaust 262, 286, 288, 290, 537, 540
Hong Kong 266, 267
Household cleaner 204
Housing 502
Humanities 410
Hungary 268–270
Iceland 271, 272
Independance, India, Burma 489
Independent documentary 553
India 273–277, 482, 489
Indian classical music 273, 274
Indonesia 278
Industry 021, 089, 095, 176, 197, 218, 257, 276, 321, 402–404, 425, 430, 479, 481, 491, 495, 571
Information science 107, 333, 469, 532
Institute of Singapore 409
Insurance 204
Iran 279
Ireland 281–285
Irish traditional music 282, 284
Israel 286–291
Italy 294, 298–300, 303
Jails 174
Jamaica 305, 306
Japan 310
Japanese cinema 511
Japanese music 267, 309
Jazz 011, 078, 134, 136, 293, 343, 353, 362, 377, 392, 425, 449, 488, 518, 520, 522, 546
Jewish history 475
Jewish life 540
Jewish subjects 559
Jewish traditional music 289
Jewry 288, 290, 537
Jewry, European 286
Jews 559
Jordan 311
Journalism 546
Jurisprudence 251
Kahn, Albert 180
Kenya 312, 313
Kiel 257
King Prajadhipok's film collection 462
Kiribati 314
Korea 010, 316, 317
Korea Democratic People's Republic 315
La Roche sur Yon 188
Labor history 095
Labor Sports Association 162
Labour movement 161, 162, 375
Lancashire 475
Landes 191

Languedoc 192
Latin American music 096
Latino culture 556
Latino history 556
Latino politics 556
Leisure 179, 204
Lesotho 318
Levy, John ethnomusicology collection 478
Librarianship 107, 333, 338, 469, 532
Library science 015, 085
Liechtenstein 319
Light music 235
Linz 035
Literature 014, 114, 203, 270, 293, 306, 348
Literature, German 250
Liturgical music 289
Live concert recordings 135
Live performances 543
Liverpool 475
Loir-et-Cher 175
Loire 213
London 500
Lorient 190
Lorraine 194
Luxembourg 320
Macedonia 574
Maine 515, 529
Maine-et-Loire 169
Majuro 327
Makkah 405
Malawi 321
Malaysia 322–326
Management 031, 148, 266, 323, 325, 326, 410, 450, 469
Manchester 475
Manitoba 095
Mannesmann 239
Maori 359, 362, 364
Maritime culture 373
Marketing 014
Mass media 546
Mathematics 053, 503
Mauritius 328, 329, 331
Mayenne 189
Medical training 332
Medicine 046, 089, 113, 122, 200, 243, 246, 287, 311, 367, 410, 453, 490, 513
Medina 405
Méliès films 514
Menaul, Air Vice Marshal 496
Metropolitan Museum of Art 539
Metropolitan Opera 536
Mexican music 334
Mexico 332, 334–338
MGM 553
Michigan 510

Middle East 260, 482
Military 154, 186, 278
Military, aviation 207
Military, Canadian 094
Military conflicts 492, 493
Military music 187
Mining 027
Missionary 321
"Mister Rogers Neighborhood" 550
Moscow 403
Motoring 470, 485
Mozart, Wolfgang Amadeus 036
Mullings, Frank 507
Museology 452
Music 358
Music hall 475
Music hall, British 485
Music history 096, 334
Musical theatre 546
Musicals 518
Muskie, Edmund S. 529
Muslim pilgrimage 405
Muslims 289
Namibia 339
Nantes 195
National collection of films 401
National disc collection 071
National film and sound collection 061
National film and video collection 029, 111, 283
National film collection 114, 145, 315, 335, 396, 565, 571, 572
National film, video and sound collection 078, 082, 374, 438, 562, 563, 569, 577
National History Museum 499
National music 129
National sound collection 030, 069, 083, 139, 150, 157, 164, 227, 229, 238, 241, 282, 456, 488, 573
National television collection 098
National video and sound collection 100, 137, 423, 457
National Women's Study Association 557
Native American music 509
Nato 496
Natural science 243, 317
Naval power 498
Navy films 439
Nazi period 537
Nazi period, emigrants 262
Nazi period, victims 262
Netherlands 340, 343, 344, 354, 356
Neuchâtel 454
New Hampshire 515
New Zealand 359–364
Newcastle University 008
News 458, 462

News collection 535
News-films 390
News reel collection 444
Newsreels 006, 011, 067, 108, 131, 145, 228, 247, 281, 310, 361, 444, 447, 455, 461, 463, 476, 484, 497, 502, 531, 563
Nigeria 368
Nigerian Institute of International Affairs 368
Nordrhein-Westfalen 240
Normandie, Basse- 167
Normandie, Haute- 212
North East England 479
North West England 502
Northern territory, Australia 018
Norway 373–377, 379, 381, 382
Norwegian dialects 384
Norwegian Labour movement 375
Norwegian-related music 379
Nova Scotia 076
Oc, Pays d' 220
Occupational safety and health 450
Ocean liners 498
Off air radio recording 488
Off air radio recording Netherlands 344
Off-air television recording 497
Off air television recording Netherlands 344
Off air video recording 488
Oil exploration 027
Ontario 088
Opera 116, 134, 250, 275, 425, 520, 522, 525, 526, 554
Opera records 379
Oral history 007–009, 017, 023, 041, 059, 092–094, 110, 156, 159, 160, 165, 270, 300, 305, 327, 344, 362, 368, 386, 408, 473, 475, 478, 488, 507, 510, 540
Oriental music 129
Orne 167
Painting 452
Papua New Guinea 386, 387
Paris 209
Parker, Charles 471
Parliament debates 576
Parliamentary sessions 447
Pas-de-Calais 184
Performing arts 022, 023, 273, 526, 533, 546
Périgueux 211
Peru 388, 389
Peruvian music 388
Photography 065
Physics 046, 053, 326, 425
Plays 275
Playwriters interviewed 523
Plzen 129
Poetry 321
Poitevin 197

Poland 391, 393
Pole missions 219
Polish music 394
Political parties 344
Politicians interviewed 125, 199, 391, 413
Pop music 392, 425, 448, 449
Pope 567
Pope John Paul II 566
Pope's speeches 568
Popmusic 357
Popular music 016, 065, 112, 117–120, 123, 125, 129, 293, 353, 362, 386, 414, 478, 488, 518, 534, 558, 569
Popular songs 167, 212
Population 179
Portillo, Jose Lopez 332
Portraits with filmmakers 453
Portugal 396–398
Portuguese music 395
Prehistory 452
Presidents of France 199
Prisoners of World War II 199
Propaganda films 299
Psychology 243, 251, 291
Public health 402
Public works 171
Pyrénées-Atlantiques 210
Quebec 080, 087
Railroad music 509
Railroad songs 509
Railways 193, 215, 475
Recreation 089
Religion 060, 260, 382, 402, 415, 425, 567
Religious music 534
Religious songs 187
Resistance 142, 262, 286
Resistance fighters 185, 199
Restoration 452
Ribéracois 211
Robinson, Francis 536
Rock music 392, 448, 449, 518
Rock'n'roll music 216, 534
Roman Catholic organisations 344
Rotterdam 352
Rumania 399
Rural employment 450
Rural life 021, 500, 515
Rural traditions 175
Russia 401, 402, 404
Russian feature films 401
Sailing 485, 498
Saints 567
San Francisco Bay Area 511
Saudi Arabia 405
Saxony 238
Schleswig-Holstein 257

Science 306, 403, 404, 497
Science fiction 114
Scientists 155
Scientists interviewed 391
Scotland 478, 480, 481
Sculpture 203, 452
Seatrade 498
Second World War, Burma 489
Seine-Maritime 212
Seine-Saint-Denis 176
Sèvres, Deux- 197
Seychelles 408
Shakespeare plays 557
Ship building 257
Ships 498
Sicily 295–297
Sign language 560
Silent films, US 514
Simmons College 517
Singapore 409–411
Singapore Broadcasting Corporation 409
Singers 554
Sites 208
Skupa, Josef 129
Slapstick comedies 131, 193, 294
Slovakia 412, 413
Slovenija 414
Social conditions 009, 015, 021, 089, 171, 179, 240, 257, 274, 276, 306, 321, 324, 328, 391, 415, 453, 461, 471
Social Democratic Party 162
Social life 489, 491, 497, 500, 502, 507, 510, 526
Social movement 045
Social science 208, 410, 503
Social work 291
Sociology 014, 176, 358
Solomon Islands 415
Songs 172, 448, 449, 554
Sound effects 120, 121
South Africa 419, 496
South Asia 260
South East England 500
Soviet animation films 401
Soviet cinema 511
Soviet feature films 401
Soviet popular scientific films 401
Soviet Union 402
Spain 423, 424, 430
Spanish cinema 424
Spanish Civil War 142, 424
Spanish folk music 426
Sport 485
Sports 004, 068, 087, 089, 114, 146, 179, 197, 237, 267, 278, 282, 328, 402, 421, 425, 453, 565, 571

Sports science 237
Sri Lanka 433–435
Stage performances 070
Stavanger 383
Steel making 027
Steiermark 032
Stock shots collection 029, 063, 089, 215, 486, 495, 500, 542, 547, 549
Stockholm 437
Strasbourg 217
Strike 173
Student films 390
Stuttgart 258, 259
Sweden 143, 160, 440–444
Switzerland 447, 453, 455–458
Syria 460
Talk shows 267
Tanzania 461
Tasmania 020
Teaching materials 012, 014, 015, 024, 025, 031, 037, 046, 049, 053, 055, 084, 090, 099, 106, 127, 249, 266, 287, 291, 334, 422, 429, 503, 512, 530, 551
Technology 114, 266, 287, 306, 311, 338, 503
Temperance movements 382
Tennessee music 534
Testimonies 178, 179, 182, 537
Textile industry 502
Thai films 462, 463
Thailand 462, 463
Theatre 002, 046, 203, 242, 250, 293, 300, 358, 471, 543
Theatre performances 437
Theatre personalities interviewed 543
Theatre plays 413
Theology 260
Thionville 218
Time-lapse photography 495
Toileterie 204
Toronto 088
Torres Strait Islands 009
Toulouse 221
Tourism 057, 087, 169, 184, 197, 217, 321, 402, 425
Towns in Spain 425
Towns in the world 425
Trade Unionism 306
Trade unions 162, 344
Tradition music 172
Traditional dances 189
Traditional music 189, 231, 264, 386
Transport 087, 089, 257, 313, 321, 402, 485, 491, 507, 571
Travel 087, 430
Tulle 222
Tunesia 464

Turin 302
Turkey 466, 467
Turkish music 466
Tyrol 034
UFA 261
Underwater archeology 219
Unesco 208
Union congresses 375
United Nations 548
Universal film and video collection 002, 039, 051, 075, 144, 152, 158, 225, 256, 361, 398, 444, 458, 472, 497, 500, 501
Universal film collection 050, 058, 062, 080, 131, 140, 177, 205, 221, 228, 234, 247, 292, 294, 320, 393, 399
Universal film, video and sound collection 011, 068, 130, 153, 181, 201, 236, 245, 259, 272, 303, 308, 412, 480, 494
Universal sound collection 028, 133, 139, 151, 226, 232, 235, 244, 253, 255, 268, 275, 349, 360, 363, 380, 381, 385, 442, 443, 487, 544
Universal video and sound collection 431
University of Antwerp 047
University of Maiduguri 370
University of Mauritius 331
University of Michigan 510
University of Toronto 092
University of Victoria 094
University Twente 347
Urbanism 171, 179
Uruguay 565, 569
US Government AV records 563
Usti nad Labem 134
Val-de-Marne 183
Valencia 430, 431
Vanderbilt University 536
Vauxhall film collection 470
Veditz, George W. 560
Vendée 187, 188
Verdi collection 546
Vermont 515
Versailles 223
Veterinary 358
Vienna 038, 042
Vietnam 010, 571
Vineyards 213
Visual arts 015, 266, 372, 539, 541
Wales 468, 474
Walsall 507
Wars 186
Washington University, St. Louis 555
Welsh dialects 474
Welsh tradition 474
West Indies 306
Western 485
Western Australia 026